New Approaches to Problem-based Learning

Problem-based learning (PBL) is a pedagogical approach that has the capacity to create vibrant and active learning environments in higher education. However, both experienced PBL practitioners and those new to PBL often find themselves looking for guidance on how to engage and energise a PBL curriculum. *New Approaches to Problem-based Learning: Revitalising Your Practice in Higher Education* provides that guidance from a range of different, complementary perspectives.

This is a professional guide that explores effective ways to initiate, design, develop, enhance and sustain (PBL) curricula in Higher Education environments. It will help Higher Education teachers, educators, education technologists, librarians and managers to explore how best to engage students using PBL. This book goes beyond a basic explanation of the PBL process and outlines from a variety of perspectives and disciplinary stances, the power, potential and practical possibilities of problem-based learning.

Leading practitioners in the field as well as new voices in PBL teaching and learning have collaborated to produce this text. Each chapter provides practical and experienced accounts of issues and ideas for PBL, as well as a strong theoretical and evidence base. Whether you are an experienced PBL practitioner, or new to the processes and principles of PBL, this book will help you to find ways of revitalising and enriching your practice and of enhancing the learning experience in a range of higher education contexts.

Terry Barrett is a Lecturer in Education Development at University College Dublin where she works with curriculum development teams to design, implement and research PBL initiatives in a range of disciplines.

Sarah Moore is Associate Vice President and Professor at the University of Limerick, where she adopts a strategic focus on optimising teaching and learning.

New Approaches to Problem-based Learning

Revitalising Your Practice in Higher Education

Edited by Terry Barrett and Sarah Moore

Routledge
Taylor & Francis Group

NEW YORK AND LONDON

First published 2011
by Routledge
711 Third Avenue, New York, NY 10017

Simultaneously published in the UK
by Routledge
2 Park Square, Milton Park, Abingdon, Oxon, OX14 4RN

Routledge is an imprint of the Taylor & Francis Group, an informa business

Typeset in Minion by Wearset Ltd, Boldon, Tyne and Wear

Library of Congress Cataloging-in-Publication Data
Barrett, Terry.
New approaches to problem-based learning: revitalising your practice in higher education/Terry Barrett and Sarah Moore.
p. cm.
Includes bibliographical references and index.
1. Education, Higher–Curricula. 2. Problem-based learning. 3. Problem-solving–Study and teaching (Higher) 4. Educational innovations. I. Moore, Sarah. II. Title.
LB2361.B36 2010
378.1'79–dc22

2010014890

ISBN13: 978-0-415-87148-8 (hbk)
ISBN13: 978-0-415-87149-5 (pbk)
ISBN13: 978-0-203-84692-6 (ebk)

"Education is an admirable thing, but it is well to remember from time to time that nothing worth knowing can be taught."

Oscar Wilde

Contents

Illustrations

Table

Editors' Preface

The painting on the cover of this book is a metaphor for the new shapes, the new contexts, and the creative combinations inherent in the problem-based learning (PBL) approaches that are presented and explored throughout this book. All of these approaches focus on the potential of PBL to revitalise our teaching and learning practice within higher education. For us, "revitalise" is an important word. Everywhere, teachers and students often talk about the experiences of being jaded and of routinisation – the excessive standardisation, and even boredom, that can too easily become a part of the formal learning environments. We believe that all teachers have a right and a responsibility to explore ways of bringing their practice alive.

It was Oscar Wilde who famously said that "Education is an admirable thing, but it is well to remember from time to time that nothing worth knowing can be taught." By focusing more on learning than teaching, by focusing more on experience and process than content and transmission and by focusing on creativity rather than control, we think that practice can be revitalised easily and innovatively. These convictions regarding practice are the values that underpin this book.

If we are focusing on learning, not teaching, then we need to reinvent, to be responsive, to hear and to see well and clearly, and to make sure that we are not getting stuck in routines. We need to give our students a rich, fertile, challenging, dynamic learning experience and we need to learn from them and from each other how we can do this, in order to re-energise ourselves as teachers and to refresh the learning experience for students.

The painting on the cover of the book by Fiona Ahern is entitled *That Childhood Country*. Can we bring some of the curiosity, questioning, creativity, colour and sense of playfulness of childhood into learning in higher education through problem-based learning?

We invite you to get immersed in and explore the ideas and the insights contained in this book. We are delighted to present to you a range of different but interconnected voices all focusing on the huge potential that PBL learning environments can realise. We are proud that so many new and established voices have come together to share their practice by contributing to this book, and we hope it will be used in a whole range of ways as a valuable resource for educators everywhere.

Acknowledgements

This book is part of the Enquiry and Problem-based Learning Project funded by the Strategic Innovation Fund of the Higher Education Authority (Ireland). We appreciate the valuable contributions to this book from the four international partners of this project, namely, the Enquiry and Problem-based Learning Project at University College Dublin, the University of Limerick, the Centre for Excellence in Enquiry-based Learning at the University of Manchester, and Probell, the Finnish Problem-based Learning (PBL) network, together with the contributions from our other international PBL colleagues.

We also want to thank Geraldine O'Neill, University College Dublin, for making possible the first writers' retreat about shaping and drafting the book proposal. A very special thank you goes to Anna Raija Numenmaa, University of Tampere, who welcomed a group of authors to her home in the beautiful Finnish countryside of Monni for two writers' retreats. The warm hospitality and exceptional natural beauty of Monni provided a wonderful environment that made a crucial contribution to the creativity and collaboration of the book. We really appreciate the great attention to detail and good humour that Jean Nee, University College Dublin, gave to the proofreading and copy-editing of this text. Thanks to Seán O'Domhnaill for his graphic design work on the figures in this book.

Part I

Stakeholders Designing Problem-based Learning Initiatives

1

An Introduction to Problem-based Learning

Terry Barrett and Sarah Moore

Introduction

Problems have always mobilised and stimulated thinking and learning; they energise our activity and focus our attention. When problems are experienced as relevant and important, people are motivated to direct their energies towards solving them. It is exactly these energising and curiosity-inducing dimensions of problems that form the basis and rationale for using problems in teaching and learning. Although problem-based learning has existed since the dawn of time, in higher education contexts we can trace problem-based learning (PBL), as a total approach to student learning, to the 1960s in North America. The basis of PBL consists of creating real-life problems for students to work on in small teams (Barrows, 1989). Now, in the 21st century, people across the globe in diverse disciplines and professions are using PBL. While some people use PBL in systematic, integrated ways, using shared methodologies across whole programmes and institutions, others use PBL in particular modules or units of a programme.

Many teachers in higher education are now highly experienced in the design and use of problems and are comfortable with the PBL methodologies that have been part of the higher education landscape for many years. However, many others are still new to the concept of PBL. This textbook brings a series of new voices to the PBL literature along with the input of people who have been practising PBL for several decades. Whether you are experienced in or are new to PBL, we believe that this mix of voices will help you to explore the following questions:

- What is the value of PBL?
- What new approaches to PBL have teachers in higher education been practising?
- How can PBL be used to energise and develop exciting and effective learning environments in higher education?
- How can we revitalise our PBL initiatives?

It is timely, given the history and the popularity of PBL, to problematise problem-based learning; indeed, it would be a contradiction in terms not to treat PBL itself as a problem. Experienced PBL practitioners need to refresh, revitalise, adapt, and keep looking at new ways of using PBL in higher education, and the voices of educators who are still new to PBL can help this form of pedagogy to develop and enhance the impact it can have on student learning.

Chapter Overview

For those who are new to PBL, this chapter will help to familiarise you with some of the key ideas, values, and principles associated with PBL, and for those of you who are familiar with PBL, this chapter will be useful in mapping out the key concepts and principles that will be explored in more detail in other parts of this text.

In order to fulfil these aims, this chapter will:

- define problem-based learning as a total, six-dimensional approach to higher education;
- outline how these key dimensions of problem-based learning will be explored in the book;
- show what the PBL tutorial process can look like in practice;
- list the success factors for PBL initiatives;
- provide an overview of the book.

Problem-based Learning as a Total, Six-dimensional Approach to Higher Education

The classical definition of problem-based learning is: "the *learning* that results from the *process* of working towards the understanding of a resolution of a *problem*. The problem is encountered *first* in the learning process" (Barrows & Tamblyn, 1980, p. 1, our emphases). Problem-based learning focuses on students learning, not on teachers teaching. It has often been defined as "a total approach", not just a teaching technique or tool. We argue that to revitalise our practice of PBL we must work on each of the six dimensions of PBL and their interrelationships. Our conception of PBL as having six dimensions is central to this book. Six key dimensions of PBL are presented in Figure 1.1.

Dimension 1: PBL Problem Design

Many teachers use problems to stimulate learning. However, a key characteristic of PBL is that problems are presented to the students at the start of the learning process rather than after a range of curriculum inputs. The PBL problem can be a scenario, a case, a challenge, a visual prompt, a dilemma, a design brief, a puzzling phenomenon, or some other trigger designed to mobilise learning.

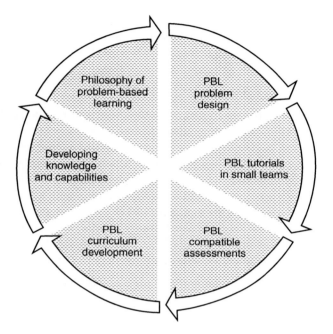

Figure 1.1 PBL as a total six-dimensional approach to higher education.

Schmidt, van der Molen, te Winkel, and Wijnen (2009) highlight three key roles of problems in PBL curricula, namely:

1. increasing levels of curiosity in domains of study;
2. experiencing relevance of the curriculum as problems are perceived as pertinent to future professions; and
3. integrating learning from all curriculum components, e.g. PBL tutorials, practice placements, lectures, and skills training.

It is important for us, as PBL practitioners, to continually find new ideas for selecting or designing relevant, motivating, challenging, interesting, multi-faceted, and up-to-date problems for our students.

Chapters That Will Help You to Explore PBL Problem Design

Design processes involve an interaction with ideas, stakeholders, and media, and the chapters in Part I of the book provide material for refreshing the design of problems in your own PBL initiatives. Part I of this book provides a range of examples of problems used in PBL initiatives. We emphasise the importance of giving the design of effective problems the serious and creative energy it deserves as a key success factor in PBL initiatives (Gijselaers & Schmidt, 1990). Chapter 2 provides some illuminative concepts for thinking about designing problems in different media and practical strategies for how to design effective problems. The importance of involving clinicians or other professionals and students is stressed in Chapters 3 and 4, respectively. Chapter 6 focuses on sharing recent research and practice on video, role-play, and compare-and-contrast problem types.

Dimension 2: PBL Tutorials in Small Teams

At the heart of PBL initiatives are small teams of students with tutors working on problems in tutorials (Silén, 2006). Often, there are about five to eight students in a tutorial team with one tutor. Where there are fewer resources, one teacher can act as a roaming tutor between two or three teams. Teams usually work together around a table with some way of capturing group discussion (e.g. a whiteboard). In the PBL tutorial, knowledge is not a process of reception, but rather a process of construction, where students generate knowledge together as they link prior learning and experience to new learning (Ausbel, 1968). The importance of the social environment of the PBL tutorial in developing individual understanding is emphasised by Savery and Duffy (1995, p. 32):

> other individuals are a primary mechanism for testing our understanding. Collaborative groups are important because we test our understanding and examine the understanding of others as a mechanism for enriching, interweaving, and expanding our understanding of particular issues and phenomena.

The functioning of the PBL tutorial is underpinned by three major principles of social constructivism that connect learning theories to problem-based learning:

1. Elaboration of knowledge at the time of learning enhances subsequent recall (Norman & Schmidt, 1992).
2. Students can learn more with capable peers than on their own (Harland, 2003; Vygotsky, 1978).
3. Learning is a dialogical process based on thought-language (Barrett, 2001; Freire, 1972).

Chapters That Will Help You to Explore the Small-Team Nature of PBL Tutorials

Chapter 9 provides ideas and strategies for maximising the potential of the PBL tutorial for learning together. The role of the tutor in developing the information literacy of the PBL students in the tutorial setting is highlighted in Chapter 10. Chapter 16 focuses on tutor development and strategies for inspiring and effective tutorial facilitation.

Dimension 3: PBL Compatible Assessments

Assessment drives student learning (Biggs, 2003). As well as designing challenging problems and facilitating effective tutorials, assessments need to be designed in such a way that they align with:

- learning outcomes;
- the development of student capabilities; and
- the problem-based learning process.

Chapters That Explore the Ways in Which Assessment Can Align and Integrate with PBL Practice

Chapter 13 provides us with ideas and examples that stimulate us to think of the ways that assessments can be used to promote student capabilities. Chapter 14 explores different ways that triple jump assessments can be designed to align assessment and learning in PBL curricula.

Dimension 4: PBL Curriculum Development

PBL curriculum development is a major, multidimensional change management project (Conway & Little, 2000). The core of a PBL curriculum is students working on PBL problems in tutorial teams. Other curriculum inputs, e.g. lectures, resource sessions, practice placements, research seminars, and skills training need to be planned and sequenced in the curriculum in order to create an integrated PBL curriculum (Kolmos, 2002).

Chapters That Focus on Developing a PBL Curriculum

In Chapter 15 crucial considerations for curriculum planning and capacity building for major PBL initiatives are discussed through drawing on three case studies. A range of curriculum development challenges that teachers new to PBL need to negotiate are explored in Chapter 17. Central questions in curriculum development are:

- What knowledge is important for graduates to develop?
- What are the key capabilities, skills, and attitudes important for graduates?

Dimension 5: Developing Knowledge and Capabilities

Problem-based learning aims to develop the students' knowledge and capabilities. In PBL curricula, students construct their knowledge of key concepts in their discipline/profession by working on problems designed around these concepts. Together, they construct their knowledge of these concepts through their dialogue in PBL tutorials, which includes sharing their independent study and together elaborating their concepts and ideas in PBL tutorials.

In addition to knowledge development, PBL explicitly aims to develop the students' capabilities in terms of key transferable skills needed for the workplace and social life (Hmelo-Silver, 2004). Employers regularly highlight the importance of key skills, which include: communications, teamwork, information literacy, critical and creative thinking, and problem solving, together with self-awareness, self-assessment, ethical behaviour, reflection, and responsibility for continuous development.

Chapters That Focus on Developing Knowledge and Capabilities

Chapter 5 discusses strategies that can be used to help students to make strong intellectual and creative connections between different concepts. Understanding theoretically and practically how knowledge can be constructed dialogically in PBL tutorials is the subject of Chapter 9.

Chapter 10 discusses a range of approaches for enhancing students' information literacy in PBL initiatives. Developing students' reflective capabilities and professionalism in academic and work contexts is the topic of Chapter 11. An exciting way of re-energising PBL is to use it in new ways that clearly signpost and make students' learning explicit. Chapter 13 shows how this can be done by using and adapting design thinking processes.

This book also explores developing knowledge and capabilities by using PBL in new contexts other than taught programmes. Chapter 19 discusses developing doctorate students' capabilities through group supervision using PBL processes. Chapter 20 looks at how knowledge was developed through writing this PBL book collaboratively using PBL and other creative processes.

Dimension 6: The Philosophy of Problem-based Learning

The contributors to this book, by exploring various dimensions of PBL, also address a range of underlying philosophical questions that are useful for all teachers to explore, which includes:

- What is the purpose of higher education?
- What is learning?
- What is teaching?
- What does it mean to practise as a professional?
- What ethical issues do we want our students to address?
- How can higher education promote critical and creative thinking?
- What is problem-based learning?
- What is the nature of problems in PBL curricula?
- What is the rationale for using problem-based learning in higher education?
- What is the purpose of the PBL tutorial?
- What new approaches, forms, and alliances are needed in PBL initiatives today?
- How can problem-based learning be re-energised and re-invented?

Margetson (1997) challenges us to change our ways of thinking both about the *problems* in PBL and the *purposes of higher education* in order to maximise the potential of PBL for facilitating the development of wholeness and educative learning. He quotes Mill (1981, p. 245): "No great improvements in the lot of mankind are possible, until a great change takes place in the fundamental constitution of their modes of thought." Problem-based learning stimulates us to think about the use of problems in different ways. How can we create problems that demand the integrated application of knowledge from different subject areas in ways that also challenge students to address the key issues of values, ethics, and professional behaviour? How can problems be constructed to reflect the different levels of uncertainty in real-life challenges?

It is useful for us to think deeply and widely about the purposes of higher education and about the potential of PBL in this context. One of the ways that PBL can integrate the purposes of higher education is through its potential to link teaching, learning, and research. In problem-based learning, students engage in research in order to explore and tackle the problems they work on. The students have to identify and articulate the features of the problem themselves and then clarify what they know already and what they do not know and need to research. They also have to engage in independent research in finding, reviewing, evaluating, and applying new information to the problem. In PBL tutorials, the students need to marshal evidence for their arguments and discuss counterarguments. Seeing PBL students as researchers may be one of the ways in which institutions can transcend different activities and functions in higher education.

How can problem-based learning help us to create more holistic approaches where theory and practice, reading and skills training, scholarship and ethical behaviour, personal and professional development, critical and creative thinking, and teaching and research form an integrated approach to learning and development? When changing to PBL or when revitalising and developing our current approaches to PBL, the range of questions posed by Margetson (1997, p. 13) is useful in helping us to focus on some of the important pedagogical considerations:

- Do our changes promote educative dialogue in an ethical community?
- Do our changes help overcome the undergraduate/postgraduate divide?
- Do our changes help overcome the opposition between vocational and liberal studies?
- Do our changes promote the integration of scholarship, teaching, and research?
- Do our changes help achieve understanding through praxis?

We hope that all of the ideas and examples in this book will stimulate you to think more deeply and creatively about PBL. We encourage you to use this book to develop your philosophy of PBL as a key element in revitalising your practice in higher education. Our aim is to encourage you to develop new ways of both thinking about and doing problem-based learning.

The PBL Tutorial Process in Practice

People new to PBL often ask what the PBL tutorial process looks like in practice. The PBL tutorial process is central to problem-based learning. In this type of tutorial, the role of the tutor is to facilitate a challenging learning process, not to give content knowledge. The students all contribute to the discussion of the problem and the work of the tutorial and some students also take on an additional role such as chairperson, scribe, reader, timekeeper, or observer. In different contexts there may be particular emphases in terms of the role of the tutorial. In some contexts, for instance, special student roles are decided on by the students, e.g. presentation co-ordinator, photographer. We now describe a summary of our current understanding of the tutor and some common student roles in PBL tutorials.

Tutor and Student Roles in the PBL Process

The role of the tutor is to:
- encourage a welcoming and challenging learning climate;
- facilitate the PBL process, not give a mini-lecture;
- listen very attentively and actively to what students are saying and observe the learning, difficulties, and fun that are taking place in the team;
- intervene, where appropriate, with process interventions based on this listening and observation;
- ask questions that encourage critical and creative thinking;
- ask students to provide the evidence for their statements and to evaluate the resources that they used;
- challenge students to link theory and practice;
- stimulate debate about major issues;
- expect students to be responsible to complete high-quality independent learning;
- facilitate students to reflect on their learning, the development of key skills, and the performance of the team;
- facilitate the review section of the tutorial.

The role of the chairperson is to:
- encourage the participation of all team members;
- facilitate the team to make and work within agreed ground rules;
- stop one person dominating the team and encourage quiet team members to contribute;
- not necessarily talk first and certainly not to talk at length;
- encourage discussion of different viewpoints;
- use the PBL process guide as a scaffold for the team to work on the problem;
- ensure that someone summarises at the end of a tutorial;
- check that everyone is clear what learning issues the team has decided to work on;
- ensure that the team have a clear action plan;

- co-ordinate the team to complete their action plan and the production of any products required for the work on the problem.

The role of the scribe/recorder is to:
- record the ideas of the team on the whiteboard so that this information can be used as a shared learning environment;
- write down clearly the learning issues that the team decide to work on;
- work both verbally and visually on the whiteboard and invite other team members to write on the whiteboard if they want to illustrate a point;
- summarise and synthesise the learning from the problem on the whiteboard as all team members contribute to this synthesis;
- co-ordinate electronic team communications.

The role of the reader is to:
- read the problem aloud at the start of the tutorial;
- re-read the problem again when the team and/or the reader decides that this would be useful;
- continue to read the problem by drawing the team's attention to key elements of the problem.

The role of the timekeeper is to:
- help the team to manage the time in tutorials;
- remind the team at key stages about how much time is left in the tutorial;
- make suggestions to the team about time management.

The role of the observer is to:
- observe the workings of the team in terms of the learning process and team dynamics;
- feedback these observations to the team;
- make suggestions based on these observations.

New approaches to student roles in PBL include students taking on specific professional roles in role-play problem types. This approach, with examples, is discussed in Chapter 6 as a new way of bringing problems to life in the tutorial. Fresh approaches to tutor development are discussed in Chapter 16.

What student roles are relevant to your context? What are your current issues about PBL tutoring?

The Tutorial Process Guide

Many PBL initiatives provide a PBL tutorial process guide in order to facilitate tutors and students in navigating the tutorial and moving forward with the problem. Barrows (1989) outlined a guided tutorial process that began with creating a suitable learning climate and defining the problem. This approach emphasises the importance of establishing an effective learning environment through establishing ground rules and clarifying tutor and student roles. In Barrows' approach, in addition to other ways that the students decide to use the whiteboard, four headings are used on the whiteboard to facilitate the initial brainstorming and the subsequent reporting tutorials: hypotheses/ideas, facts, learning issues, and action plan. The hypotheses/ideas section of the whiteboard is a space for all of the ideas to be recorded initially. Subsequent discussion might mean that some of these ideas are eliminated or that new ideas are added. The facts are the particulars of the problem contained in the case and the other things that the group decide on are facts about the problem. The students decide what they need to learn about in order to work on the problem and can phrase these learning issues as questions. In this process, learning issues are vital and the action plan involves deciding who is doing what when. Barrows' approach also stresses the importance of the review phase of the tutorial, where the team have another look at what they have learned and reflect on the team dynamics. The review of learning can also happen by the team synthesising their learning visually on the whiteboard.

Schmidt and Moust (2000, p. 23) outline the Seven Jump Approach used in Maastricht University as follows:

1. Clarify unknown terms and concepts in the problem description.
2. Define the problem: that is, list the phenomenon to be explained.
3. Analyse the problem: "brainstorm" – try to produce as many different explanations for the phenomenon as you can. Use prior knowledge and common sense.
4. Criticise the explanations posed and try to produce a coherent description of the processes that, according to what you think, underlie the phenomenon.
5. Formulate learning issues for SDL (self-directed learning).
6. Fill in the gaps of your knowledge through self-study.
7. Share your findings with the group and try to integrate the knowledge acquired into a comprehensive explanation of phenomenon.

Some PBL initiatives use or adapt one of these process models and some have invented one that suits their own profession. The Royal Canadian Mounted Police (RCMP) (2008, p. 1) have developed a community policing problem-solving model called CAPRA:

C = Client
A = Acquiring and Analysing Information
P = Partnerships
R = Response
A = Assessment of Action Taken

CAPRA is more than a problem-solving model. It is designed to assist the police officer or other members of the workforce to anticipate problems and to prevent problems from arising, where appropriate, in consultation with partners, as much as it is to resolve problems through multidisciplinary, interagency, and consultative processes. It applies to enforcement as much as it does to prevention. It applies to every aspect of police internal organisational service delivery. It is a method of service delivery that focuses on providing the best quality service by reflecting an understanding of clients' needs, demands, and expectations, and, where possible, using partnership approaches.

To understand the PBL process and to choose or devise a PBL process guide, it is important to have clarity about the difference between *PBL* tutorials and other types of tutorials. Based on a discourse analysis study of a PBL tutorial, Koschmann, Glen, and Conlee (2000, p. 63) stress that:

> Whereas the goal from the tutor's perspective in a conventional tutorial is to bring the tutee to a negotiated level of understanding, the primary objective of the PBL tutorial is just to make deficiencies in the learner's understanding evident. These deficiencies need not, and usually are not, immediately redressed but instead are deferred as LIs [learning issues] for later independent study. Further, it can be seen that the PBL tutor is attempting to effect a more global change in the tutees' orientation toward learning and knowing.

For each problem, there needs to be a minimum of two tutorials and an independent study session so that the students can work through the PBL process. At the other end of the spectrum, it is sometimes appropriate and effective to have one large problem for a unit or module. Chapter 7 encourages PBL practitioners to adapt or invent PBL process models that are compatible with discipline-specific ways of thinking and acting professionally. What type of PBL tutorial process guide is most appropriate to your contexts? In this chapter, we present a customised PBL process guide for a PBL module on Problem-based Learning in Higher Education which is part of a Diploma in University Teaching and Learning at University College Dublin as an example of an adaptation of existing PBL process models for a specific context.

Success Factors for Implementing PBL

A key way of revitalise PBL initiatives is to be aware of the success factors of PBL and to plan strategies for work on specific factors.

Book Overview

This book is organised into three parts and explores new approaches to problem-based learning where the six key dimensions of PBL are taking innovative forms. It discusses recent strategies being used to work on important success factors in problem-based learning.

We hope that you will get many novel ideas from this book that you can adapt for your own PBL initiatives.

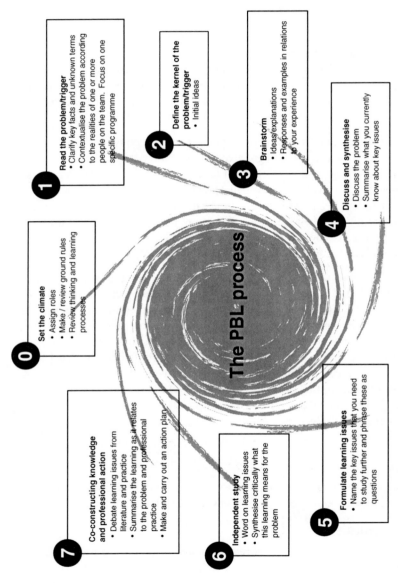

Set the climate
- Assign roles
- Make / review ground rules
- Review thinking and learning processes

1 Read the problem/trigger
- Clarify key facts and unknown terms
- Contextualise the problem according to the realities of one or more people on the team. Focus on one specific programme

2 Define the kernel of the problem/trigger
- Initial ideas

3 Brainstorm
- Ideas/explanations
- Responses and examples in relations to your experience

4 Discuss and synthesise
- Discuss the problem
- Summarise what you currently know about key issues

5 Formulate learning issues
- Name the key issues that you need to study further and phrase these as questions

6 Independent study
- Word on learning issues
- Synthesise critically what this learning means for the problem

7 Co-constructing knowledge and professional action
- Debate learning issues from literature and practice
- Summarise the learning as it relates to the problem and professional practice
- Make and carry out an action plan

The PBL process

Figure 1.2 PBL process guide used in a module on Problem-based Learning in Higher Education at University College Dublin (adapted from Barrows, 1989 and Schmidt, 1983).

Philosophical factors
- An understanding of the philosophical principles underpinning PBL, and
- A commitment to the philosophy of PBL (Barrett, 2001; Margetson, 1997, 2001).

Design factors
- Comprehensive curriculum design (Conway & Little, 2000; Kolmos, 2002; Savin-Baden, 2000).
- Well designed problems (Gijselaers & Schmidt, 1990; Jonassen & Hung, 2008; Mauffette, Kandlbinder, & Soucisse, 2004).
- Assessment compatible with PBL and the specific discipline/ profession (Macdonald & Savin-Baden, 2004; Raine & Symons, 2005).
- Scheduled independent study time (Fincham & Schuler, 2001).

PBL tutoring factors
- Small group size (Wilkerson, 1996).
- A realistic acceptance of the role change (Kolmos, 2002; Little, 1997).
- Effective tutoring skills (Barrett, 2004; Hmelo-Silver & Barrows, 2006; Poikela, 2005; Savin-Baden, 2003).
- The ability to model and review PBL tutorial process skills (Barrett, 2010; Papiczak, Tunny, & Young, 2009; Silén, 2006).
- Frequent opportunities for students to gain feedback (Little, 1997).

Staff and student induction factors
- Student induction to PBL and student support (Hoad-Reddick & Theaker, 2003; Little, 1997).
- Substantial appropriate staff development (Conway & Little, 2000; Farmer, 2004; Murray & Savin-Baden, 2004; Richardson, 2005)

Management factors
- A pragmatic and realistic approach (Little, 1997).
- Institutional and management support (Kolmos, 2002).
- A PBL co-ordinator and administrative support (McLoughlin, 2005).

Figure 1.3 Success factors for implementing PBL (adapted from Barrett, 2005, p. 22).

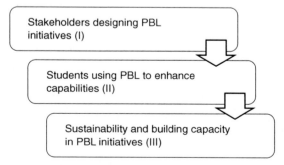

Figure 1.4 Overview of the three parts of this book.

References

Ausbel, D. (1968). *Educational psychology: A cognitive view.* New York: Holt Reinhart & Winston.

Barrett, T. (2001). Philosophical principles for problem based learning: Freire's concepts of personal development and social empowerment. In P. Little & P. Kandlbinder (Eds.), *Refereed proceedings of the 3rd Asia Pacific Conference on PBL: The power of problem-based learning* (pp. 9–18). Newcastle, Australia: PROBLARC.

Barrett, T. (2004). Researching the dialogue of PBL tutorials: A critical discourse analysis approach. In M. Savin-Baden & K. Wilkie (Eds.), *Challenging research into problem-based learning* (pp. 93–102). Buckingham: Open University Press.

Barrett, T. (2010). The problem-based learning process as finding and being in flow. *Innovations in Education & Teaching International, 47*(2), 167–174.

Barrows, H. (1989). *The tutorial process.* Springfield, IL: Southern Illinois University School of Medicine.

Barrows, H., & Tamblyn, R. (1980). *Problem-based learning: An approach to medical education.* New York: Springer.

Biggs, J. (2003). *Teaching for quality learning at university* (2nd ed.). Berkshire: The Society for Research into Higher Education & Open University Press.

Conway, J., & Little, P. (2000). From practice to theory: Reconceptualising curriculum development for problem-based learning. In O.S. Tan, P. Little, S.Y. Lin, & J. Conway (Eds.), *Problem-based learning. Educational innovations across disciplines: A collection of selected papers* (pp. 169–179). Singapore: Temasek Centre for Problem-based Learning. Retrieved from: http://pbl.tp.edu.sg/Curriculum%20Planning/Articles/JaneConwayPennyLittle.pdf.

Farmer, E. (2004). Faculty development for problem-based learning. *European Journal of Dental Education, 8,* 59–66.

Fincham, A., & Schuler, C. (2001). The changing face of dental education: The impact of PBL. *Journal of Dental Education, 65*(5), 406–421.

Freire, P. (1972). *Pedagogy of the oppressed.* Harmondsworth: Penguin.

Gijselaers, W., & Schmidt, H. (1990). Towards a causal model of student learning within the context of problem-based curriculum. In Z. Nooman, H. Schmidt, & E. Ezzat (Eds.), *Innovation in medical education: An evaluation of its present status* (pp. 95–114). New York: Springer.

Harland, T. (2003). Vygotsky's zone of proximal development and problem-based learning: Linking a theoretical concept with practice through action research. *Teaching in Higher Education, 8*(2), 263–272.

Hmelo-Silver, C. (2004). Problem-based learning: What and how do students learn? *Education Psychology Review, 16*(3), 235–266.

Hmelo-Silver, C.R., & Barrows, H.E. (2006). Goals and strategies of a problem-based facilitator. *Interdisciplinary Journal of Problem-based Learning, 1,* 21–39.

Hoad-Reddick, G., & Theaker, E. (2003). Providing support for problem-based learning in dentistry: The Manchester experience. *European Journal of Dental Education, 7*(3), 3–12.

Jonassen, D., & Hung, W. (2008). All problems are not equal: Implications for problem-based learning. *The Interdisciplinary Journal of Problem-based Learning, 2*(2), 6–28.

Kolmos, A. (2002). Facilitating change to a problem-based model. *The International Journal of Academic Development, 7*(1), 63–74.

Koschmann, T., Glen, P., & Conlee, M. (2000). When is a problem-based tutorial not a tutorial? Analyzing the tutor's role in the emergence of a learning issue. In D. Evenson & C. Hmelo (Eds.), *Problem-based learning: A research perspective on learning interactions* (pp. 53–74). London: Lawrence Erlbaum Associates.

Lewin, K. (1952). *Field theory in social science: Selected theoretical papers by Kurt Lewin.* London: Tavistock.

Little, S. (1997). Preparing tertiary teachers for problem-based learning. In D. Boud & G. Feletti (Eds.), *The challenge of problem-based learning* (pp. 117–124). London: Kogan Page.

Macdonald, R.F., & Savin-Baden, M. (2004). *A briefing on assessment in problem-based learning.* LTSN Generic Centre Assessment Series. Available on the Higher Education Academy's Resource Database at: www.heacademy.ac.uk/resources.asp?process=full_record&section=generic&id=349.

McLoughlin, J. (2005). Coordinating and managing PBL programmes: Challenges and strategies. In T. Barrett, I. Mac Labhainn, & H. Fallon (Eds.), *Handbook of enquiry and problem-*

based learning: Irish case studies and international perspectives (pp. 189–196). Galway: Centre for Excellence in Learning and Teaching, National University of Ireland Galway and All Ireland Society for Higher Education.

Margetson, D. (1997, September). *Wholeness and educative learning: The question of problems in changing to problem-based learning.* Keynote paper presented at the International Conference on Problem-based Learning, Changing to PBL, Uxbridge, London.

Margetson, D. (2001, September). *Can all education be problem-based? Can it afford not to be?* Paper presented at the Hong Kong Centre for Problem-Based Learning, Problem-based learning Forum, Hong Kong.

Mauffette, Y., Kandlbinder, P., & Soucisse, A. (2004). The problem in problem-based learning is the problems: But do they motivate students? In M. Savin-Baden & K. Wilkie (Eds.), *Challenging research into problem-based learning* (pp. 11–25). Buckingham: Society for Research into Higher Education and Open University Press.

Mill, J.S. (1981). Autobiography and literary essays. In J.M. Robson (Ed.), *Collected works of John Stuart Mill.* Toronto: University of Toronto.

Murray, I., & Savin-Baden, M. (2004). Staff development in problem-based learning. *Teaching in Higher Education, 5*(1), 107–126.

Norman, G., & Schmidt, H. (1992). The psychological basis of problem-based learning: A review of the evidence. *Academic Medicine, 67*(9), 557–565.

Papiczak, T., Tunny, T., & Young, L. (2009). Conducting the symphony: A qualitative study of facilitation in problem-based learning tutorials. *Medical Education, 43*(4), 377–383.

Poikela, S. (2005). Learning at work as a tutor: The processes of producing, creating, and sharing knowledge in a work community. In E. Poikela & S. Poikela (Eds.), *PBL in context: Bridging work and education* (pp. 177–193). Tampere: Tampere University Press.

Raine, D., & Symons, S. (2005). Experiences of PBL in physics in UK higher education. In E. Poikela & S. Poikela (Eds.), *PBL in context: Bridging work and education* (pp. 67–78). Tampere: Tampere University Press.

Richardson, J.T. (2005). *The future of research in problem-based learning.* Paper presented at Problem-based Learning: A Quality Experience. Conference held University of Salford, 15–17 September.

Royal Canadian Mounted Police (RCMP) (2008). *RCMP CAPRA Problem Solving Model.* Retrieved from: www.rcmp-grc.gc.ca/ccaps-spcca/capra-eng.htm.

Savery, J., & Duffy T. (1995). Problem-based learning: An instructional model and its constructivist framework. *Educational Technology, 35*(5), 31–38.

Savin-Baden, M. (2000). *Problem-based learning in higher education: Untold stories.* Buckingham: Society for Research into Higher Education and Open University Press.

Savin-Baden, M. (2003). *Facilitating Problem-based learning: Illuminating perspectives.* Buckingham: Society for Research into Higher Education and Open University Press.

Schmidt, H.G. (1983). Problem-based learning: rationale and description. *Medical Education, 8,* 59–66.

Schmidt, H., & Moust, J. (2000). Factors in small group tutorial learning: A review of research. In D. Evensen & C. Hmelo (Eds.), *Problem-based learning: A research perspective on learning interactions* (pp. 19–51). Mahwah, NJ: Lawrence Erlbaum.

Schmidt, H.G., van der Molen, H.T., te Winkel, W.W.R., & Wijnen, W.H.F.W. (2009). Constructivist, problem-based learning does work: A meta-analysis of curricular comparisons involving a single medical school. *Education Psychologist, 44*(4), 227–249.

Silén, C. (2006). The tutor's approach in base groups (PBL): A phenomenological approach. *Higher Education, 51*(3), 373–385.

Vygotsky, L.S. (1978). *Mind in society: The development of higher psychological processes.* Cambridge, MA: Harvard University Press.

Wilkerson, L. (1996). Tutors and small groups in problem-based learning: Lessons from the literature. *New Directions for Teaching & Learning, 68,* 23–22.

Further Resources

Maastricht University PBL site: www.unimaas.nl/pbl.

McMaster University Canada, where problem-based learning started: www-fhs.mcmaster.ca/mhsi/problem-.htm.

2

Designing Problems and Triggers in Different Media

Challenging All Students

Terry Barrett, Diane Cashman, and Sarah Moore

Introduction

Designing high-quality problems is a key success factor for problem-based learning (PBL) curricula (Gijselaers & Schmidt, 1990) as the problem is the starting point and the driving force for learning. The role of the problem-designer is to construct or select the presenting problem to be given to the students at the beginning of the learning process. It is then the students' role to define the kernel of the problem. As problem-based learning practitioners, we have benefited from much advice from the literature that tells us that quality problems should be:

- engaging and motivating;
- authentic, real-world, from professional and social life;
- ill-structured, open to multiple ideas/hypotheses, sustaining discussion;
- multidimensional with physical, cognitive, social, emotional, ethical, and other dimensions;
- a stimulus for the generation of a web of collaborative enquiry;
- challenging students to achieve learning outcomes, gain an understanding of key concepts, and acquire an ability to work on common practice problems;
- graduate attributes-focused, i.e. enhancing the development of transferable skills, e.g. teamwork, information literacy, critical thinking, and creative problem-solving.

  (Barrett, 2005; Barrows & Tamblyn, 1980; Conway & Little, 2000;
  Gijselaers, 2005; Jonassen & Hung, 2008; Margetson, 1997)

This chapter focuses on designing problems in different media in order to meet the criteria listed above and other criteria. We argue that it is important for curriculum designers to negotiate a range of important interrelationships. These interrelationships include the links between problems and challenges from practice and the real world, desired graduate attributes, key concepts, learning outcomes and choice, and variety of media in problem design. We strongly assert that, when designing problems, it is important to incorporate inputs from a range of stakeholders, including: lecturers, employers, workplace supervisors, education developers, education technologists, students, librarians, and information technologists. Together the stakeholders can negotiate the construction of effective problems for their PBL curricula (Azer, 2007).

Strategies for involving various stakeholders in problem design are discussed in Chapters 3, 4 and 7. The student voice can often be omitted from the problem design process. Therefore, it is vital to recognise that students and recent graduates have a particular role in bringing their understanding of the student experience, learning, and motivation to the design process and this issue is discussed further in Chapter 4.

Barrows defined problem-based learning as: "the learning that results from the process of working towards the resolution of a problem. The problem is encountered first in the learning process" (Barrows & Tamblyn, 1980, p. 10). A problem, understood traditionally, is something to be solved, e.g. working on the diagnosis and treatment of a patient presenting with specific symptoms and case history, or the investigation of a crime. However, in PBL, the term "problem" has a broader meaning. In this chapter, and throughout this volume, "problem" is the umbrella term for a range of problem types, including scenarios, dilemmas, and triggers. The word "trigger", in itself, is useful as it conjures up the notion of something that stimulates, motivates, and provokes learning.

So, in helping a team of stakeholders to design a "problem", it is important to encourage them to define the notion of "problem" in this broader way. A problem might be:

- a scenario;
- a story;
- a dilemma;
- a challenge;
- a trigger derived from any media; or
- a starting point for learning.

Its main focus could involve:

1. understanding a perplexing phenomenon;
2. working on a challenge, e.g. a design brief, creating a work of art;
3. finding a more effective, appealing or environmentally friendly way to do something;
4. learning more about a key concept through working with a trigger; or
5. producing a product for a client group.

These are all ways of learning and developing through working on a variety of problem types and this chapter explores how this learning and development can be achieved.

Chapter Overview

This chapter discusses:

- *why* it is important to design problems in different media;
- *what* kinds of alternative media you might consider using in designing and developing problems;
- *how* to design problems effectively, and what considerations need to be applied to different types of media.

In tackling these issues, we highlight three concepts that we think are helpful when thinking about designing PBL problems: "liminal spaces", "threshold concepts", and the notion of "hard fun". Inspired by these concepts, we provide examples of problems in different media in a variety of disciplines. We also provide a range of practical resources to help you in constructing problems for your curricula.

Illuminative Concepts for Understanding Problem Design

The three illuminative concepts for understanding problem design are:

1. the problem as a provoker of a liminal space;
2. the problem as a trigger for tackling threshold concepts; and
3. the problem as a stimulus for hard fun.

These concepts provide ways for thinking creatively and critically about problem design and they shed light on both theory and practice. This section will discuss each of these concepts in turn and a further section will give samples of problems inspired by these concepts and presented in different media. Recent qualitative research on how students talk about problem-based learning has clearly

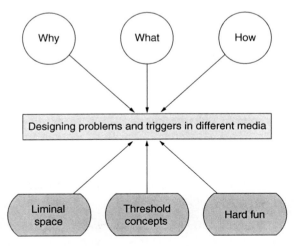

Figure 2.1 Chapter overview: Designing problems and triggers in different media.

identified the emergence of two of these illuminative concepts: the problem as a provoker of a liminal space and the problem as a stimulus for hard fun (Barrett, 2008). Other recent work on the increasingly popular notion of "threshold concepts" (Lucas & Madenovik, 2007; Meyer & Land, 2006) is also clearly relevant for PBL curricula. The notion of threshold concepts encourages us to think of the problem as a trigger for tackling vital concepts within particular disciplines.

The Problem as a Provoker of a Liminal Space

The theory of "liminality" tells us that, sometimes, particularly when we are learning new knowledge or competences, we cannot go directly from an old state to a new state. Rather, we need first to go to an intermediary state that is neither completely old nor completely new. Sometimes people need to locate themselves in liminal spaces in order to learn. By entering a sort of "transitory phase" we may be more likely to grow, to explore identities, to work through problems, and to be creative. Liminal spaces can become a place of transition, transformation, stagnation, or attempted regression. In a critical discourse analysis study of PBL students' talk in PBL tutorials, the students talked about the PBL problem as a provoker of a liminal space (Barrett, 2006, 2008).

Participants on PBL programmes talked about PBL problems as provokers of liminal spaces. These spaces can be described as bridges, doorways, or access points that link established ways of thinking and fresh ways of thinking

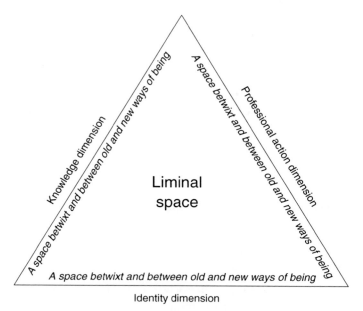

Figure 2.2 The problem as a provoker of a liminal space (Barrett, 2008, p. 149).

and move learners from satisfaction with current identities to a desire to explore other possible identities. Liminal spaces facilitate the transition from habitual professional action to new forms of professional action. This concept of liminality encourages us, as PBL practitioners, to design problems that provoke students to create and to learn in transitional spaces and to work on all three dimensions: knowledge, identity, and professional action.

The Problem as a Trigger for Tackling Threshold Concepts

Following on from understanding the problem as a provoker of a liminal space, one way for stimulating students to new levels of knowledge is to design problems focusing on threshold concepts. Threshold concepts are the difficult to understand, important concepts in a discipline; the concepts that, once you understand them, you are enabled to think and act in new ways. They are "akin to a portal opening up a new and previously inaccessible way of thinking about something. It represents a transformed way of understanding or viewing something without which the learner cannot progress" (Meyer & Land, 2006, p. 3). Threshold concepts are the conceptual gateways to the discipline and are considered to be transformative, irreversible, integrative, and troublesome (Meyer & Land, 2006). If problem-designers identify the threshold concepts within their disciplines and construct problems and triggers around these, they are much more likely to create problems from which students will learn in effective and challenging ways.

Examples of threshold concepts include depreciation in accounting, object-oriented programming in computer science, and the piezoelectric effect in ultrasound. What are the threshold concepts in your own discipline? What are your ideas for designing problems around these threshold concepts?

The Problem as a Stimulus for Hard Fun

When students talked about PBL, they often described the process as being both "hard" and "fun" at the same time (Barrett, 2009). The three dimensions of fun identified were:

1. laughter and joking;
2. freedom and creativity; and
3. playfulness.

The "hardness" of learning had three dimensions:

1. intense activity;
2. high difficulty level of problem; and
3. the transformation of changing beliefs and values.

This insight, derived from PBL students themselves, prompts us, as designers, to construct problems that are both hard and fun and to use different media to do this creatively.

Why Design Problems and Triggers in a Variety of Media?

In addition to meeting the quality criteria discussed earlier, there are a number of other reasons for designing problems and triggers in different media:

- Real-life problems present in different media.
- Variety and challenge are important in learning.
- Students have different preferred modes of communication and learning styles.
- Working in different media is an important element in developing creativity and multiple intelligences.
- Different modalities shape student learning.
- Problems can be worked through critically and creatively using different media.
- Many students are familiar with working and communicating in a range of technologies and media.
- Working effectively in different media is a key transferable skill for work.

Problems and challenges in real life present themselves in a range of media, e.g. a phone call, a discussion with a client, an email; thus, in a PBL curriculum, the presentation of problems to students should reflect this diversity. Variety and challenge are very important in PBL (Mauffette, Kandlbinder, & Soucisse, 2004). Students may become bored or under-stimulated if all or most of the problems are presented in the same format, e.g. written scenarios.

> People seem to concentrate best when the demands on them are greater than usual and they are able to give more than usual. If there is too little demand on them, people are bored. If there is too much for them to handle, they get anxious. Flow occurs in that delicate zone between boredom and anxiety.
>
> **(Csikszentmihalyi, 1986, in Goleman, 2006, pp. 91–92)**

Presenting problems in a variety of media and encouraging the students to work using different media is part of the process of making the problems more challenging than usual and encouraging students to move towards a state of flow. Problems can be designed to stretch students to develop new knowledge and skills. In this state of flow students are engaged in optimal performance.

It is useful to design problems in ways that recognise that students have different learning styles which include activists, pragmatists, theorists, and reflectors (Honey & Mumford, 2006). Traditional teaching focuses on the development of two forms of intelligence: verbal-linguistic and mathematical-deductive reasoning. Multiple intelligence theory (Gardner, 1993) encourages PBL practitioners to design problems that also develop other intelligences including interpersonal, intrapersonal, kinaesthetic, spatial, musical, and environmental intelligences. The cognitive theory of multimedia learning suggests that students are more likely to integrate prior knowledge and recall new learning by utilising the two sensory channels: auditory-verbal and visual-pictorial (Mayer, 2002). Finally, in a knowledge society, digital competences are crucial in workplaces. The global citizen is required to work with existing, new, and emerging technologies as part of their daily practice (Tapio, 2004).

What is the Range of Media that Can Be Used in Problem Design?

In PBL, the idea is that problems will be based on the experiences that students will meet in professional practice and experiences that challenge them to understand key concepts. The different media formats for problem design can be classified into three major categories:

- lived experiences;
- simulated experiences; and
- digitised experiences.

The range of problem formats is only limited by our creativity, which is limitless when you consider the creativity of a group of stakeholders collaborating together to design problems.

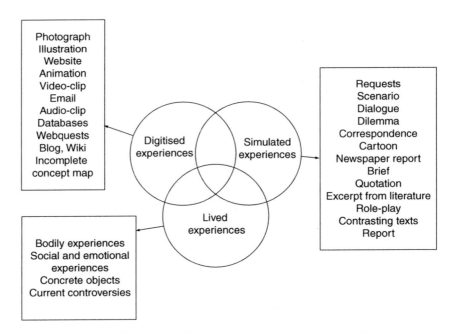

Figure 2.3 Using different media formats to present experiences to students.

Lived Experiences

Problems where students can manipulate and experience concrete objects can be very effective. For example, students who were doing a master's course in ultrasound, while working full-time as radiographers or midwives, were given a brown paper bag with Technology 1, the name of the module, printed on it. Inside the bag was a pair of children's trainers with flashing lights in the heels.

This trigger stimulated the students to think about the piezoelectric effect, a threshold concept which underpins the understanding of both how the light flashes on the trainer when a force is applied to it and how the physics of ultrasound works. If a student can explain this physics principle in both the trainer and in an ultrasound image, then they have really tackled this threshold concept. Being able to explain a threshold concept in two contrasting media can provoke deep levels of understanding.

Another way of designing problems is to use genuinely experiential, physical, bodily experiences as a trigger. For example, in Finland, a physiotherapy lecturer takes her students swimming in the ice-hole of a lake; they use the reaction of their own bodies to develop a comprehensive understanding of physiological reactions to cold. In engineering, a lecturer in engineering gets students to hold a brick at different distances from their bodies in order for them to develop a demonstrated understanding of levers.

Figure 2.4 Problem using a physical object (source: Marie Stanton et al., University College Dublin).

Simulated experiences

Giving students a brief from a client can be a way of getting them to see themselves in professional roles. First-year English Literature students were presented with the following problem:

Debating the Renaissance

The Globe Theatre in Southwark, London, is seeking a PR team to promote its activities, and you have been invited to pitch an idea for a promotional campaign based on an issue, character, idea or theme found in Shakespearean drama. The campaign must be based directly on a speech (or speeches), dialogue or scene from one of Shakespeare's plays and the excerpt must be, in your opinion, key to understanding the play as a whole. It must be suitable for an international (but English-speaking) audience of teenagers, and is intended to engage their interest in the theatrical culture of Renaissance London as well as in Shakespearean drama specifically. You can consider a variety of formats for your campaign, such as conventional drama, a storyboard, a cartoon, a website design, a blog, an advertisement or a networking site, but it must be based directly on the original language of the play, although you may depart creatively from it or adapt it to a new setting.

Danielle Clarke, University College Dublin
(Clarke, 2010, p.34)

It was hard work for students to expand their knowledge of Shakespeare and to explore themes that would be interesting and engaging for teenagers. It was also fun to play creatively with the interaction of their ideas and their choice of a combination of media. These are the types of problems that combine difficulty with fun – reflecting the "hard fun" phenomenon. In subsequent presentations the students demonstrated high levels of creativity and engagement with the literature. The range of media used in the presentations included posters, computer games, flyers, drama, and PowerPoint presentations.

A dialogue can be a very effective format. The following dialogue was designed for a first-year interprofessional module on collaborative learning for health professions.

Lunch-time Chat

JANE: I filled out my application form for college last night.

KEVIN: What did you put down?

JANE: Medicine.

KEVIN: What! You hate blood, you can't even watch Grey's Anatomy without getting sick!

JANE: Yah but my Dad says you make loads a money…

KEVIN: I thought running on to Rugby pitch rubbing some Rugby player with a sponge would be more your style?

JANE: No, no … I did think about radiography … medicine with no blood … but Mum says they are just well educated photographers…

KEVIN: That must make your Mum a well educated "bed maker" then…

JANE: Don't let the "Director of Nursing" hear you saying that or she'll never let you see her daughter again … see ya later…

KEVIN: Yah see ya…

Tara Cusack et al., University College Dublin

This problem was designed to provoke a liminal space for the students, between their current sense of the identity of health professionals and a more developed sense of identity. It gave them a space to work on their professional and personal identities and to learn more about the role and identities of other health professionals.

Digitised Experiences

Digitised problem formats include photographs, illustrations, websites, animations, video-clips, audio-clips, databases, webquests, blogs, wikis, and incomplete concept maps. A way of using digitised experiences is to reuse PBL problems that are open access, e.g. SONIC (Sonic Students On-line in Nursing Integrated Curricula). An example of SONIC is the following problem called "Peter", which is an online case scenario that allows students to view and interact with simulations of Peter's symptoms (www.uclan.ac.uk/health/schools/school_of_nursing/studying_in_school_of_nursing/sonic/scenarios/peter/peter.php).

Peter (www2.uclan.ac.uk/fachealth/sonic/scenarios/uclananim/wholebodysymptoms.html)

Peter Murphy is 76 years old; his wife died six months ago and he has no other family. He lives alone. Since becoming a widower he frequently visits his local pub for company, although he is not an alcoholic. The pub landlord raised the alarm after Mr Murphy had not been seen at the pub for three days. His GP was alerted and, on visiting his home, found him in a confused and neglected state. Mr Murphy was conscious, but it was apparent he was unaware of his surroundings and had clearly been incontinent. He continuously repeated that he did not feel well and was alternately verbally abusive and passive. He is admitted onto the hospital ward, where you are working as a student, with a provisional diagnosis of urinary tract infection and inability to cope.

On admission you notice Mr Murphy's skin was dry and flaky; he "looked" dehydrated and his dentures were "loose". An aphthous ulcer was present on his lower jaw, under his dentures, and his tongue was coated; his mouth was sore at the corners (angular cheilitis). The preliminary diagnosis remained that of urinary tract infection and confusion, but he was also described as a "social problem". Blood samples were taken for biochemical and haematological analysis. The need for findings was not regarded as urgent and the results were not available for two days. An eventual dietetic assessment revealed Mr Murphy weighed only 58 kg and had lost 11.7% of his usual body weight in the last six months. His height was 1.72 m and his estimated current calorie intake was 600 kCal per day.

A further problem about an elderly women, Doris, can be accessed from the SONIC project at: www.uclan.ac.uk/health/schools/school_of_nursing/ studying_in_school_of_nursing/sonic/scenarios/doris/doris.php. The accompanying DVD clip can be accessed at: http://breeze01.uclan.ac.uk/p71955463.

How Do You Develop Problems Effectively Using Different Media?

This section outlines a five-step approach to the practical design of problems in a variety of media. The strategy is based on the concept of reusable learning objects (Littlejohn, 2003) and is illustrated in Figure 2.5. We recommend undertaking a developmental process that involves starting with a brainstorming

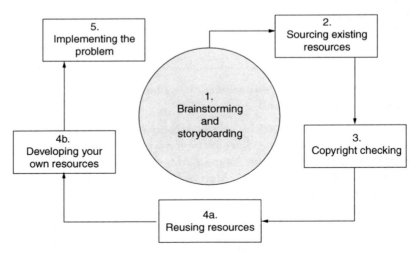

Figure 2.5 A five-step approach to developing problems in different media.

session with key stakeholders, detailing the problem on paper, sourcing and repurposing existing resources, reusing or developing your own media, and then implementing the problem in your curriculum.

Step 1: Brainstorming and Storyboarding

The first crucial stage in this strategy is the brainstorming and storyboarding session. By the end of this stage, you should have completed a detailed paper-based design of your problem and identified a range of factors that will need to be addressed in order to develop and implement the problem.

Brainstorming

Remember that, by involving a wide range of stakeholders in this stage of the process, idea generation can be richer, the problem can be contextualised more effectively, and, finally, implementation issues from a range of viewpoints can be highlighted (Azer, 2007). Once you have assembled your stakeholder group, the first step is to identify the learning outcomes clearly and the key concepts of the module or unit of study for which the problem is intended (Drummond-Young & Mohide, 2000; Hung, 2006).

Next, the team should begin to brainstorm ideas for problems. They should try to be as creative as possible at this stage, jotting down or drawing all suggestions on a shared learning environment, e.g. poster or whiteboard. At this point, try to mix and match ideas to come up with combined alternatives that were not already suggested and do not exclude anything. The group should then select which idea should be used and put other ideas aside for possible future use.

Storyboarding

The initial tendency for many designers will be to create the problem straight away. However, it is much better to flesh out ideas completely in the form of a storyboard. The storyboard should be a complete paper-based design that identifies all aspects of the problem development and implementation and helps you to address any issues that may be encountered. A storyboard can take many forms, but, inevitably, the final version will depend on the type of problem you intend to develop. You could include details suggested in the following template.

At this stage, for any type of storyboard, key decisions must be made on the format of the problem. Take, for example, a problem that is text-based and/or contains an image. Sketch down what you have visualised in your mind's eye.

If your problem relates to a bodily or a physical experience, write down what the students will be required to do. If your problem is an audio-clip, ask yourself questions such as "what sounds do you need to capture?" and "how will the students need to interact with the audio trigger?" If you intend to

Problem design template

Title of problem
Authors
Date
Module/unit
Learning outcomes and concepts/incidents
Problem presentation (exactly as it will be presented to students)
Media use
Problem overview
Problem implementation
Learning resources

Figure 2.6 Problem design template.

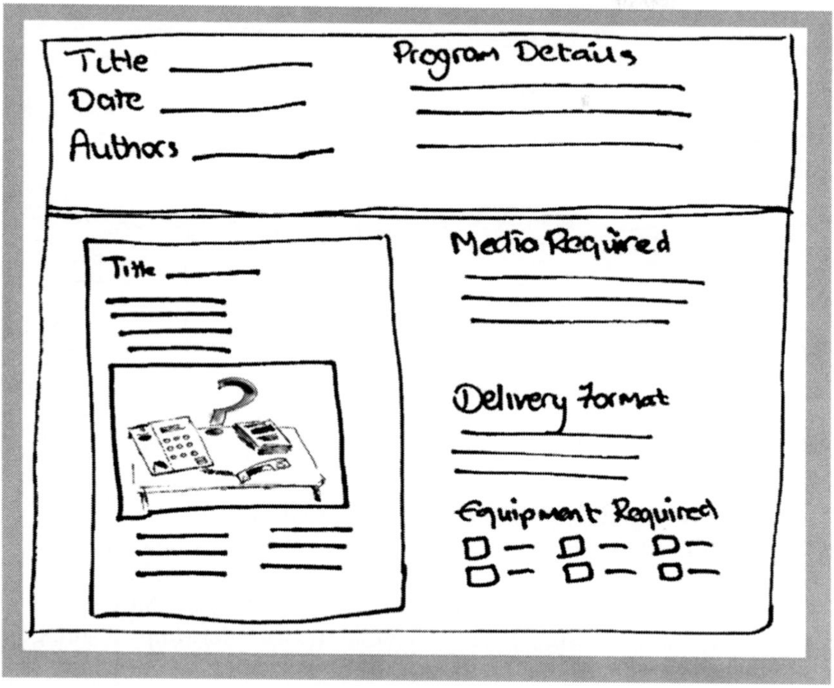

Figure 2.7 Storyboard example.

create a short video-clip, a storyboard will need to illustrate the flow of the key scenes. Can you identify what props, actors, or backgrounds you will require in order to complete the video? You should include details such as potential locations and specialist equipment required. Will you need a budget? Do you have technical support available from your institution?

Sketch the problem exactly as it will be presented to the students in the formats that you have chosen. This should be explicit enough to be clear to someone external to your design group. Key questions must be answered during storyboarding:

1. What is the rationale for the choice of media?
   Choices for the inclusion or exclusion of media must be rationalised. Can you explain why a certain format is chosen over another? Base your decisions on learning outcomes. Remember, when designing problems in different media, it is often the case that "less is more".
2. What supports can you avail yourself of to design, create, and use this problem?
   Keep in mind how feasible it will be to create your problem within your timeframe, budget, and institutional supports.

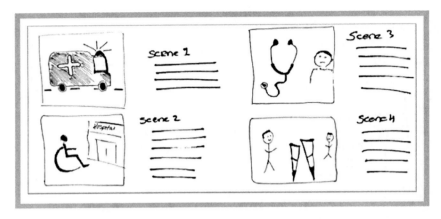

Figure 2.8 Video storyboard example.

3. How will this type of trigger be delivered to students?
   Will the trigger be presented to the students as a whole or will a
   progressive-disclosure approach be adopted, with the students being
   presented with parts of the problem in stages? What are the logistical
   and operational issues that need to be addressed before implementing
   the problem?

The key point of making a storyboard is to identify how the problem links in
with the learning outcomes, how will it be presented to students, and how you
have addressed any logistical issues. Finally, bear in mind that the illustrations
in a storyboard can be simple; they are not meant to be masterpieces! Use
stick men, if you must, as you only need a rough representation of the
problem at this stage.

Step 2: Sourcing Existing Resources

By the time you have completed your storyboard, you should have a very clear
idea of the resources you require for your trigger. You should try, as far as
possible, to locate existing resources, rather than investing in the development
of new materials – keep in mind that multimedia development, in particular,
can be a time-consuming task. Reusing or repurposing existing content could
save you large amounts of time and effort.

Considerable advances in technology have supported the sharing of digital
resources via social networking sites and repositories. Development in the
field of Open Access has enabled a range of resources to be accessed easily
and used without the constraint of passwords or subscription costs.
Additionally, you may have access to your institutional repository and,
possibly, your colleagues' personal collections of resources, which may also be
a valuable source of materials that you can reuse. Figure 2.9 lists a range of
sources that can help you to get started in your researching of reusable objects.

Title	URL	Description
Creative Commons	http://creativecommons.org	Search for reusable resources under a creative commons licence
Wiki Commons	http://commons.wikimedia.org	Media repository
MERLOT – Multimedia Educational Resource for Learning and Online Teaching	www.merlot.org	Teaching and learning repository
YouTube – Video broadcasting website	www.youtube.com	Popular video sharing and broadcasting website
MIT Open Courseware	http://ocw.mit.edu/OcwWeb/web/home/home/index.htm	Massachusetts Institute of Technology online lecture notes, exams and videos
Flickr – Online photo-sharing website	www.flickr.com	Popular photograph-sharing website
OpenDOAR – OpenAccess Repository Directory	www.opendoar.org	This site contains listings for Open Access repositories
PBL Clearing-house	https://chico.nss.udel.edu/Pbl	Delaware University Problem-based Learning Clearinghouse. This website provides a range problem examples

Figure 2.9 List of open-access resources.

Step 3: Copyright Checking

Copyright protects the intellectual rights of a variety of works including creative and artistic works. With the wide availability of easily accessed material on the Internet there is a common misperception that this content can be reused without due acknowledgement or permissions granted by the original author. The principles of plagiarism apply in this regard and it is not acceptable to take credit for other people's work. Copyright checking need not be an arduous and daunting task as simple strategies can enable you to use third-party resources and protect the intellectual property of others. Here

are some simple steps that you should undertake before reusing any
third-party material.

1. Look for licences at the origin of the resource that give permission
   statements, e.g. Creative Commons Licences: http://creativecom-
   mons.org.
2. If you cannot find a licence or permission statement, seek written
   permission before use. Alternatively, you could choose another
   resource that clearly states permissions for use.
3. When reusing the resource, always cite the author and source.
4. If in doubt, consult with your institutional copyright officer for further advice.

Step 4a: Reusing Resources

If you have found existing resources and ensured that you have copyright
clearance for reuse, the next stage is to incorporate the resource into a usable
format that can be delivered to your students.

Step 4b: Developing Your Own Resources

If you have been unsuccessful in locating a previously developed resource,
you will have to consider creating your own resources at this stage. You have
a range of options, from traditional methods that rely on "pen and paper" and
other common art materials, to readily available objects, or using digital
media. Again, this is dependent on the needs identified in your storyboard.

Step 5: Implementing Your Problem

After you have worked out the practical and logistical issues, the problem can
be implemented. You should evaluate the problem in order to continuously
develop the PBL initiative.

Conclusion

Designing high-quality problems is hard, interesting, intellectually stimulating,
important, creative work. We argue strongly for involving a range of
stakeholders in problem design. The next chapter explores working with
clinicians and/or other professionals in developing problems. Different
stakeholder perspectives play a key role in the development of problems that
provide the variety that is vital to engaging students in rich learning
environments. Designing problems in different media will both challenge all
students and increase the repertoire of problem-design formats for
programme teams. Three particular problem formats, namely, video-based
problem components, role-plays, and compare-and-contrast problems are
explored in detail in Chapter 6.

References

Azer, A.S. (2007). Twelve tips for creating trigger images for problem-based learning cases. *Medical Teacher, 29*(2–3), 93–97.

Barrett, T. (2006). The problem as a space betwixt and between old and new ways of knowing. In E. Poikela & A. Raija Nummenmaa (Eds.), *Understanding problem-based learning* (pp. 33–50). Tampere: Tampere University Press.

Barrett, T. (2005). Understanding problem-based learning. In T. Barrett, I. Mac Labhainn, & H. Fallon (Eds.), *Handbook of enquiry and problem-based learning: Irish case studies and international perspectives* (pp. 13–25). Galway: CELT, National University of Ireland and All Ireland Society for Higher Education. Retrieved from: www.nuigalway.ie/celt/pblbook/chapter2.

Barrett, T. (2008). *Students' talk about problem-based learning in liminal spaces.* Unpublished doctorate thesis, Coventry University.

Barrett, T. (2009, June). Invited paper: What can we learn about learning from how problem-based learning students talked about it in PBL tutorials? In G. O'Grady (Ed.), *The 2nd International PBL Symposium proceedings: What are we learning about learning?* (pp. 96–111). Singapore: Republic Polytechnic, Centre for Education.

Barrows, H., & Tamblyn, R. (1980). *Problem-based learning: An approach to medical education.* New York: Springer.

Conway, J., & Little, P. (2000). From practice to theory: Reconceptualising curriculum development for problem-based learning. In O.S. Tan, P. Little, S.Y. Lin, & J. Conway (Eds.), *Problem-based learning. Educational innovations across disciplines: A collection of selected papers* (pp. 169–179). Singapore: Temasek Centre for Problem-based Learning. Retrieved from: http://pbl.tp.edu.sg/Curriculum%20Planning/Articles/JaneConwayPennyLittle.pdf.

Clarke, D. (2010). Engaging 500 first year students of English through enquiry-based learning. In T. Barrett & D. Cashman, *A practitioner's guide to enquiry and problem-based learning: Case studies from University College Dublin*, (pp. 32–35). Dublin: UCD Teaching and Learning.

Drummond-Young, M., & Mohide, A.E. (2000). Developing problems for use in problem-based learning. In E. Rideout (Ed.), *Transforming nursing education through problem-based learning* (pp. 165–191). Mississauga, ONT: Jones & Bartlett.

Gardner, H. (1993). *Frames of mind: The theory of multiple intelligences.* London: Fontana.

Gijselaers, W. (2005, June). *Putting minds at work.* Keynote paper presented at the International Conference on Problem-based Learning, PBL in Context: Bridging Work and Education, Lhati, Finland.

Gijselaers, W., & Schmidt, H. (1990). Towards a causal model of student learning within the context of problem-based curriculum. In Z. Nooman, H. Schmidt, & E. Ezzat (Eds.), *Innovation in medical education: An evaluation of its present status* (pp. 95–114). New York: Springer.

Goleman, D. (2006). *Emotional intelligence: Why it can matter more than IQ.* New York: Bantam Books.

Honey, P., & Mumford, A. (2006). *The learning style helper's guide.* Maidenhead: Peter Honey.

Hung, W. (2006). The 3C3R model: A conceptual framework for designing problems in PBL. *The Interdisciplinary Journal of Problem-based Learning, 1*(1), 55–77.

Jonassen, D., & Hung, W. (2008). All problems are not equal: Implications for problem-based learning. *The Interdisciplinary Journal of Problem-based Learning, 2*(2), 6–28.

Littlejohn, A. (Ed.). (2003). *Reusing online resources: A sustainable approach.* London: Kogan Page.

Lucas, U., & Madenovik, R. (2007). The potential of threshold concepts: An emerging framework for educational research and practice. *London Review of Education, 5*(3), 237–248.

Margetson, D. (1997, September). *Wholeness and educative learning: The question of problems in changing to problem-based learning.* Keynote paper presented at the International Conference on Problem-Based Learning, Changing to PBL. Uxbridge, London.

Mauffette, Y., Kandlbinder, P., & Soucisse, A. (2004). The problem in problem-based learning is the problems: But do they motivate students? In M. Savin-Baden & K. Wilkie (Eds.), *Challenging research into problem-based learning* (pp. 11–25). Buckingham: Open University Press.

Mayer, E.R. (2002). Cognitive theory and the design of multimedia instruction: An example of the two-way street between cognition and instruction. *New Directions for Teaching & Learning, 89*(Spring), 55–71.

Meyer, J.H.F., & Land, R. (2006). *Overcoming barriers to student understanding: Threshold concepts and troublesome knowledge.* New York: Routledge.

Sonic Students On-line in Nursing Integrated Curricula. Retrieved from: www.uclan.ac.uk/health/schools/school_of_nursing/studying_in_school_of_nursing/sonic/index.php.

Tapio, S. (2004). *Key competencies for lifelong learning: A European reference framework.* Brussels: Directorate General for Education and Culture, European Commission.

3

Designing Authentic PBL Problems in Multidisciplinary Groups

Marie Stanton and Majella McCaffrey

Introduction

This chapter explores the question:

> How can we involve academics and workplace experts in the design of authentic PBL problems?

We provide a practice example involving a range of stakeholders. We hope that you find this chapter informative and helpful for constructing problems in your own PBL contexts.

Chapter Overview

This chapter will:

- discuss the literature related to effective problem design that guided our problem design strategies;
- provide guidelines on how to organise a multidisciplinary problem design day, based on one used by the authors, to optimise authenticity;
- link theory and practice of problem design by discussing the authors' experience of designing and using problems in a PBL programme designed for radiographers and midwives studying ultrasound at master's level.

Designing Authentic, Ill-structured, Engaging Problems

Watson (2004, p. 188) provides a useful definition of PBL as follows: "At its most fundamental, PBL is characterised by the use of real world problems as a context for students to learn critical thinking skills and problem solving skills and to acquire knowledge of the essential concepts of the course." Critical thinking skills involve the ability to interpret, analyse, and evaluate information and ideas, and develop independent opinions and judgements based on sound evidence and reasoning (Facione, 1990).

This section of the chapter considers the key features that make problems effective in developing specialist ultrasound knowledge and generic graduate attributes including team working and critical thinking skills. Features identified in the literature, which contribute to effective PBL problems, are discussed in the context of a Master's of Science (MSc) PBL programme in clinical ultrasound. In particular, the following aspects of problem design are discussed in turn: authenticity, learning issues generation, activation of prior knowledge, complexity, optimal structure, quality of self-directed learning, and problem cues.

What Do We Mean By Authenticity?

Programmes which prepare students for a profession should construct problems that are true to the students' future work. Van Berkel and Schmidt (2000) describe problem-based learning as being contextually valid because the problems are taken from professional practice and students acquire knowledge organised around these triggers. Abrandt, Dahlgren, and Oberg (2001, p. 263) discuss the intention of problems or scenarios which get the students to associate the scenarios with real-life situations; in their opinion, the scenarios "provide a meaningful context for the concepts and principles that relate to future professional work". In ultrasound education, optimising the authenticity of the problems includes making the problems realistic, accurate, and consistent with current practice. Our students are already in clinical practice and will, therefore, notice quickly if problems do not meet these criteria. Multidisciplinary design days were planned to make our problems as authentic as possible. This innovative approach will be described and discussed in the next section of this chapter.

What Factors Influence the Learning Issues Generated by the Students?

By the end of the first group meeting, the students are expected to generate learning issues that reflect what they feel they need to learn in order to "solve" the problem. Dolmans, Gijselaers, Schmidt, and van der Meer (1993) recommend evaluating problems according to their effectiveness in generating appropriate learning issues. Kjellgren, Ahlner, Dahlgren, and Haglund (1993, p. 23) go so far as to define a problem as "constituted by the questions, that can be asked about a situation or a concept, of which one or more are particularly relevant to one's education". Dolmans, Snellen-Balendong, Wolfhagen, and van der Vleuten (1997) suggest that effective problems stimulate self-directed learning by encouraging students to generate learning issues and conduct literature searches.

The process of developing problems for the MSc ultrasound programme included predicting the learning issues the students would create. The design team evaluated the problems to ensure that appropriate cues were included. In general, the student-generated learning issues matched those predicted by the staff. Dolmans et al. (1997) consider this match to be a sign of an effective problem. In our programme, insisting that students allocate sufficient time for a thorough discussion of the problem cues and suggesting that learning issues be phrased as questions seemed to help the students refine their learning issues. If the students did not get all of the learning issues, the facilitators used their own judgement and either asked the students to reconsider their learning issues with reference to the problem or decided that the students were likely to come across the missing issues as they did their individual study on the existing issues. Intervening too regularly to suggest or amend learning issues could lead to students making less effort to discuss the problem and generate their own learning issues.

How Can Problems Be Designed to Activate Prior Knowledge?

Problems should be designed to activate prior knowledge in order to facilitate the comprehension of new knowledge (Dolmans et al., 1993; Jacobs, Dolmans, Wolfhagen, & Scherpbier, 2003). Problem designers must obtain an accurate knowledge of the students' previous learning in order to include appropriate cues which will help students recognise the relevant previous knowledge that they possess from diverse sources including formal learning, experiential learning, and life experience. As postgraduate students, with at least one year of clinical experience, our students have relevant prior knowledge to draw on. For example, students have prior knowledge of general anatomy, physiology, and pathology. Problems must activate this knowledge in order to develop new knowledge related to the representation and interpretation of anatomy, physiology, and pathology in an ultrasound image.

How Complex Should Problems Be?

Abrandt et al. (2001) investigated problems in terms of the structure and content of the questions that the problems evoked, and concluded that complexity is an important feature of a well-functioning scenario. Within our context, problems could include a range of issues which reflect the complexity of clinical practice, for example, patient history, ultrasound images, protocols, technology, management, communication, infection control, and medico-legal issues. Clinicians do not deal with one issue at a time. However, care must also be taken to avoid making problems overly complex, as noted by Jonassen (2000), a very complex problem, with too many components, can over-burden the working memory and make it impossible to solve. Designers of problems must resist the temptation to "cover" too much by including too many issues in a single problem. The evaluation and refinement of problems should include an assessment of how the module or programme outcomes are addressed across a range of problems. This assessment reduces the temptation to include too many issues in any one problem.

The use of resource sessions following the completion of a problem also lessens the fear inherent in reducing "coverage". In our programme, resource sessions typically involve a clinical expert interacting with the students. The focus is on giving students information that is not readily available to them in textbooks, in particular, on viewing normal and abnormal ultrasound images and having an opportunity to discuss these images and other aspects of practice with a clinical expert.

Overly simple problems are easily solved without students engaging in an in-depth discussion. An overly simple problem will not stimulate student learning because it is not challenging enough and is not well linked to "real life" (Jacobs et al., 2003). Consequently, the students' learning issues, their self-directed learning, and the depth of their discussion in the feedback group meeting are all compromised.

Abrandt et al. (2001) studied problems in relation to the structure and content of the questions that the problems evoked; their observation that a single-line provocative statement functioned very well seemed to contradict their analyses of other problems which had suggested that complexity is an important aspect in problem design. They interpreted the success of this simply presented problem as follows: problems that contain a provocative statement or evoke emotions also act as powerful triggers.

We introduced provocative statements into a number of our problems. For example, although ultrasound of the thyroid is a very common examination in general ultrasound departments, the students were presented with a quotation from an interview with an endocrinologist in which it was suggested that ultrasound should rarely be used for examining the thyroid. This provocative statement motivated students to defend ultrasound, to investigate its advantages and disadvantages in comparison with other imaging technologies, and provoked a good depth of discussion and reconsideration of student perspectives on a number of issues. This simply presented, provocative statement contained a range of complexities that students identified and teased out for themselves as part of their PBL learning process.

How Structured Should Problems Be?

Biggs (2003, p. 234) differentiates three structures which may be found in problems. First, an overly tight structure which provides all the necessary information to solve the problem. He suggests that this type of structure cannot be considered truly PBL. A second type of structure includes problems that provide some facts and students have to find the remaining facts. This structure, referred to as BIG learning, encourages students to go beyond the information given. The final structure type is one in which problems are open or ill-defined, that is, they present no data and require that students research the case themselves. In the third problem structure, referred to as WIG learning, students work without being given any information. Although the PBL literature often advocates ill-structured problems that represent the reality of professional working contexts, the level of structure needs to be considered carefully. In a study by Jacobs et al. (2003), students described some problems as too ill-structured, that is, they could be solved or addressed in too many ways. The same study criticised problems that were too structured as they often contain one simple solution, which could be found through the application of a limited number of predictable and prescriptive strategies.

Dolmans et al. (1997) state that effective problems integrate basic science knowledge with clinical knowledge. In ultrasound education, problems are designed to integrate basic sciences, such as anatomy, physiology, pathology, and physics, with the clinical practice of ultrasound. Many scenarios trigger students to consider the theory and research underlying everyday practice in clinical ultrasound departments. These scenarios encourage students to question traditional techniques and seek evidence-based practices.

Jacobs et al. (2003) suggest that the concepts of complexity and structuredness should be considered together, and discuss the need to optimise levels of complexity and structuredness, for example, if a problem is too complex or too ill-structured it is difficult for students to activate prior knowledge. A high degree of complexity makes it difficult for students to engage in active discussion and this, in turn, limits the development of useful learning issues. Equally, if problems are too simple or too well-structured, the students will not be sufficiently challenged to engage in active discussion and, again, useful learning issues will be compromised. The aim of our problem design days was to design problems which accurately reflected clinical practice. Inherently real-life clinical scenarios are at the appropriate level of complexity and structuredness for our programme aims.

What Influences Self-Directed Learning (SDL)?

Gijselaers and Schmidt (1990) found that the quality of problems has a major influence on the time spent on self-study. Van Berkel and Schmidt (2000) investigated the extent to which problems encouraged SDL activities and found that the quality of problems influenced academic achievement and intrinsic interest. Jacobs et al. (2003) also concluded that, in PBL, the quality of student learning activities depends greatly on the quality of the problems. Feedback from our facilitators suggests that the best problems produced in-depth discussion, appropriate learning issues, evidence of conscientious efforts on the students' part to understand the issues needed to "solve" the problem, and consideration of alternative approaches. In our experience, information literacy is a key determinant of the students' success at SDL. Our librarians provide multiple information literacy resource sessions and individual access to a librarian with specialist knowledge of health sciences resources. See Chapter 10 for strategies for embedding information literacy in PBL initiatives.

How is Group Discussion Stimulated?

A number of studies highlight that the stimulation of group discussion is a measure of the effectiveness of a particular problem (Gijselaers & Schmidt,

1990; Van Berkel & Schmidt, 2000). Dolmans et al. (1997) emphasise the importance of cues in starting the discussion and in stimulating the students to elaborate. Both Dolmans et al. (1997) and van den Hurk, Wolfhagen, Dolmans, and van der Vleuten (1999) suggest that effective problems stimulate interest in the subject matter because they sustain discussion and encourage consideration of alternatives. In our programme, the problems that did not stimulate a lively discussion tended to be those that the students had the least prior knowledge of. This finding underscores the need to design problems carefully, that is, to link the students' prior knowledge by using cues in order to guide them to new knowledge. If students do not have any prior knowledge of a particular topic, we need to ask ourselves whether this topic should be on the curriculum as, perhaps, the topic is outdated or very rarely practised in the clinical environment. The inclusion of clinicians in our problem design process minimised the risk of incorporating inappropriate issues in our problems.

The concepts illuminated in this section include some of the predominant views in the literature related to the criteria that can be used to evaluate problems designed for PBL programmes. These criteria are useful considerations in the planning stages of problem design. These criteria can also be used retrospectively after the facilitators and students have experienced a problem and have provided feedback on its quality.

The next section adds to the literature on problem design by presenting a method of optimising problems prior to using them with students. It is based on the authors' experience of designing problems for an MSc programme in clinical ultrasound.

Guidelines for Facilitating Problem Design Days with a Range of Stakeholders

In our curriculum design process, a key strategy was to invite a multidisciplinary group of stakeholders to write authentic and challenging triggers to stimulate student learning. The participants in the multidisciplinary group included clinical specialist radiographers, clinical midwife specialists, lecturers in ultrasound, librarians, and an educational developer with a specialism in PBL. The clinicians were asked to bring ultrasound problems or cases with them. The aim of the problem design days was to use the skills of the participants to develop the clinical cases to direct student learning towards particular programme outcomes. These outcomes included developing specific ultrasound knowledge and clinical competence, together with more generic outcomes related to developing the students' team working, higher-order thinking skills, and information literacy.

The main purpose of this chapter is to use the authors' experiences and evaluation of problem design days for a PBL MSc-level programme in ultrasound to develop guidelines which could be transferred to other contexts. This section outlines 13 guidelines which could be applied or adapted to your PBL context.

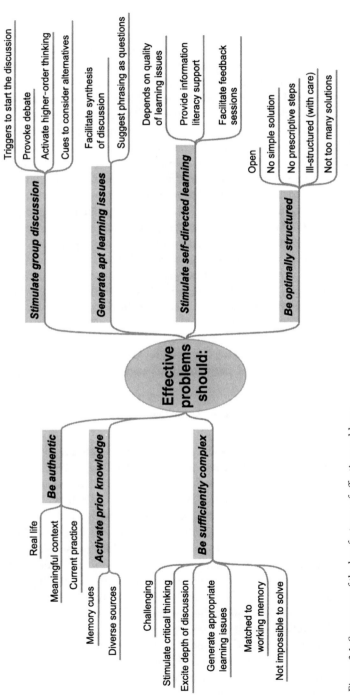

Figure 3.1 Summary of the key features of effective problems.

Identify the Briefs and Elements Required for the Problems in Your Programme

It is important to consider both the knowledge acquisition and the types of learning that your problems should encourage. For example, this could include using information literacy skills to develop multidisciplinary knowledge which is well linked to the appropriate workplace. The programme designers should agree on the key issues to be addressed in the problems and the discussion should include aligning the cues and desired learning issues to the objectives or graduate attributes of the PBL programme. In the MSc's ultrasound programme, we wanted the problems to motivate a range of knowledge and skills in our graduates, including ultrasound-specific knowledge and clinical skills and generic objectives such as information literacy, team working, and critical thinking. It is important to send this information to the participants, in advance, as part of the preparation pack.

Identify the People Within and Outside Your Organisation Who Can Contribute to Designing Problems with the Required Elements

You should consider lecturers in the relevant disciplines, workplace experts, librarians, students, educational developers with PBL expertise, and graduates. The use of a multidisciplinary team provides a variety of perspectives on what should be included in each problem and a better prediction of how students will respond to them. For example, in designing ultrasound problems, the multiple disciplines represented in our participants meant that advice was provided on many relevant aspects of current ultrasound practice including indications for ultrasound, current protocols, typical ultrasound appearances of normal and abnormal anatomy, communication skills, ultrasound physics, infection control, and medico-legal issues. Feedback from our focus group participants was unequivocally positive regarding the effectiveness of the multidisciplinary teams employed. The following are three typical comments from these participants:

"Very useful as non-subject experts could stand back and see other issues."

"Reassuring to hear how PBL has worked in veterinary education."

"Great insight for librarians into the needs of the student."

Construct a Preparation Pack

You might consider including a timetable for the day, appropriate introductory articles, useful websites, sample problems, programme summary, and travel instructions. At our problem design days, most of the participants considered the items listed above to be very useful, however, one participant felt that some of this material was too abstract and suggested that we add a two-page summary of PBL, customised to the ultrasound context, which we will do for future problem design days.

Set the Tone

One way to set the tone for the day is to have a welcoming reception; this provides an opportunity for the local and visiting participants to get to know each other and aids in developing a friendly, relaxed atmosphere, which is conducive to problem design. Many of our participants stated that, initially, they were very apprehensive about presenting the problems they had brought, but they became more relaxed and open due to the way that the day was structured.

Provide a Keynote Address

A keynote address by a senior member of the academic staff can convey how important the university considers the input of clinicians to problem writing. Our Vice Principal for Teaching and Learning, who had experience of PBL in veterinary medicine, agreed to deliver this address; he spoke about the rationale for using PBL and the performance of veterinary students in PBL modules. This demonstrated to the participants that PBL had been used for a significant length of time, in a high-profile programme, and that senior university staff had a high opinion of its effectiveness. During focus group discussions, the participants stated that hearing how PBL worked in veterinary medicine helped them to believe in the PBL process.

Describe the Context

It is important to present participants with an overview of the curriculum, particularly if it is a new programme. Presenting an overview of the curriculum provided our participants with an opportunity to understand the purpose of the problems and how they linked with other learning and assessment strategies. Participants used this session to voice their opinions regarding the structure of the course. At the time, this session was uncomfortable for us as some opinions were strongly against PBL. However, feedback during the focus groups showed that opinions regarding PBL had shifted to being unequivocally positive. This change in opinion was an unexpected benefit of our problem design days.

Explain the Key Characteristics of PBL Problems

Prior to developing problems, participants need to be informed of the characteristics of effective problems and the variety of approaches which can be used. An educational developer with extensive experience of PBL presented a comprehensive outline of these characteristics and approaches to our participants and a lecturer in ultrasound presented some problems that were being developed by the course team. The participants created a wide variety of problem types, the majority of which fulfilled the criteria for effective problems that were summarised in Figure 3.1. The creation of diverse problem types suggests that this strategy was effective.

Select Small Multidisciplinary Groups

The groups were multidisciplinary with five to six participants – typically, three clinicians and two to three other staff from a variety of academic backgrounds. The use of small groups helped to generate an intimate atmosphere for the exchange of knowledge and opinions. The participants stated that the small groups helped them to be open and communicative.

Manage the Groups

It is important to appoint a group facilitator who will make sure that everyone is respected and that each clinician has an opportunity to present at least one problem. All participants should be invited to contribute to each problem designed. In our case, two ultrasound lecturers, who were members of the curriculum design team, facilitated the two groups. Each group summarised their problems on a template. The template included sections on how the problem is presented to students, how the students' performance will be judged, learning resources the students may need, the expected learning issues, and advice for the facilitator. In addition, it is useful to keep a record of the location of any electronic data relevant to the problem or any missing data, which needs to be added during editing.

Provide an Opportunity for Small-Group Feedback

Small-group feedback can highlight issues which can be used to improve future problem design days and can also increase understanding between academics and clinicians. If you plan to record these sessions and use the data for development and/or publication purposes you must obtain permission from the participants.

Provide an Opportunity for Whole-Group Feedback

Bringing the small groups back into a larger group provides an opportunity for viewing the types of problems developed within the smaller groups. This session can facilitate the sharing of a variety of approaches to designing problems. In our session, a contrast in the approach of the two groups became apparent. Although one group produced more problems, but in less depth than the other group, we valued both approaches, as each group produced problems that we could complete and use.

Select and Refine the Problems

The course team needs to review the proposed problems and select a range which will trigger authentic learning and will match the module and programme aims and outcomes. Problem templates must be refined and completed, for example, contact participants to supply any outstanding material or information. Templates that are clearly written will guide the facilitators and ensure that each student group gets similar learning opportunities for each problem.

	Problem name	**Please evaluate this problem with reference to its impact on your learning**
1.		
2.		
3.		
4.		

MSc Ultrasound: Problem evaluation by students

Module _____ **Date** _____

Do you agree with the problems used to motivate learning in this module? _____ If you answered no please state:

1. Which problems you disagree with and why

2. What alternative problems you feel should be included

Figure 3.2 Problem evaluation template.

Evaluate and Publish

It is important to evaluate your problem design day and publish recommendations to develop this strategy further. Following the PBL problem design day, the curriculum design team worked on the problems in order to collect any outstanding information or artefacts. The team also evaluated the draft problem templates with particular consideration given to authenticity, complexity, structure, students' prior knowledge, and the links between the cues given in the problem to provoke discussion and the likely learning issues.

At the end of each semester, the students evaluated the problems and the feedback was generally very positive. The template that we designed for the evaluation of problems is presented in Figure 3.2.

The following figure summarises the organisation of a multidisciplinary problem design day.

Before the day
- Identify briefs and elements for problems
- Identify and invite contributors
- Construct a preparation pack and send it to participants

During the day
- Set the tone
- Provide a keynote address
- Describe the context
- Explain the requirements for designing quality problems in different formats
- Construct small multidisciplinary groups
- Manage the groups
- Seek small-group feedback
- Summarise the outcomes and experience with the whole group

After the day
- Select and refine the problems
- Evaluate the problems against the programme or module outcomes
- Evaluate the problem design day
- Use the problems
- Document learning issues generated by the students and facilitators feedback
- At the end of the semester ask the students to evaluate each problem
- Modify any problems you will reuse
- Organise further problem design days for your next programme

Figure 3.3 Organisation of a multidisciplinary problem design day.

Conclusion

We created authentic problems through our multidisciplinary problem design days. Evaluations of the problems by the students and facilitators were generally very positive and some unexpected benefits were also realised. For example, the opinions of PBL sceptics were transformed and some of these former sceptics became very supportive advocates of PBL in the clinical context and some of the participants volunteered to offer resource sessions in their areas of expertise to the new programme. All of the participants had an increased understanding of the students' needs and the two problem design days were very useful as a public relations exercise.

There is great emphasis on evidence-based practice (EBP) in healthcare today. In clinical practice, the foundation for such EBP must be laid during academic programmes in order for it to be more than a catchphrase (Distler, 2007). Well-designed PBL problems have the potential to develop the students' core knowledge and their ability to learn and think critically, thus preparing them for lifelong learning. In healthcare, this critical thinking enhances the graduates' ability to offer high-level clinical services to their patients.

This chapter discussed a multi-stakeholder approach to problem design. The next chapter focuses on students as key stakeholders in PBL initiatives and explores how students can take on an expanded role in designing, implementing, and evaluating PBL in your context.

References

Abrandt Dahlgren, M., & Oberg, G. (2001). Questioning to learn and learning to question: Structure and function of problem-based learning scenarios in environmental science education. *Higher Education, 41*, 263–282.

Biggs, J. (2003). *Teaching for quality learning at university* (2nd ed.). Berkshire: Society for Research into Higher Education and Open University Press.

Distler, J.W. (2007). Critical thinking and clinical competence: Results of the implementation of student-centred teaching strategies in an advanced practice nurse curriculum. *Nurse Education in Practice, 7*, 53–59.

Dolmans, D.H., Gijselaers, W.H., Schmidt, H.G., & van der Meer, S.B. (1993). Problem effectiveness in a course using problem-based learning. *Academic Medicine, 68*(3), 207–213.

Dolmans, D.H., Snellen-Balendong, H., Wolfhagen, I., & van der Vleuten, C. (1997). Seven principles of effective case design for a problem-based curriculum. *Medical Teacher, 19*(3), 185–189.

Facione, P.A. (1990). *Critical thinking: A statement of expert consensus for purposes of educational assessment and instruction "the Delphi Report"*. Millbrae, CA: California Academic Press.

Gijselaers, W.H., & Schmidt, H.G. (1990). Development and evaluation of a causal model of problem-based learning. In Z.H. Nooman, H.G. Schmidt, & E.S. Ezzat (Eds.), *Innovation in medical education: An evaluation of its present status* (pp. 95–113). New York: Springer Publishing Company.

Jacobs, A.E., Dolmans, D.H., Wolfhagen, I.H., & Scherpbier, A.J. (2003). Validation of a short questionnaire to assess the degree of complexity and structuredness of PBL problems. *Medical Education, 37*, 1001–1007.

Jonassen, D.H. (2000). Toward a design theory of problem solving. *Educational Technology Research & Development, 48*(4), 63–85.

Kjellgren, K., Ahlner, J., Dahlgren, L.O., & Haglund, L. (Eds.). (1993). *Problem-based learning: Experiences from the Faculty of Health Sciences*. Lund: Studentlitteratur.

Van Berkel, H.J., & Schmidt, H.G. (2000). Motivation to commit oneself as a determinant of achievement in problem-based learning. *Higher Education, 40*, 231–242.

van den Hurk, M.M., Wolfhagen, I.H., Dolmans, D.H., & van der Vleuten, C.P. (1999). Student-generated learning issues: A guide for individual study? *Education for Health, 12*(2), 213–221.

Watson, G. (2004). Integrating problem-based learning and technology in education. In O.S. Tan (Ed.), *Enhancing thinking through problem-based learning approaches* (pp. 187–201). Singapore: Thompson.

Further Resources

Hung, W. (2009). The 9-step problem design process for problem-based learning: Application of the 3C3R model. *Educational Research Review, 4*, 118–141.

4

Students as Essential Partners

Karen O'Rourke, Louise Goldring, and Marcia Ody

Introduction

This chapter explores the question:

> How can we work with students as essential partners to support the development of PBL curricula and make connections with other student-centred initiatives?

Student engagement and activity is a fundamental principle of problem-based learning, as is the notion of a collaborative and co-operative "community of learners". This chapter argues that active student engagement can connect PBL with other institutional student-centred initiatives and, thus, lead to a range of effective partnerships between members of the wider university community. These partnerships provide students with opportunities to make significant contributions to the design, facilitation, and evaluation of PBL curricula, ensure that the environments for successful PBL are developed and maintained, and, consequently, achieve the vital connections between "persons with knowledge, understanding, feelings and interests who come together in a shared educational process" (Margetson, 1997, p. 39). Students are often described as "stakeholders" in PBL, but there are many other stakeholder groups involved; indeed, the authors of this chapter are representatives of one of those groups – educational developers – a role with its own set of priorities, expectations, demands, and deliverables. Each author was inspired to undertake formal educational development roles as a result of personal participation in student support schemes. For example, as an undergraduate student in Manchester, Karen was proactive in encouraging other students to take a more collaborative role in their learning experience; one of her main voluntary projects being the instigation of a new and highly successful peer mentoring scheme in the Department of English and American Studies. In her final year, Karen was awarded an internship to enable her to champion and co-ordinate peer mentoring activities throughout the department in a more structured and formal way, and, in this role, she addressed issues such as mentor recruitment and training, in addition to preparing a continuation strategy to enable the scheme to be taken forward in future years. During the first year of her master's degree, Karen was employed on a part-time basis as Student Enterprise Officer for the University of Manchester and the university's Institute of Science and Technology (UMIST), supporting a wide range of innovative student-centred projects, as well as implementing cost-effective teaching and learning innovations through involving students in the initiation, promotion, and development of their ideas. She was later offered the post of Research Assistant to one of the first UK National Teaching Fellows and was responsible for enhancing student learning through investigation, development, implementation, and evaluation of appropriate PBL methods and systems in Literary Studies. Karen continued to research the "student experience" of PBL curricula, took up a centralised post as the university's Curriculum Development Officer and went on to become a key member of the team that developed Manchester's successful bid for a Centre for Excellence in Teaching and Learning (CETL) in Enquiry-based Learning. She is able to draw heavily on the strong track record for PBL developed at the university over a number of years and in a wide range of disciplines.

Never intending to pursue a career in higher education, Marcia's philosophy and enthusiasm grew from her early engagement in student activity as a Students' Union Sabbatical Officer where she developed a passion for the design and delivery of creative approaches to co-curricular activity. As a student, she was often frustrated by others' apathy to engage in union activity, and so, in her role as President, she set about establishing a student development programme. Marcia then succeeded Karen as Student Enterprise Officer in Manchester, where she further expanded and enhanced the peer support schemes and implemented and embedded the now established "Students as Partners" programme. Currently a Teaching and Learning Manager, Marcia has strategic responsibility for the widespread programme and, having become the UK National Peer Assisted Study/Supplemental Instruction Certified Trainer, she disseminates, trains, and supports implementation in other institutions.

This chapter aims to highlight the role of students, not only as learners, but as agents of change and as a mechanism for the effective integration of diverse stakeholder needs.

We should point out that the University of Manchester uses Enquiry-based Learning (EBL), as a broad umbrella term, to describe those approaches to learning that are driven by a process of research and investigation, and we see PBL as a form of EBL as Figure 4.1 illustrates.

Savin-Baden (2003) observes that PBL can take many different forms and our experience is that it can *feel* very different too. Kahn and O'Rourke (2003) stress that the way in which students are equipped to take on the challenges of EBL can be a crucial factor to its success. They also argue that, for tutors, the shift from content expert to facilitator may require as much, if not more,

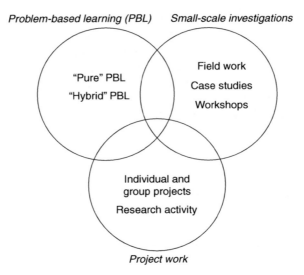

Figure 4.1 Approaches to learning covered by the term Enquiry-Based Learning (EBL) (Kahn & O'Rourke, 2005, p. 4).

preparation as that given to the students. Add to that the idea that each specific discipline has to interpret PBL according to its own insights and adopt models and forms of PBL that are appropriate (Hutchings & O'Rourke, 2006) and the constant evolution of PBL becomes apparent and necessary to meet the changing needs of learners and their teachers, professional practice, and society. "For the students who are professionals of the future, developing the ability to investigate problems, make judgements on the basis of sound evidence, take decisions on a rational basis, and understand what they are doing and why is vital" (Brew, 2007, p. 7). The increasing use of PBL, as a vehicle to support interdisciplinary learning, emphasises the flexibility and applicability of such approaches as "integral to learning in the world that lies outside institutionalised academic learning … a world of unpredictability, a world in which knowledge is shared and grown within small group work" (Jackson, 2003, p. 1). This interpenetration of the different disciplines mirrors the interpenetration of different approaches to student-centred change that the authors propose as crucial to effective PBL practice, and so a range of subject areas and student-focused initiatives are utilised in this chapter. In an attempt to provide a sharp focus on the role of the student, we have selected specific snapshots of student activity and commentary to emphasise particular examples of students as partners and co-consultants in the overall development and implementation of PBL curricula. What we hope shines through in these examples is the students' willingness and desire to get involved, their readiness to offer support and the sheer quality of their valuable contributions to the wider PBL environment.

Chapter Overview

This chapter discusses:

- creating a climate for PBL to flourish;
- organising formal approaches to student involvement; and
- engaging students in the development and delivery of PBL.

Creating a Climate for PBL to Flourish

There is increasing recognition of the value of student engagement at all levels within higher education, acknowledging that students can be/are active participants in and directors of their own educational experience. This philosophy encourages responsibility, empowerment, and control, as well as offering opportunities for research and collaboration and supporting students to develop their own personal goals, aspirations, and expectations to become autonomous, self-directed learners.

Developing an institutional culture of student engagement requires strategic change and involves welcoming students as partners in the wider learning community. The University of Manchester has a well-established "Students as Partners" programme of activity which has evolved from student development activity (formerly Student Enterprise (SE), Enterprise in Higher Education (EHE)). SE had considerable success in promoting student-centred learning, enabling students to become actively involved in both their departments and their disciplines, while, at the same time, developing themselves as individuals; it provided evidence of efficient, effective methods of involving students in devising, implementing, and evaluating improvements in the learning experience. Notable examples of these activities include peer mentoring, Peer Assisted Study Sessions (PASS), student-led induction, post-graduate conferences and symposia, discussion fora, study skills guides, and online journals. In spite of widespread recognition of the importance of the holistic student experience and the value of student-led approaches, these activities were traditionally perceived to be peripheral to the academic experience and often aligned themselves directly with the Students' Union.

In time, at the University of Manchester, the evidence of the value of student enterprise activity and the importance of student engagement, in relation to academic and social integration at an institutional level, created a climate for further expansion and the embedding of a more cohesive co-curricular programme of work. As mainstream integral activity, the Students as Partners programme was managed by the central Teaching and Learning Support Office in liaison with all faculties, helping to shape and support the institution's strategic goals. The programme recognised the need to be proactive in facilitating partnerships between academic staff, professional support services, and students in order to develop a supportive climate in which opportunities for student engagement in all aspects of university life could be enhanced.

The Students as Partners initiative sought to:

- encourage students to adopt a holistic approach to their learning and development;
- value the student voice;
- create opportunities for student initiatives and student-led projects;
- support transition into and through higher education;
- increase autonomy and engagement in learning;
- enhance and develop curricula; and
- inform and develop policy and strategy.

As it became more established, the programme developed a culture which has been conducive to engaging students as co-consultants, leaders of change, generators of ideas, and contributors to strategy. Students are valued as members of consultation groups, working parties, and committees, and have helped bring about a shared vision on all matters that affect them including curriculum review, quality enhancement, and pedagogy.

> I was pleased to have the opportunity to contribute to major changes within the University and it was nice to be able to voice my opinions in a fun and inspiring way ... as students we were able to suggest a number of recommendations and to discuss these with staff ... you feel like you are part of the University decision-making process.
> **(3rd-year Physics student, University of Manchester, 2008)**

At discipline or programme level, discussion often takes place through facilitated focus groups. Student representatives are also engaged at all levels in regular Student–Staff Liaison Committees and other related meetings.

> Being proactive and working with staff and students enhances the student learning experience in a variety of ways, for us at the time of studying but also for future students. Being involved has helped me to become organised in my own learning but it has also built a really social side to my studies ... I have developed and benefited so much...
> **(final-year Combined Studies student, University of Manchester, 2008)**

The continued effective engagement of students as co-consultants requires the development of a series of up-to-date opportunities that allow them to acquire skills and knowledge, to build their trust in others, and discover how much they can contribute to the development of staff and other students.

Organising Formal Approaches to Student Involvement

Supporting the transition into higher education and the provision of a personalised learning experience are key factors in student retention, motivation, and achievement. As part of an integrated approach to student support and development, the University of Manchester engages students in two formalised, complementary initiatives: Peer Mentoring and Peer Assisted Study Sessions (PASS). Both schemes have been running since 1995 and, while distinct, can and do overlap. These schemes are "discipline-owned and student-led", organised and maintained by student leaders. By accepting responsibility for its own scheme and utilising the Students as Partners team (along with faculty staff, for guidance, training, and evaluation), a course can ensure that the scheme meets the specific needs of the students.

Peer Mentoring is a widely recognised voluntary support scheme and primarily has a social/pastoral focus. The higher-year students involved (Peer Mentors) are generally more active at the start of the academic year when new students are adjusting to life in Manchester and getting to grips with the demands of their chosen discipline. Mentors assist with orientation and socialisation. However, the scheme can continue throughout the year and this is highly encouraged as it fosters a greater sense of cohesion and community for all students involved. Mentoring schemes can offer additional support sessions at critical periods in the student life-cycle, such as campus orientation, using the library effectively for a first assignment, understanding tutor feedback, exam revision strategies, and selecting courses for subsequent years of study. In addition, the student-produced guides providing information about the city, the university, accommodation, and the skills required for study are usually well-received.

It must be stressed that PASS is *non-remedial* and is attached to particularly challenging courses within a degree programme, providing a safe environment for students to discuss ideas, review lecture notes, ask questions, share problems, and resolve issues in a setting that supplements core delivery. Higher-year students volunteer and are trained as PASS leaders, operating in pairs to facilitate regular, timetabled study groups usually comprising 6–12 lower-year students. Sessions generally take place in weekly one-hour slots and attendance is encouraged though by no means compulsory. PASS sessions are intended to promote collaborative learning through exploratory discussion and provide opportunities for leaders to share their own experiences of the course, thus de-mystifying the higher years of study and building confidence and positivity among the attendees. Leaders do not re-teach material but, instead, encourage attendees to compare notes, clarify what they have read and heard, analyse, criticise, question, and seek verification of ideas. In addition to consolidating knowledge of the subject and gaining deeper conceptual understanding, study and learning strategies are integrated into the PASS sessions.

PASS leaders undertake comprehensive facilitation training, and benefit from ongoing peer observation and weekly de-briefs after each session. Leaders come together regularly to share best practice and discuss the challenges and successes of their individual sessions. PASS leaders provide valuable feedback to academic staff on common problems experienced by attendees and offer an insight into how lecture material, seminars, and labs are being received.

> A good reason for me being a PASS leader in the first place is the motivation I get from the students; the feedback from a good session where they've actually left having learnt something, or having helped them solve their problems, and them coming back with more things to say and more things to share...
>
> **(Zoe Drymoussi, PASS Leader, Biological Sciences, 2008)**

The established Students as Partners programme has informed the successful development of EBL at the University of Manchester both in terms of student motivation and through the structures that provide support and consultancy to those implementing EBL and PBL. The institution in policy and practice has recognised the harmonious relationship between EBL/PBL and Students as Partners. In 2003, Hoad-Reddick and Theaker outlined the crucial connection between peer support and students' adaptability to PBL, in describing PASS in Dentistry they commented:

> The aim was for senior students to disseminate study skills and working methods for PBL rather than to provide facts. The [PASS] session was obviously very successful – some students had to be asked to leave after 3.5 h as the dental hospital had to be closed! Not only were the sessions popular with first year students, they were also very popular with the senior students leading the groups. These students developed a very strong group identity and were intensely proud of their input into the first year [PBL] course.
>
> **(p. 7)**

Engaging Students in the Development and Delivery of PBL

The University of Manchester's Centre for Excellence in Enquiry-based Learning (CEEBL) is one of the Higher Education Funding Council for England (HEFCE)-funded centres recognised as excellent in teaching and learning. From its early development stages, CEEBL considered "Students as Partners" to be at the core of its values. Engaging PBL students on the bid-writing team provided crucial first-hand evidence and a unique selling point at the competitive bidding stage, sending a clear message to the HEFCE that students would be at the heart of the proposed five-year initiative, which eventually received over £5 million in 2005 to fund teaching and learning activity specifically related to EBL and PBL.

Part of the CEEBL funding was used to set up a formal Student Intern Programme, so that each academic year a team of cross-faculty students could be recruited to work collaboratively with academic staff developing EBL. The student interns also worked closely with the core CEEBL team to deliver, evaluate, and disseminate various aspects of EBL. It was interesting to note that almost all students applying for intern positions with CEEBL had acted as Peer Mentors or PASS leaders at some point, and it was encouraging to hear them speak knowledgeably about the benefits of these schemes in relation to the skills required from them as interns. The internships were seen as an amalgamation of Peer Mentoring and EBL – the environments and skills were easily mapped across each other and students could clearly articulate the relationships between these schemes and approaches. The student interns were actively encouraged to support curriculum development and to help students and staff to make the transition to EBL approaches. The intern programme was structured so that students could work on a flexible basis, approximately five hours per week, managing their own time and organising their own workloads in negotiation with each other and the CEEBL team. The interns were integrated into all aspects of CEEBL's programme of activity but naturally developed closer relationships with academic staff in their own faculty, who were engaged in embedding and enhancing EBL in specific courses and modules familiar to the interns.

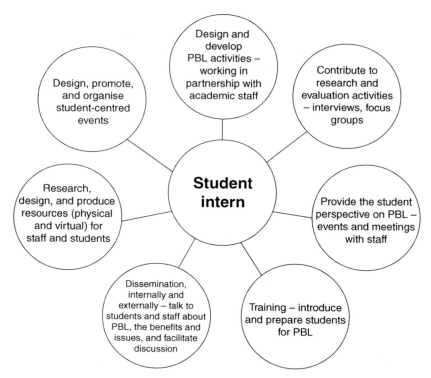

Figure 4.2 A transferable model of the CEEBL Student Intern Programme – kinds of activities the students can support and lead.

The intern programme instigated a growing network of students enthusiastic about the ways in which people learn, and with a passion for shaping their own and other students' learning experiences. They produced useful resources and guides, facilitated workshops, co-authored case-studies and conference presentations, and contributed to the CEEBL research and evaluation strategies.

To illustrate the benefits of the CEEBL student programme further, it is useful to include an intern's story:

CEEBL Project

Development of a guide for online group work for Pharmacy and Mid-wifery students on Inter-Professional Education (IPE) modules, and to support module evaluation.

Context

The IPE online module has had mixed evaluation over the past two years and this year it is hoped that a structured EBL approach will help to create coherence for this online group module. I have worked very closely with the academic member of staff to design the EBL problems used. Once the course started I kept a reflective journal, submitted weekly to the academic so that adjustments could be made. I facilitated two focus groups during the module to analyse the effect the changes were having on the students' experience. I am a current student on this module and have been particularly focused on the support structures in place for students working on e-EBL. As part of my evaluation of the module I identified the need for a guide to go on the VLE (Blackboard) and I also support students through their group work and EBL processes.

Outcome

Unlike typical feedback students provide about their courses, such as end of module questionnaires, the students on this course unit could see that their feedback was directly affecting the current module that they were on, rather than improving it for the next cohort. My influence on the course development has resulted in good feedback from students, which in turn has ensured that this module will continue next academic year.

The fact that students knew that there were improvements being made throughout the module was a positive thing for them as they felt that the changes were being put in place to benefit their experiences. In the focus group students found it easier to voice their opinions to another student instead of a staff member.

I also intend to make the guides more generic so that they can be made available as a resource for all students on the CEEBL website. I will also look at developing a staff equivalent for online facilitators.
Kate Jones, Faculty of Medicine and Human Sciences, 2008–2009

This chapter's co-author Louise Goldring would, at this point, like to share her own EBL journey:

I have been interested in student development throughout my education. During sixth form, I requested volunteer work as a classroom assistant for English lessons and found it fascinating and rewarding to encourage participation and interaction from students. As an undergraduate at the University of Manchester I continued this interest by volunteering as a Peer Mentor for 2 years supporting 1st-year English students, where I had the opportunity to lead sections of EBL tutorials. During this time I also took part in various focus groups to share my opinions about my university experience as a whole. I found the mentoring experience very enjoyable, especially the responsibility of guiding students to think and learn for themselves, which was an integral part of the role. It was the facilitation of these processes that really interested me.

When applying for my master's in the Faculty of Humanities in 2006 I found out about the Centre for Excellence in Enquiry-based Learning and applied to be an Intern. The empowerment and enjoyment I felt when actually having the chance to shape student development and experience was incredibly rewarding. I felt that my position as a current student, able to reflect on my own experiences and act as a representative for others, was recognised and valued by CEEBL and academics across the HE sector and I could see first-hand the effect the Intern team was having on learning at Manchester.

During my Internship I worked on a collaborative project with another Intern and an academic member of staff, developing a guide for EBL facilitators (available at www.manchester.ac.uk/ceebl). When developing this resource we identified the need for a visual representation of the EBL process, as we felt that this would help staff and students understand it. We created the EBL Process/Skills wheel (see the guide) and this has now been used widely across the University of Manchester and further afield.

In my subsequent roles at CEEBL as Sabbatical Officer and, now, Student Engagement Officer, supporting, training, coordinating, and then managing the Intern team, I have actively promoted the practice of using Interns as full collaborators in the learning process, rather than simply a method of feedback. I strongly encourage staff to work with

Interns when designing and developing their course modules, as well as evaluating them. I am a strong advocate and exemplar for students shaping their own experience and becoming full, valid, and active members of learning communities, having the chance to gain the skills and advantages I had while working as an Intern.

As emphasised above, the Student Intern Programme at CEEBL has strongly promoted student empowerment in the learning environment and demonstrated that the EBL approach is ideal for actively involving students in shaping their own learning, as well as being an exemplary vehicle for supporting students through that process. The strong platform provided by the long-standing and credible Students as Partners schemes ensured that the environments for EBL to flourish were in place and was conducive to *real* student engagement. It has been found that empowering a few enthusiastic students to support and develop EBL has been a wide-reaching and worthwhile initiative. The relatively small-scale investment required for developing Student Interns has had a much wider impact for the entire institution.

As demonstrated by the authors' own journeys (described above), there are many benefits, rewards, and opportunities to be gained through active support and engagement in the PBL process in its widest sense. Tutors wise enough to work closely and collaboratively with students in this way reap many benefits. The following blog by an undergraduate student intern almost explodes with sheer enthusiasm and it highlights a true passion for learning, and for educational development.

Last friday i met up with Sally Freeman in pharmacy to discuss how the medicinal chemistry project funded by CEEBL last year is developing. I will be working on this project again this year and hope to put a draft together of a paper to go into Pharmacy Education over the next few weeks. There may also be the possibility of presenting a poster on the project at the RPSGB conference. Meanwhile, I met with Liz Theaker this afternoon and I will be running some focus groups over the next few weeks to review how the new curriculum is being recieved in dentistry. I am also planning to redesign the personal development records within pharmacy following on from our workshop on the 22nd November. I have found an expert in the field of continuing professional development and am meeting with her next monday. Hopefully we will be able to come up with some solutions to make it more student friendly and also correlate more with the records we will have to keep when we are practicing pharmacists.

This undergraduate Pharmacy student went on to co-author a published paper with an academic, gained a First Class degree and was awarded Student of the Year – who says students are apathetic, selfish and lazy?!

Conclusion

It has been stressed that problem-based learning is not the sole solution to all curriculum design problems that we encounter in different contexts (Boud & Feletti, 1997). We would similarly emphasise that the embracing of students as partners is not the solution to all PBL implementation problems. The blurred boundaries, which such partnership working encourages, throw up a whole new range of issues for the PBL community. A sensitive balance needs to be achieved if all stakeholders are to benefit from this collaborative approach. There are many challenges, many demands, and getting to the point where a true community of learners is achieved can require going through the pain threshold – developing student partnership initiatives can seem complicated and uncomfortable at times, but it is worth it! The shared values and processes between "Students as Partners" and PBL are encapsulated by this student:

> it was the skills we learned from this [PBL] experience ... listening, communication, empathy, tolerance, negotiation, patience, time-management, focus ... everyone feels they have got a role or some part and there is equal power relationship ... we learned how to step back from things sometimes, to see things from other people's views ... and we just changed our way of thinking a bit ... we have all been taught to think but now we see a different way to think.
>
> **(2nd-year student, Engineering, University of Manchester)**

Shouldn't that be what we are trying to achieve for students and *all* stakeholders in PBL?

This chapter focused on the importance of students as partners in shaping PBL curricula. The next chapter discusses the important role that student feedback can play in supporting students' ability to make crucial connections between concepts in a PBL module.

References

Boud, D., & Feletti, G. (Eds.). (1997). *The challenge of problem-based learning* (2nd ed.). London: Kogan-Page.

Brew, A. (2007). *Research and teaching: Beyond the divide.* London: Palgrave Macmillan.

Hoad-Reddick, G., & Theaker, E. (2003). Providing support for problem-based learning in dentistry: The Manchester experience. *European Journal of Dental Education, 7*, 3–12.

Hutchings, B., & O'Rourke, K. (2006). *A study of enquiry-based learning in action: An example from a Literary Studies third year course.* Manchester: Centre for Excellence in Enquiry-Based Learning, University of Manchester.

Jackson, N. (2003). *Learning based on the process of enquiry.* Imaginative Curriculum Working Paper. Retrieved from: http://enquirylearning.pbworks.com/f/Learning+through+enquiry+HE+Academy+paper.rtf.

Kahn, P., & O'Rourke, K. (2003). *A guide to enquiry-based learning*. Retrieved from: www.heacademy.ac.uk/resources/detail/id359_guide_to_curriculum_design_ebl.
Kahn, P. & O'Rourke, K. (2005). Understanding enquiry-based learning. In T. Barrett, I. Mac Labhainn, & H. Fallon (Eds.), *Handbook of enquiry and problem-based learning: Irish case studies and international perspectives* (pp. 1–12). Galway: CELT and AISHE. Retrieved from: www.nuigalway.ie/celt/pblbook/chapter1.
Margetson, D. (1997). Why is problem-based learning a challenge? In D. Boud & G. Feletti (Eds.), *The challenge of problem-based learning* (2nd ed., pp. 36–44). London: Kogan-Page.
Savin-Baden, M. (2003). *Facilitating problem-based learning: Illuminating perspectives*. Buckingham: Society for Research into Higher Education and Open University Press.

Further Resources

University of Manchester. (2009). *PASS at the University of Manchester*. www.campus.manchester.ac.uk/tlso/studentsaspartners/peersupport/pass.
University of Manchester, Centre for Excellence in Teaching and Learning (CEEBL): www.manchester.ac.uk/ceebl.
Leeds Metropolitan University, Centre for Excellence in Teaching and Learning (The Institute for Enterprise): www.leedsmet.ac.uk/enterprise.
The Learning Through Enquiry Alliance (LTEA): www.ltea.ac.uk.

5

Making Strong Learning Connections

Students' Involvement in Improving the Interconnections of Concepts in a PBL Module

Geraldine O'Neill and Woei Hung

Introduction

How can PBL help students to make strong intellectual and creative connections between different concepts?

This chapter should help you to answer the question stated above by presenting practical, evidence-based strategies that facilitate students to achieve "conceptual integration" in their discipline knowledge base. We will discuss three strategies that we have found to be particularly helpful in integrating discipline knowledge in a single-module PBL context.

This chapter explores our experiences with a PBL module on education theories in a Postgraduate Diploma in University Teaching and Learning that was taken by a group of academic staff. We will draw specifically on both our research study of this group (O'Neill & Hung, 2010) and a theoretical model (Hung, 2006) in order to suggest practical strategies that you can use to help students make strong connections in their learning.

Clearly, student involvement in their learning activities is important and this involvement is actively and explicitly supported by the PBL learning process. In our module, we found that the students actively engaged in the PBL process and provided us with some very useful feedback on their experience of the module. In particular, the students explained how they had struggled with making conceptual connections in the disciplinary knowledge and gave us some ideas on how we might, and did, improve this situation for similar modules in the future (O'Neill & Hung, 2010). Our students were not unique in this struggle to seek and find interrelationships among the concepts and pieces of information that they had studied (Drummond-Young & Mohide, 2001; Songer & Linn, 1991). We argue that, with the appropriate guidance, it is possible to facilitate a stronger, more interconnected learning orientation, with positive results.

Chapter Overview

This chapter will:

- explore some literature about facilitating students' connection of disciplinary concepts in PBL curricula;
- provide practical examples of tools that we have found to be useful in developing the students' ability to make connections in PBL initiatives;
- describe three practice strategies that will help you to think about how your students can make conceptual connections within your own discipline. These strategies are:

    1. attending to the design of the problems;
    2. considering the role and sequence of the different learning resources; and
    3. integrating assessment by using both an integrated assessment process and finishing with an explicit integrative assessment task.

Connections, Integration, and Conceptual Understanding

Very often, students do not proactively integrate what they have learned (Dolmans, Gijselaers, Schmidt, & van der Meer, 1993; Drummond-Young & Mohide, 2001; Hung, 2003; Lieux, 2001; Songer & Linn, 1991). Hung (2006) voiced the importance of helping learners to integrate the knowledge that they have learned by understanding and establishing their conceptual connections among the problems within a PBL curriculum. Therefore, we believe that PBL curricula should be designed in ways that will both explicitly and implicitly facilitate students to engage in such cognitive processes. With this facilitation, we could prevent what Hung (2006, p. 61) cautioned against, that is, "problem-packaged" knowledge becoming "compartmental" knowledge (Linn & Hsi, 2000; Kali, Orion, & Eylon, 2003).

Developing connections between and within the problems in a PBL curriculum is a critical but under-discussed issue. The facilitation of the students' knowledge integration process and a well formed conceptual knowledge base, as we and others have discovered (O'Neill & Hung, 2010; Vardi & Ciccarelli, 2008), can be even more challenging with a single PBL module.

Keep in mind that, in the PBL processes, students are required to engage actively in the process of solving real-life problems (Dolmans & Schmidt, 1994). By tackling a series of individual, authentic, and highly contextualised problems (Gallagher, 1997), the aim is that learners will:

- acquire,
- comprehend,
- apply,
- structure, and
- integrate their emerging knowledge.

We cannot assume that PBL automatically solves the dilemma of "disconnected thinking", or eliminates the risk of students learning in fragmented, un-integrated ways. We argue that it is very important to devise specific strategies for helping students to integrate their understanding of the connection between concepts across (not just within) problems.

So, in order to facilitate the establishment of strong conceptual connections, we propose three strategies for PBL practice (see Figure 5.1). These strategies involve paying attention to the design of the problems, the role and sequence of all of the learning resources used by students to tackle the problem, and integrating assessment processes and tasks.

Practice Strategy 1: Attention to the Design of the Problems

PBL problems should be pre-designed in such a way that the students will naturally engage in making conceptual connections between concepts learned during the problem-solving processes. Our advice to you on problem design is being guided by Hung's (2006) 3C3R PBL problem design model, specifically the connection component. We found that this model was very useful in designing the module in our study. The 3C3R PBL problem design model is "A systematic method specifically designed to guide instructional designers and educators to design effective PBL problems. ... The 3C3R model consists of two classes of components: core components and processing components" (Hung,

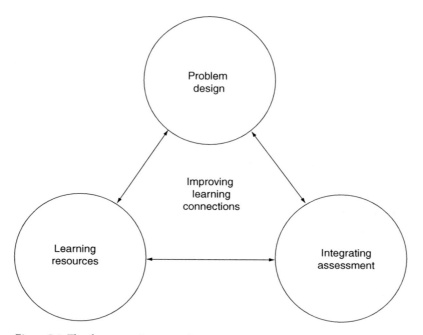

Figure 5.1 The three practice strategies.

2006, p. 56). The core components, including content, context, and *connection*, are more focused on the content/concept learning, whereas the processing components relate to the learner's cognitive processes, i.e. problem solving.

Connection, one of the 3C components in this model, addresses the importance of facilitating students to interconnect related concepts and information within the discipline knowledge through appropriate PBL curriculum design (for more information about the 3C3R model, please refer to Hung, 2006). Depending on the type and the stage of concept integration (e.g. connecting individual concepts at the early stage or forming a conceptual framework at the later stage), the connection component of PBL problems can be divided into two categories: interweaving and holistic. The interweaving connection in PBL problems helps the learners to develop the interconnections among the individual concepts, principles, procedures, and information within the sub-topics of the domain knowledge; while the holistic connection aids the learners in establishing a holistic view or conceptual framework of the discipline knowledge.

The Interweaving Category

Prerequisite, overlapping, and multi-facets are three approaches that you can use to design the interconnections among the problems in a PBL curriculum. These three approaches address the different types of conceptual interconnections that are often determined by the nature of the disciplines.

Prerequisite Approach

The prerequisite approach helps the learners to establish these connections in a conceptually logical order from simple/basic to complex/advanced. The problems at the more complex level should build on the prerequisite concepts and information that appear in the preceding problems. This approach should help you guide learners to see the interconnected relationships among different levels of concepts by engaging them in problem-solving activities in a sequential manner. The prerequisite approach is a particularly appropriate design choice for learning sequential or hierarchical concepts, for example, learning mathematical procedures.

Overlapping Approach

Another approach is overlapping concepts between problems. Hierarchical relationships do not always exist among the concepts in a discipline. With this approach, the problem design should ensure that the concepts appear in several problems so that the learners can study each concept in relation to other concepts. By understanding multiple sets of concepts involved in several problems, the learners can link these sub-networks into a larger and more complete network. The overlapping approach would suit disciplines such as History or Literature.

Multi-facets Approach

The characteristics or nature of the concepts could change from one context to another or over time. Incorporating a given concept in multiple problems with different contexts helps the learners to understand the multi-faceted effect of variables, for example, the difference between the concept of "ethical behaviour" in classroom, business or clinical placement contexts.

The Holistic Category

In the holistic category, the connection component is usually utilised in one problem that requires the learners to study the subject domain holistically. Top-down and bottom-up are two approaches that you could use in the timing of a holistic problem.

Top-down Approach

The top-down approach enables the problem to serve as an advance organiser (Ausubel, Novak, & Hanesian, 1978). The PBL curriculum that utilises this approach should start the PBL curriculum or module by giving the learners a problem that requires them to focus on the overall picture of the domain (e.g. a problem that requires the learners to survey the contemporary topics in marketing in an introduction to marketing course). This first problem would function as an overview of the PBL curriculum or module. Thus, the top-down approach will equip the learners with an overall conceptual map about the domain as the first step in their studies.

Bottom-up Approach

Conversely, PBL curricula that utilise the bottom-up approach would give the learners a problem that functions as an overall review and summary of the domain. This approach helps the learners to conceptually organise, integrate, and summarise what they have learned from all of the PBL problems through-out the curriculum or module, including the individual concepts and the interconnections. For example, in the final problem in our PBL module, implemented at University College Dublin, the students were asked to make a presentation to a group of new academic staff in an induction programme on connecting educational theories to teaching practice.

By using a combination of the holistic and/or the interweaving approaches to design PBL problems, the learners can be guided to naturally (implicitly) engage in the concept integration processes.

Practice Strategy 2: The Role and Sequence of the Different Learning Resources

Our students alerted us to the importance of paying attention to the role and sequence of the different learning resources in order to help them to make connections. Problem-based learning is a curriculum where the problem (one learning resource) is placed at the beginning of the learning process; it differs from other curricula where problems are often encountered only after the students have been taught the necessary knowledge (Moust, van Berkel, & Schmidt, 2005; Vardi & Ciccarelli, 2008). In PBL settings, the problem is usually presented to students in a group and is often described as the "Group Brainstorm" or Maastricht Steps 1–5 (Davis & Harden, 1999). Following the presentation of the problem, students carry out independent study (Maastricht Step 6, see Figure 5.3) drawing on other resources (Moust et al., 2005). A vast range of resources can be used including literature and textbooks, people's experiences, online resources, lectures, laboratories, field-work, and practicals (Fyrenius, Bergdahl, & Silén, 2005; Moust et al., 2005). After a period of independent study, the group then reconvenes to consolidate their knowledge with the benefit of these other resources; we have called this stage the "Group Academic Debate" (Maastricht Step 7, see Figure 5.3).

In our module, the module material was very new to the students; these students had little prior theoretical knowledge in this area. We discovered that when the group discussion on the problems was the primary learning resource, the students struggled with developing connections. One student reported that s/he did not have the language to engage in the initial group discussion and that some early support, often described as "scaffolding" (Hill & Hannafin, 2001), was crucial. The concept of scaffolding student learning implies that there is a need to give some structured points in the process, that is, the students' self-directed learning is supported and the level of challenge is increased incrementally. For example, throughout the semester, as group discussion became challenging and, at times, confusing, there was a need to "drip feed" some expert knowledge by other scaffolds using a variety of resources.

This use of different resources is highlighted in the literature, particularly in the e-learning literature. For example, Littlejohn and Pegler (2007, p. 78) describe the process of using various resources as "orchestrating the blend" and advocate that, at the start of the process, "it is useful to have access to a short synopsis. Its purpose is to outline the ideas and abstract the pattern behind the activity". In addition, they state that "no single representation can convey the whole story at every level" (p. 79). We have used Littlejohn and Pegler's (2007) representation of the different resources to highlight the sequence of the module in our study (see Figure 5.3). Moust et al. (2005), on the other hand, caution against pulling away from the emphasis in PBL of the student doing the learning and information seeking.

The students involved in our module believed that the lecture had a role in scaffolding the learning and consolidated some of their emerging connections. The lecture gave the students a glimpse of the full picture and, as also noted by Margetson (2000), was an efficient use of their time. However, the majority of our students believed that a lecture should be mid-way through or towards the end of the semester. Moust et al. (2005, p. 673) advocate that: "Lectures are given only after students have immersed themselves in a particular area. In that way the teacher's role can play an <u>integrative</u> and clarifying role."

Fyrenius et al. (2005, p. 62) discuss the role of the lecture in the PBL sequence and suggest that care should be taken not to revert to the more traditional lecture with "passive listeners". Instead, they suggest that the lecture, if used, should be interactive and mirror the PBL process by the incorporation of individual reflection, group discussion (in pairs, threes, etc.), and the brief explanation of new or complicated areas. In addition, they suggest that the students should have an input into the content of the lecture based on their needs.

Video Resource: Ball et al. (2009)

This video resource highlights the views of some medical staff and students, in the University of Nottingham, on the role of the lecture in PBL curricula. In particular, they note how the lecture reinforces the students' prior learning and it scaffolds the boundaries of the self-directed learning on the topic.

Our students did not want to be spoon-fed by a lecture at the beginning, but they did seek some means of engaging with the new language of the module, in this case, the educational theories. It was decided, based on their feedback, to provide the students with some key overview articles (another resource) to read prior to the first problem and, in the second action research cycle of our study, the students stated that these resources had been very helpful. Moust et al. (2005) argue that the use of prescribed literature can lead to all students reading the same material for the group discussion, with a negative effect on the synthesis in the discussion. In our case, these readings were not associated with a particular problem but with the whole module.

Practice Strategy 3: Integrating Assessment – Using an Integrated Assessment Process and Integrative Assessment Task

Our students suggested that, in addition to the learning resources in our module, an integrated assessment process was also essential in developing strong connections (see Figure 5.1). In addition to this sequencing of assessments, in order to support the connections of concepts, it appeared that we needed to ask students to make these connections explicitly in their final "summative" assessment (a summative assessment is an assessment that counts towards the student's grade). This assessment task, with its associated criteria, explicitly highlighted the fact that we were seeking the students' understanding of the connection between discipline concepts. We have called this type of task an integrative assessment task. Therefore, we shall deal with this idea of both an ongoing integrated assessment process and a final integrative assessment task.

Current good practice in the assessment literature in PBL (MacDonald & Savin-Baden, 2004) and in other curricula (Juwah et al., 2004) emphasise the increasingly important role in higher education of the ongoing integrated use of tutor, peer, and self "formative" assessment. Juwah et al. (2004, p. 7) describe how formative assessment, with its primary focus on feedback, encourages teacher and peer dialogue on learning and helps the students "to check out and correct misunderstandings and to get an immediate response to difficulties".

As the students struggled with some of the relationships between the connections on our module, we were able to give ongoing feedback (formative assessment) on their knowledge integration during the group discussions, using formative tutor assessment initially, developing later into self- and peer-formative assessment (see Figure 5.3). This integration process was also assisted by the two ongoing summative assessments, handed up in Weeks 5 and 8, which contributed to their grade (see Figure 5.2).

This early tutor-assessed summative assessment actively encouraged the students to integrate their thoughts and work on the problem that they had completed in their self-study with the comments made in the discussion by the other group members (see Figure 5.2, Section 3). In summary, this ongoing embedded approach to integrating assessment appeared to be well received by the students in our study and in other studies (Gijbels, van de Watering, & Dochy, 2005).

A final assessment that encourages a synthesis of concepts is often described as a synoptic assessment (Patrick, 2009). We have described this type of final assessment as an integrative assessment task. For example, in many higher education programmes, the research or design project is intended to develop an integration of concepts across the programme. In the second cycle, we used a more project-oriented assessment in that we specifically (explicitly) asked that, in presenting their group projects to the whole class, the students would explain their overview of the connections. The connections are often usefully presented in a visual manner and without prompting; in our module, the students used concept maps to represent the connections. Concept maps have been recommended as an approach to improve connectivity in PBL (Hsu, 2004; Rendas, Fonseca, & Pinto, 2006). In relation to Moust et al.'s (2005) concerns over reverting to teacher-oriented

---

Student assignment template:

"Independent Study Summary and Additional Insights from your Group"

Section 1: Your ideas:

Using the structure of <u>your</u> group's learning objectives, summarise the findings from your independent study of the literature/other resources: (500 words, excluding references).

Section 2: Your references:

Give the complete references of at least two key journal articles/book chapters and one relevant website that support your summary above.

Section 3: The additional insights from the group:

Fill this section in <u>by hand</u> after the Academic Debate, i.e. while still in the seminar room.

What additional (not in section 1 and 2) insights into this problem did you learn from the group discussion?

Figure 5.2 Summative assignment template for Weeks 5 and 8.

approaches in PBL, in our module, these concepts maps were student-generated and the students were able to observe multiple interpretations of the connections. Representing connections was both an assessment and a learning task, which supported Gijbels et al.'s (2005) view that these tasks should no longer be viewed as separate.

Conclusion

We found that our students benefited greatly from this single-module PBL experience. However, we found that conceptual integration did not happen by accident; it required some additional strategies to help make the connections between disciplinary concepts in the module. Our students were involved in highlighting some of these strategies to us. In summary, if you are considering using a single-module PBL approach, you may find it useful to ask yourself some of the questions listed below, based on our three strategies, in order to support your own students in making stronger learning connections.

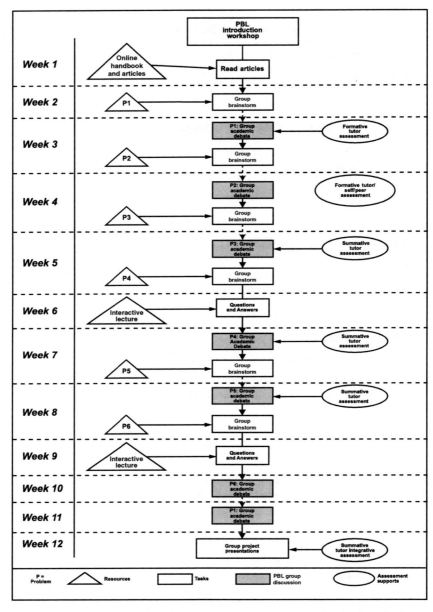

Figure 5.3 The sequence of scaffolding in the module (adapted use of Littlejohn & Pegler's, 2007, coding).

REFLECTIVE EXERCISE
Ask Yourself:

1) Giving attention to the design of the problems:
- Would it help the students to start with a holistic (overview) problem?
- Can you revisit some concepts by repeating them in other problems, possibly different contexts?

2) Considering the role and sequence of the different learning resources:
- What information, ideas, resources are crucial at the very start of the process?
- What can you introduce as the problem-focused activity unfolds over time?
- How can the sequencing of group-work, lectures, and practicals assist with the students' capacity to make connections between different concepts within your discipline?

3) Using both an integrated assessment process and finishing with an explicit integrative (synoptic) assessment task:
- How can you support the students by the continued use of formative and summative assessments throughout the process that explicitly assess conceptual connections?
- Is there a final integrative assessment that would engage them in making their own version of these connections?

Acknowledgements

Many thanks to the students involved in the original study. Thanks also to Diane Cashman for the artwork in Figures 5.1 and 5.3.

References

Ausubel, D.P., Novak, J.D., & Hanesian, H. (1978). *Educational psychology: A cognitive view* (2nd ed.). New York: Holt, Rhinehart & Winston.

Ball, J., Donegan, D., Garrud, P., Leary, A., & Lyle, S. (2009). *How does problem-based learning fit with lectures and seminars?* Retrieved from: www.nottingham.ac.uk/pesl/themes/learning/howdoesp455.

Davis, M.H., & Harden, R.M. (1999). AMEE Guide – AMEE Medical Education Guide No. 15. Problem-based learning: A practical guide – Practical hints on implementing PBL in your teaching programme. *Medical Teacher, 21*(2), 130–140.

Dolmans, D.H.J.M., & Schmidt, H.G. (1994). What drives the student in problem-based learning? *Medical Education, 28,* 372–380.

Dolmans, D.H.J.M., Gijselaers, W.H., Schmidt, H.G., & van der Meer, S.B. (1993). Problem effectiveness in a course using problem-based learning. *Academic Medicine, 68*(3), 207–213.

Drummond-Young, M., & Mohide, E.A. (2001). Developing problems for use in problem-based learning. In E. Rideout (Ed.), *Transforming nursing education through problem-based learning* (pp. 165–191). Boston, MA: Jones and Bartlett.

Fyrenius, A., Bergdahl, B., & Silén, C. (2005). Lectures in problem-based learning: Why, when and how? An example of interactive lecturing that stimulates meaningful learning. *Medical Teacher, 27*(1), 61–65.

Gallagher, S.A. (1997). Problem-based learning: Where did it come from, what does it do, and where is it going? *Journal for the Education of the Gifted, 20*, 332–362.

Gijbels, D., van de Watering, G., & Dochy, F. (2005). Integrating assessment tasks in a problem-based learning environment. *Assessment & Evaluation in Higher Education, 30*(1), 73–86.

Hill, J.R., & Hannafin, M.J. (2001). Teaching and learning in digital environments: The resurgence of resource based learning. *Educational Technology Research and Development, 49*(3), 37–52.

Hsu, L. (2004). Developing concept maps from problem-based learning scenario discussions. *Journal of Advanced Nursing, 48*(5), 510–518.

Hung, W. (2003). *An investigation on the role of causal reasoning methods in facilitating conceptual understanding of college students in physics.* Doctoral dissertation, University of Missouri, Columbia.

Hung, W. (2006). The 3C3R Model: A conceptual framework for designing problems in PBL. *The Interdisciplinary Journal of Problem-based Learning, 1*(1), 55–77.

Juwah, C., Macfarlane-Dick, D., Matthew, B., Nicol, D., Ross D., & Smith, B. (2004). *Enhancing student learning through effective formative feedback.* Retrieved from www.heacademy.ac.uk/resources/detail/id353_effective_formative_feedback_juwah_etal.

Kali, Y., Orion, N., & Eylon, B. (2003). Effect of knowledge integration activities on students' perception of the earth's crust as a cyclic system. *Journal of Research in Science Teaching, 40*(6), 545–565.

Lieux, E.M. (2001). A skeptic's look at PBL. In B. Duch, S.E. Groh, & D.E. Allen (Eds.), *The power of problem-based learning: A practical "how to" for teaching undergraduate courses in any discipline* (pp. 223–235). Sterling, VA: Stylus Publishing.

Linn, M.C., & Hsi, S.H. (2000). *Computers, teachers, peers: Science learning partners.* Hillsdale, NJ: Erlbaum.

Littlejohn, A., & Pegler, C. (2007). Documenting e-learning blends. In A. Littlejohn and C. Pegler (Eds.), *Preparing for blended e-learning* (pp. 70–93). New York: Routledge.

Macdonald, R.F., & Savin-Baden, M. (2004). *A briefing on assessment in problem-based learning. LTSN Generic Centre Assessment Series.* Retrieved from: www.heacademy.ac.uk/resources/detail/id349_A_Briefing_on_Assessment_in_Problem-based_Learning.

Margetson, D.B. (2000). Depths of understanding and excellence of practice: The question of wholeness and problem-based learning. *Journal of Evaluation in Clinical Practice, 6*(3), 293–303.

Moust, J.H.C., van Berkel, H.J.M., & Schmidt, H.G. (2005). Signs of erosion: Reflections on three decades of problem-based learning at Maastricht University. *Higher Education, 50*, 665–683.

O'Neill, G., & Hung, W. (2010). Seeing the landscape and the forest floor: Changes made to improve the connectivity of concepts in a hybrid problem-based learning curriculum. *Teaching in Higher Education, 15*(1), 15–27.

Patrick, H. (2009). *Synoptic assessment: Report for QCA.* Retrieved from: www.ofqual.org.uk/files/synoptic_assessment_report_for_qca_pdf_05_1620.pdf.

Rendas, A.B., Fonseca, M., & Pinto, P.R. (2006). Toward meaningful learning in undergraduate medical education using concept maps in a PBL pathophysiology course. *Advances in Physiology Education, 30*(1–4), 23–29.

Songer, N.B., & Linn, M.C. (1991). How do students' views of science influence knowledge integration? *Journal of Research in Science Teaching, 28*, 761–784.

Vardi, I., & Ciccarelli, M. (2008). Overcoming problems in problem-based learning: A trial of strategies in an undergraduate unit. *Innovations in Education and Teaching International, 45*(4), 345–354.

Further Resources

Fink, L.D. (2005). *Integrated course design: Idea paper 42.* Retrieved from: www.ben.edu/programs/faculty_resources/IDEA/Papers/Idea_Paper_42%20Integrated%20Course%20Design.pdf.

6

Bringing Problems to Life Using Video, Compare/Contrast, and Role-play

Applying Experience from Medical Education to Your PBL Context

Tatum Langford Korin and LuAnn Wilkerson

Introduction

This chapter explores the following key questions:

How can I bring problems alive for my students?

How can I use the experience and research of problem types in medicine to design problems for my own PBL initiatives?

In 1969, the McMaster Medical School in Canada was the first to assert that students could learn basic science content without sitting in a lecture hall 8 hours a day for 2 years. The medical school transformed the curriculum so that small-group problem-based learning (PBL) tutorials, with a trained faculty member, became the forum for content enquiry, shared learning, and knowledge transfer. Time spent in passive learning environments, such as lectures, took a back seat to problem-focused, learner-centred, enquiry-based small-group discussions (Barrows & Tamblyn, 1980). It was not until 1985, when Harvard Medical School made the bold decision to revise its curriculum to reflect a hybrid model which involved limited lecture and laboratory time balanced with problem-based learning tutorials (Moore, 1994; Wilkerson, Steven, & Krasne, 2009), that many medical schools worldwide began adopting a problem-based pedagogical approach to address knowledge integration across courses and years (Cooke, Irby, Sullivan, & Ludmerer, 2006; Harden, Sowden, & Dunn, 1984; Irby and Wilkerson, 2003; Woods, 2007). In 2005, Kincade estimated that, in the United States, 70% of all medical schools had implemented PBL to some degree. It is precisely because of this "prevailing trend in basic science curriculum change around the world ... towards integration, both horizontally among disciplines and vertically, between basic and clinical sciences, often including PBL as an integrative function" (Wilkerson et al., 2009, p. 813) that innovative case design and delivery methods are a top priority.

Most schools that use PBL over extended periods of the curriculum find themselves experimenting with problem types and formats in response to faculty or student feedback or changing societal and professional needs. Early Problem-based Learning Module packs created by Barrows and Tamblyn (1977) have given way to multi-page paper cases, computer simulations, or standardised (simulated) patients which progressively reveal the problem. Trigger images have grown from large bulky radiographs to digital images of all types, including video encounters with the patient or situation. Problems have been developed with multiple endings that depend on decisions made by the group or that extend over multiple years to create a virtual panel of patients seen again and again by the student physician. Exercises such as concept mapping, evidence-based medicine activities, project design, patient charting, and computerised manikin simulations have been used to supplement more traditional paper problems.

These innovative educational techniques expand the learning goals that can be addressed with PBL, help to maintain student engagement, increase problem complexity, and serve to shift the balance between basic science and clinical content. Such variations in PBL can also be used to target problems to the differing levels of learners, to the learning objectives of different courses or clerkships, or to reignite the students' commitment to self-directed learning.

Chapter Overview

In this chapter, we will illustrate three variations designed to bring the PBL problem to life by engaging students in what Lave and Wenger (1991) term "legitimate peripheral participation" (LPP). In LPP, the learner is provided with increasingly greater opportunities to use resources and participate in productive activities central to the community that they are preparing to enter; here, it is the community of physicians.

> Learners inevitably participate in communities of practitioners and ... the mastery of knowledge and skill requires newcomers to move toward full participation in the sociocultural practices of a community. Legitimate peripheral participation provides a way to speak about the relations between newcomers and old-timers, and about activities, identities, artefacts, and communities of knowledge and practice. A person's intentions to learn are engaged and the meaning of learning is configured through the process of becoming a full participant in a sociocultural practice. This social process, includes, indeed it subsumes, the learning of knowledgeable skills.
>
> **(Lave & Wenger, 1991, p. 29)**

The three problem variations that we have chosen to illustrate require students to act and think like physicians: *video-based problem components*, *role-plays*, and *compare-and-contrast problems*. In describing each variation, we will identify one or more of the PBL learning goals that can be addressed, link the variation to a dimension of LPP, and provide evidence of effectiveness. The goals summarised by Hmelo-Silver (2004) in her review of PBL outcomes include the development of a flexible, integrated knowledge base; skills in problem solving and reasoning; attitudes and skills to support self-directed, lifelong learning; skills in effective collaboration; and intrinsic motivation for and persistence in learning. In medical education, there is the added goal of developing professional practice skills such as taking a medical history, counselling a patient, or negotiating a treatment plan.

Problem Types: Three Popular Options drawn from Medical Education

Video-based Problem Components

> *Learning goals*: development of a flexible, integrated knowledge base; skills in problem solving and reasoning; skills for professional practice; intrinsic motivation.
>
> *Legitimate Peripheral Participation*: listening to and observing patients, families, and other healthcare situations.
>
> *Effectiveness*: Balslev, de Grave, Muijtjens, Eika, and Scherpbier, 2008; Balslev, de Grave, Muijtjens, and Scherphier, 2005; de Leng, Dolmans, van de Wiel, Muijtjens, and van der Vleuten, 2007; Kamin, O'Sullivan, Deterding, and Younger, 2003; Kamin, O'Sullivan, Younger, and Deterding, 2001.

Most PBL curricula use cases that closely mirror actual clinical or medical science experiences. Patient cases, in particular, provide a learning environment that is motivating to medical students by engaging them in the process of diagnostic reasoning and/or treatment planning, even when the underlying basic mechanisms of health and disease are a primary focus. However, the use of paper (or text)-based cases, which is the *modus operandi* for many medical schools, does not closely simulate the real patient experience. It is difficult for text-based cases to convey the behavioural, psychosocial, and visual elements that are part of the patient's story. Short of having actual or standardised patients visit every PBL small-group session to tell their stories and be subjected to questions and physical exam manoeuvres, which is costly and labour-intensive, video is the next best thing. Videos also remind students of the human or social dimensions of healthcare and can be of actual patients or scripted to recreate a patient encounter. De Leng and colleagues (2007) conducted focus groups with 24 2nd-year Dutch medical students who had just completed a series of video-enriched PBL cases. Students agreed that video cases added authenticity, gave a more comprehensive view of the patient, motivated their involvement with the problem, and made the case more memorable. In a comparative study of three PBL case formats, two of which included video, Kamin and colleagues (2003) found that American students noted similar benefits of the video experience, adding that the video provided an effective role model for professional practice. The following examples from the video-enriched cases at the University of California, Los Angeles (UCLA) School of Medicine help to illustrate these benefits.

Authentic

In an interview with an actual patient suffering from cystic fibrosis, the sound of the patient's laboured breathing, long, strained pauses, and the sight of the oxygen tank to which she is tethered via nasal prongs gives students a sense of what it means to live with this disease.

Comprehensive

A case focused on embryology begins with a scripted video of a young woman who has come to her primary care physician, excited that using her boyfriend's acne medicine (a possible teratogen, unknown to her) has improved her complexion. She wants a prescription of her own. The physician conducts a sexual history and learns that the patient is sexually active without constant contraception. Exploring these issues, students develop learning issues that cover embryological development, teratogenicity of isotretinoin, contraception, adolescent behaviour, health policy, and pre-natal care. The visual nature of this story also provides the opportunity for students to watch and listen to a physician take a sexual history of an adolescent.

Motivating and Challenging

When students watch an interview with an actual couple and their infant son suffering from Tay Sachs disease, they are confronted with many questions and emotions. The child is enrolled in an experimental clinical study and the parents hold out hope of his cure. Students are challenged to consider physiological mechanisms of stem-cell treatment, the patient's prognosis, and the ethical issues of clinical research in addition to the basic biology of the disease.

Memorable

In a case involving actual newborn twins developed by Kamin and colleagues (2003), the physician is videotaped examining both infants. One infant appears small and lethargic with little muscle tone on passive movement, while the other is larger, active, and responsive. This striking comparison triggers instant curiosity and may create a lifelong image of what is meant by the term "floppy baby".

Several studies suggest videos may be advantageous in promoting aspects of clinical reasoning. In a qualitative analysis of critical-thinking categories that involved comparing audiotapes of 6 hours of PBL discussion of a video and a text case, students engaged in more data-gathering and problem-description activities in the video group than in the text group (Kamin et al., 2001). In a comparison of a video versus a text case, using discourse analysis, paediatric residents used significantly more instances of data exploration, theory building, and theory evaluation in the video condition (Balslev et al., 2005).

Reflective Exercise

What video-based material could you consider using, designing, or developing within your own PBL initiative?

Do you plan to use existing video material, film a real situation, or script your video?

In the design or selection of video components, what features would you need to include in order to ensure they are:

authentic;
comprehensive;
motivating and challenging;
memorable?

Role-playing Problem Types

Learning goals: development of skills in problem solving and reasoning; skills in collaboration and teamwork; skills for professional practice.

Legitimate Peripheral Participation: learning from members of a healthcare team, assuring clear communication and understanding, participating in the clinical team.

Effectiveness: Prince, van Eijs, Boshuizen, van der Vleuten, and Scherpbier, 2005; Willis, Jones, McArdle, and O'Neill, 2003.

The small group nature of PBL offers the opportunity for students to develop skills through collaboration and teamwork. However, results are mixed on the usefulness of PBL in producing this outcome (Willis et al., 2003). A survey of graduates of one Dutch PBL school and four non-PBL schools on perceived competencies, including teamwork, found that both groups reported the same level of teamwork skills 18 months after graduation; however, a higher percentage of PBL graduates (19.4%) reported that they had learned teamwork skills in medical school than did non-PBL graduates (5.8%) (Prince et al., 2005). The majority of both groups indicated that teamwork had been largely learned on the job and not in school! Just placing students in small groups for PBL or any other type of discussion may not guarantee that they will develop skills in teamwork.

How might the PBL experience be modified to emphasise teamwork skills? Several suggestions appear in the medical education literature. At the University of Manchester, PBL cases include specific references to non-physician members of the healthcare team caring for the patient (Willis et al., 2003). Role-playing teamwork situations as part of PBL is another possible approach and, as part of PBL, it is not new (Menahem & Paget, 1990). It has generally involved the use of standardised patients or the "tutor plays patient", in which the tutor is charged with providing answers in response to enquiries from members of the group (Barrows & Tamblyn, 1977) or, more recently, from a computerised database (Kamin et al., 2003). Role-playing, in this context, is focused on students developing skills for professional practice.

Role-playing can also be used to reinforce the importance of peer learning and collaboration. PBL requires students to learn from one another, listening carefully in discussion, understanding one another's individual learning issues, and asking questions to clarify their own understanding or that of others in the group. In order to assist students in making this shift to peer learning at UCLA, we have written a new section into many of the PBL cases for 1st-year medical students that occurs after the discussion of learning issues during a return tutorial. This new section informs the group members that they are the medical team caring for this patient and are about to be visited by a family member, the patient, or a physician who wants to know more about the disease, its diagnosis, treatment, or possible outcomes, and outlines a number of questions that this visitor might ask. The questions represent major learning goals for the case and, when well selected, are closely linked to the issues that students have just pursued during their previous discussion in tutorial. Students are given 10 minutes for a period of co-operative learning in which the goal is for everyone to reach a common level of understanding of these central issues. In these 10 minutes, the students ask one another about areas of uncertainty or remaining confusion, so that everyone is ready to address each of these questions should he or she be asked by the "visitor". During this co-operative period, the tutor remains uninvolved, but after the 10 minutes has elapsed, the tutor takes on the role of the visitor and poses questions to individual members of the group. The following illustrates this section of a case of cystic fibrosis as part of an introductory course for 1st-year medical students.

Use of Role-play to Stimulate Cooperative Peer Learning (Author: Sally Krasne, UCLA)

Day 2, Part 1, Case of the Leaking Lung

(This is a section of a case of cystic fibrosis as part of an introductory course for 1st-year medical students.)

The results of the DNA test confirmed that Herman suffered from cystic fibrosis (CF) but that he did not have the most severe form of it since he had a severe genetic mutation in only one allele of the CFTR gene and a more mild mutation on the other allele. Herman arranged to meet Dr Grady (the geneticist), the attending physician, the respiratory therapist, and other members of the team. He told them that he had a number of questions that he wanted to ask them.

1. How did the sweat test that you gave me work? Why does CF cause my sweat to be so salty?
2. How do my particular CFTE mutations differ from other CF mutations in CFTR gene? Was I at greater risk because my family is from Israel?
3. Why does having CF cause me to have all this congestion in my lungs? Is there anything I can do to avoid so much bronchitis?
4. Is there a cure for CF, and if not, might there be one soon?
5. How will you treat my CF? Do I need to be careful about what I eat or what I do? Can I do anything to make myself less likely to get sick?

Role-playing is also used during later courses in the pre-clerkship phase to help students develop skills needed to work successfully in the type of clinical team that they will encounter during their clinical assignments. In this variation, the first session on a new case occurs as usual until the students are ready to finalise their learning issues. At this point, the group considers how each of the issues might be relevant to the healthcare team during discussion with a patient using the following prescribed roles:

- *The Patient's Student Physician – Presenter*: This student is responsible for presenting the case to the team at the beginning of the return tutorial. In order to prepare, the student is expected to have read broadly on the possible diagnoses represented on the learning issue list.
- *Postgraduate Trainee – Patient Educator*: This student is expected to be able to explain the clinical condition and plan to the "patient" using jargon-free language and to ensure the patient's understanding. The student also needs to be prepared to answer any questions from the patient about his/her condition and to obtain informed consent.
- *Patient*: The student in the role of patient will ask difficult questions about his or her condition, treatment risks and benefits, or other learning issues drawn from the list. This student is also expected to check the Internet for information that a patient with this condition might easily have found.
- *Attending Physician*: This student will lead the discussion with the care team and the patient. This role requires broad preparation across shared learning issues.

Three additional roles are added to the team in relation to evidence-based medicine. In the hospital, these roles might be taken on by any member of the clinical team, from student to attending physician.

- *Evidence-based Consultant #1*: This student is to prepare a comparative chart of primary sources to answer one of the learning issues related to diagnostic or treatment decisions, using the Best Bet format found at www.bestbets.org.
- *Evidence-based Consultant #2*: This student is to identify a primary article related to a question about clinical outcomes in the case. If an outcome does not appear on the learning issue list, one is added at the end of the first session.
- *Guideline Consultant*: This student is responsible for searching for and summarising any clinical guidelines that would be applicable for this patient.

Some learning issues offer the opportunity for other roles, for example, nutritionist, nurse, social worker, or family member. The remaining students take on individual learning issues from the list that have not been covered by the previous roles, usually basic science questions.

During the return tutorial, the "attending physician" guides the team in organising its work, presenting the case, discussing the possible diagnoses, determining the next steps in work up or treatment, and discussing the decisions with the patient. The evidence-based consultants will offer the resources that they have identified as relevant to the decision-making process as it unfolds. Students have found that playing these different roles helps them to appreciate the importance of each member of the team and prepares them for the next stage of their medical education, clinical immersion.

Despite the challenges associated with designing and facilitating role-plays of these types, our students have evaluated them as helpful, particularly the clinical team roles, in preparing them for clinical work and stressing the importance of peer learning.

Reflective Exercise

- What role-plays could you identify, develop, and use within your own PBL initiative?
- How do you plan to assess the efficacy of the role-plays you implement?

Compare and Contrast Problem Types

Learning goals: development of a flexible knowledge base, skills in problem solving, and reasoning.

Legitimate Peripheral Participation: engaging in analytic and non-analytic reasoning in making diagnostic decisions.

Effectiveness: Ark, Brooks, and Eva, 2007; Eva, Hatala, LeBlanc, and Brooks, 2007; Patel, Arocha, and Leccisi, 2001.

A stated goal of PBL is the development of skills in problem solving and reasoning. The hope is that, by practising the reasoning process during PBL case discussion, students will be able to apply this approach in the clinical setting. Several concerns have been expressed over the desirability of relying on PBL alone in teaching students how to approach problems. Patel and colleagues (2001) warn that the hypothetico-deductive analytic reasoning process used in PBL may result in students with a limited approach to new problems compared to students trained in more traditional curricula. More recently, studies have demonstrated that purposefully teaching students to use both an analytic and a non-analytic reasoning approach, the latter relying on pattern recognition, are associated with greater diagnostic accuracy (Ark et al., 2007; Eva et al., 2007). PBL also raises concerns that learning core concepts in relation to a single case, called context specificity, makes transfer to new cases and situations more difficult than if those same concepts had been learned using multiple examples (Coulson, Feltovich, & Spiro, 1997). The addition of a new feature to PBL may be useful in addressing both of these concerns.

The value of contrast and compare in increasing transfer is one of the most studied strategies in the field of transfer research (Catrambone & Holyoak, 1989). By having to compare and contrast features across multiple instances, students can be guided to develop the deep structures of a concept or to construct a generalised schema for use in new situations rather than relying on the similarity of surface features (e.g. clinical symptoms) between the learned problem and the new problem. Drawing on their theory of cognitive flexibility, Coulson et al. (1997, p. 142) used four cases of hypertension to demonstrate how being able to compare the underlying physiologic mechanisms at work in each would lead to different treatments and outcomes:

> For learners to develop cognitive flexibility and acquire complex knowledge structures that support flexible cognition, the same items of knowledge must be represented in memory in a variety of different ways, including those that reflect their use in many different contexts (commensurate with their complex and irregular structure).

Various approaches have been added to PBL to stimulate compare-and-contrast discussion. First, the first section of a case can be written to purposively create a broad set of hypotheses that can be compared and contrasted during the reasoning process before additional sections of the case are distributed. This approach requires faculty development so that the tutors systematically induce the contrastive reasoning process (Bowen, 2006). For example, individual students might be asked to use the initial patient data to argue for one hypothesis over another. Alternatively, students might be asked to diagram the process by which mechanisms produce symptoms or vice versa. When contrastive thinking is not explicitly set as a goal, the tutor may or may not engage students in this activity. Second, a PBL problem can actually consist of two or three cases selected purposefully to stimulate comparison and contrast across deep features. For example, two patients with a rash are presented; an older adult with a reactivation of a former viral infection and a child with an acute viral infection. Rather than focusing solely on symptoms, students are encouraged to explore viral mechanisms, particularly those that allow for the latency after resolution of the acute episode of infection. Third, an in-depth PBL case can be followed by several short "vignettes", illustrating the same surface features as the main case, but possessing very different causal mechanisms. Vignettes might be introduced in a subsequent laboratory or lecture or embedded at the end of a PBL case. For example, the PBL case of a young man with bradycardia and irregular heartbeats who is an avid exerciser is paired with four vignettes of patients having the same heart rate and blood pressure but very different pathophysiologies. These vignettes are an engaging way to stimulate contrastive thinking while promoting pattern-recognition.

In confronting the same concepts in multiple situations, students are encouraged to construct differing representations in memory. Research in learning for transfer suggests that the construction of high-quality schema is associated with greater accuracy in accessing and applying prior instances to new situations. However, research by Catrambone and Holyoak (1989) suggests that three or more initial instances and specific instructions are needed to support the student's development of a high-quality schema. Thus, faculty development for tutors is essential in order to maximise the effects of this approach on students' reasoning.

Reflective Exercise

- How might multiple problems be linked to your PBL problem to stimulate compare-and-contrast discussion?
- What underlying features should you use in determining the appropriate choice of compare-and-contrast problems?
- Where, in your curriculum, will compare-and-contrast problems have the most impact?

Implications for PBL Practice

There are many more decisions to be made in constructing PBL problems in medical education, some of which may be relevant in other disciplines as well.

Should PBL cases represent common diseases or problems seen in the population? When are simple, rather than more complex, problems appropriate? How might preventive medicine and non-medical cases be constructed to engage students when the mystery of diagnosis is missing? How can problems be shaped to motivate persistence in learning? Is there a developmental sequence of case features that would logically move students from more peripheral participation to more central participation in the work of being a physician? In this chapter, we have sought to address just a few of the variations in problem design that can contribute to bringing cases to life. Each of these features was selected for its promise in engaging the learner in accomplishing one or more central PBL learning goals while learning to use the types of resources and skills needed for lifelong learning in their chosen community of practice. Implementation will require the involvement of multiple stakeholders to provide the right balance of goals for the specific programme and a commitment to ongoing faculty development for tutors who may find such variations daunting to facilitate. Additional research will be needed to determine whether these variations in PBL problems will produce more than student enthusiasm.

Acknowledgements

We wish to acknowledge the contributions of Sally Krasne, Carl Stevens, Matthew Leibowitz, and Janet Pregler along with the multiple course directors at the David Geffen School of Medicine at UCLA in the initial design, implementation, and refinement of these PBL variations.

References

Ark, T.K., Brooks, L.R., & Eva, K.W. (2007). The benefits of flexibility: The pedagogical value of instructions to adopt multifaceted diagnostic reasoning strategies. *Medical Education, 41*, 281–287.

Balslev, T., de Grave, W.S., Muijtjens, A.M.M., & Scherphier, A.J.J.A. (2005). A comparison of text and video cases in a postgraduate problem-based learning format. *Medical Education, 39*, 1086–1092.

Balslev, T., de Grave, W., Muijtjens, A.M.M., Eika, B., & Scherpbier, A.J.J.A (2008). The development of shared cognition in paediatric residents analyzing a patient video versus a paper patient case. *Advances in Health Sciences Education, 14*(4), 557–565.

Barrows, H.S., & Tamblyn, R.M. (1977). The portable patient problem pack: A problem based learning unit. *Journal of Medical Education, 52*, 1002–1004.

Barrows, H.S., & Tamblyn, R.M. (1980). *Problem-based learning: An approach to medical education.* New York: Springer Publishing.

Bowen, J.L. (2006). Educational strategies to promote clinical diagnostic reasoning. *New England Journal of Medicine, 355*, 2217–2225.

Bransford, J.D., Sherwood, R.D., & Hasselbring, T.S. (1990). Anchored instruction: Why we need it and how technology can help. In D. Nix & R.J. Spiro (Eds.), *Cognition, education and multimedia: Exploring ideas in high technology.* Hillsdale, NJ: Lawrence Erlbaum Publishers.

Catrambone, R., & Holyoak, K.J. (1989). Overcoming contextual limitations in problem-solving transfer. *Journal of Experimental Psychology, Learning, Memory & Cognition, 15*, 1147–1156.

Cooke, M., Irby, D.M., Sullivan, W., & Ludmerer, K.M. (2006). American medical education 100 years after the Flexner report. *New England Journal of Medicine, 355*, 1339–1344.

Coulson, R.L., Feltovich, P., & Spiro, R.J. (1997). Cognitive flexibility in medicine: An application to the recognition and understanding of hypertension. *Advances in Health Science Education, 2*, 141–161.

De Leng, B.A., Dolmans, D.H.J.M., van de Wiel, M.W.J., Muijtjens, A.M.M., & van der Vleuten, C.P.M. (2007). How video cases should be used as authentic stimuli in problem-based medical education. *Medical Education, 41*, 181–188.

Eva, K.W., Hatala, R.M., LeBlanc, V.R., & Brooks, L.R. (2007). Teaching from the clinical reasoning literature: Combined reasoning strategies help novice diagnosticians overcome misleading information. *Medical Education, 41*, 1152–1158.

Harden, R.M., Snowden, S., & Dunn, W.R. (1984). Some educational strategies in curriculum development: The SPICES model. *Medical Education, 18*, 284–297.

Hmelo-Silver, C.E. (2004). Problem-based learning: What and how do students learn? *Educational Psychology Review, 16*, 235–266.

Irby, D.M., & Wilkerson, L. (2003). Educational innovations in academic medicine and environmental trends. *Journal of General Internal Medicine, 18*, 370–376.

Kamin, C., O'Sullivan, P., Deterding, R., & Younger M. (2003). A comparison of critical thinking in groups of third-year medical students in text, video, and virtual PBL case modalities. *Academic Medicine, 78*, 204–211.

Kamin, C.S., O'Sullivan, P.S., Younger, M., & Deterding, R. (2001). Measuring critical thinking in problem-based learning discourse. *Teaching & Learning in Medicine, 13*, 27–35.

Kenny, N.P., & Beagan, B.L. (2004). The patient as text: A challenge for problem-based learning. *Medical Education, 38*, 1081–1082.

Kincade, S. (2005). A snapshot of the status of problem-based learning in U.S. medical schools, 2003–04. *Academic Medicine, 80*, 300–301.

Lave, J., & Wenger, E. (1991). *Situated learning: Legitimate peripheral participation*. Cambridge: Cambridge University Press.

Menahem, S., & Paget, N. (1990). Role play for the clinical tutor: Towards problem-based learning. *Medical Teacher, 12*, 57–61.

Moore, G.T. (1994). *The first curriculum: Content and process*. In D.C. Tosteson, S.J. Adelstein, & S.T. Carver (Eds.), *New Pathways to medical education: Learning to learn at Harvard Medical School* (pp. 470–479). Cambridge, MA: Harvard University Press.

Patel, V.L., Arocha, J.F., & Leccisi, M.S. (2001). Impact of undergraduate medical training on housestaff problem-solving performance: Implications for problem-based curricula. *Journal of Dental Education, 65*, 1199–1218.

Prince, K.J.A.H., van Eijs, P.W.L.J., Boshuizen, H.P.A., van der Vleuten, C.P.M., & Scherpbier, A.J.J.A. (2005). General competencies of problem-based learning (PBL) and non-PBL graduates. *Medical Education, 39*, 394–401.

Wilkerson, L., Steven, C.M., & Krasne, S. (2009). No content without context: Integrating basic, clinical, and social sciences in a pre-clerkship curriculum. *Medical Teacher, 31*, 812–821.

Willis, S., Jones, A., McArdle, P., & O'Neill, P.A. (2003). A qualitative study of the attitudes towards teamwork of graduates from a traditional and an integrated undergraduate medical course. *Advances in Health Sciences Education, 8*(2), 139–148.

Woods, N.N. (2007). Science is fundamental: The role of biomedical knowledge in clinical reasoning. *Medical Education, 41*, 1173–1177.

Further Resources

Azer, S. (2007). Twelve tips for creating trigger images for problem-based learning cases. *Medical Teacher, 29*, 93–97.

Eva, K.W. (2005). What every teacher needs to know about clinical reasoning. *Medical Education, 39*, 98–106.

Neville, A.J., & Norman, G.R. (2007). PBL in the undergraduate MD program at McMaster University: Three iterations in three decades. *Academic Medicine, 82*, 370–374.

7

Employers' Perspectives on Problem-based Learning Initiatives

Siobhán Drohan, Yves Mauffette, and Jean-Louis Allard

Introduction

This chapter addresses the following key question:

> How do we promote and facilitate the design of realistic problems that will help PBL students develop a range of skills relevant for their lives and their work?

If one of the key goals of educators is to prepare students to work in their professions, then listening to the perspectives of employers is a crucial activity. Higher education environments are not always good at doing this, but we do know that employers want to be listened to and have their ideas incorporated into tertiary education syllabi.

In this chapter, we argue particularly for the role of realistic problem design and the benefits of problem-based learning (PBL) for the development of the much sought-after transferable skill set. This argument will draw on a combination of the research, academic practice, and industrial experience of the authors.

Chapter Overview

The focus of this chapter is to present three interrelated key principles:

1. Employers' perspectives stress the indispensability of transferable skills for successful recruitment, integration into work roles, and promotional capabilities for all professions.
2. Employers' viewpoints of the effectiveness of PBL programmes can shape the development of these transferable skills.
3. Employers desire the types of PBL problems that develop these transferable skills in addition to technical skills.

The employers' perspectives on each key principle will be discussed, in turn, in the following section.

Illuminative Concepts on Employers' Perspectives

There are three interrelated ideas that help us, as PBL practitioners, to integrate employers' perspectives into our initiatives, namely: transferable skills, effectiveness of PBL, and realistic problem design.

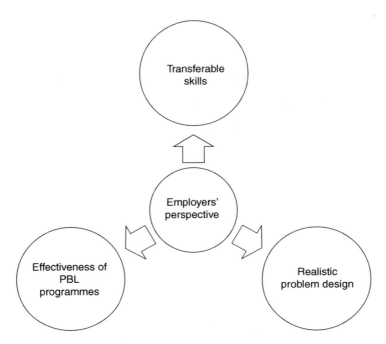

Figure 7.1 Employers' perspectives on PBL initiatives.

One of the challenges in designing any given curriculum lies in understanding the set of skills required by its future graduates. Numerous studies assert the growing need for transferable skills in a variety of disciplines including business (Bennis & O'Toole, 2005), engineering (Shuman, Besterfield-Sacre, & McGourty, 2005), and information technology (IT) (Swanson & Phillips, 2004), to name a few. As well as subject knowledge and discipline-specific competences, there are more generic skills that higher education environments need to foster among students, skills that will assist learners in a whole range of ways within their lives and at work. Such generic, transferable skills are highly valued by future employers but are often lacking in recent graduates (Klaus, 2008). Academia calls for all graduates, irrespective of discipline, to possess better critical-thinking, problem-solving, and communication skills (Skilbeck, 2001). Employers often cite collaboration, time-management, multi-tasking, and customer service skills (Curry, Sherry, & Tunney, 2003).

Employers assert that the presence of transferable skills facilitates the integration of graduates into their new roles (McMurtrey, Downey, Zeltmann, & Friedman, 2008), while also enhancing career progression and promotional capabilities (United States Department of Commerce, 2003). When recruiting graduates, many employers identify transferable skills as more important than technical skills (Curry et al., 2003; Uden & Moran, 2007) and these skills often become the deciding factor for hiring successful candidates (Branine, 2008; Byrne, 1996). Consequently, many authors have called for the examination and enhancement of current curricula to concentrate more on developing transferable skills (McMurtrey et al., 2008; Yen, Chen, Lee, & Koh, 2003).

We argue here that many of the transferable skills that employers seek are a by-product of PBL initiatives. Glasgow (1997) and Duch, Groh, and Allen (2001) assert that PBL imparts domain-specific knowledge in tandem with a suite of transferable skills that are sought by employers, academia, and policy makers.

In the IT discipline, as a case in point, the transferable skills that PBL fosters are beneficial for the professional development of graduates (Bentley, Lowry, & Sandy, 1999). In addition, the skills developed in PBL programmes closely match the transferable skills identified in the 2008 curriculum guidelines of the Association for Computing Machinery (ACM) and the Institute of Electrical and Electronics Engineers Computer Society (IEEE-CS). There is also a close alignment between the PBL approach and the IT workplace, as both are multidisciplinary, problem-driven entities that require teamwork and self-directed learning (Ellis et al., 1998). Bentley et al. (1999) suggest that these similarities could be exploited to simulate a realistic IT problem domain in an undergraduate learning environment. Hence, the virtues of PBL in preparing students to acquire transferable skills such as problem solving is a major asset for developing truly educated individuals (Knowlton, 2003).

Effectiveness of PBL Programmes

The medical profession has a longer tradition of training their students using PBL and it has been argued that PBL may have relative advantages (Sanson-Fisher & Lynagh, 2005). For example, Williams and Day (2009) found that, within the workforce, nurses trained in a PBL programme were perceived to have a better grounding in theory than those in traditional programmes and that the PBL graduates showed more initiative. Anecdotal evidence provided by former PBL students suggests that they continue to use the PBL approach to tackle problems in their workplace (Uden & Moran, 2007). However, despite this positive and promising evidence, more comprehensive meta-analyses of employers' perceptions of PBL graduates are still scarce.

The following case study of employers' perspectives regarding the transferable skill set of PBL students provides some insight into the effectiveness of PBL in this context.

Case Study: What Employers Seek and How Students from PBL Initiatives Are Perceived

eXia is a French computer science school created in 2004 within the Cesi group. It prepares students for the current IT world and specialises in software and network development. In creating this school, the challenge that eXia faced was the new knowledge demands of industries to keep up with the fast-changing nature of IT and to prepare students with a broad range of expertise. Employers sought technically skilled IT graduates who, as argued earlier in this chapter, possessed, as individuals, a series of transferable skills, such as a lifelong learner, and had the ability to work in groups and could communicate effectively. These industrial demands led the programme developers to use PBL as an approach to educate their students. A programme was set up using the PBL method (see Allard & Mauffette, 2006a for a complete description). The first two years of this PBL programme provide a generalised course of study and the final years allow the students to acquire more autonomy and develop their individual skills. At specific times, the students are also required to complete internships.

In this PBL programme, the eXia school's first cohort of students in computer science was required to complete an internship in various companies. These 1st-year students had to complete a two-and-a-half month internship. A total of 80 students were placed in 10 different cities in France and were required to complete duties relating to software development. At the end of the internship, the workplace supervisors completed an evaluation questionnaire and gave their opinion on the student's abilities and competence. The questionnaire was designed to measure the students' autonomy, team work, communication, technical skills, and other abilities sought in the programme. The results indicated that the internship supervisors awarded higher grades to the PBL students than were previously observed in traditional programmes (90% of the students were awarded an A to A+). The supervisors recognised that the PBL students could easily understand and analyse complex situations and were able to quickly act on them. Within this survey, the supervisors were asked the following question: "If you judge the intern's capacity to successfully accomplish the given tasks, what is the quality that contributed the most?" The supervisors responded that, for these PBL interns, the quality that contributed most was autonomy and adaptability (see Figure 7.2). The supervisors also recognised that the PBL interns demonstrated team work, initiative, communication, integration within the work group, and time-management skills. In addition, the supervisors were astonished by the efficacy of the PBL method in training the students. These results are somewhat surprising since they applied to all of the students in their first internship and suggest that the PBL method attained the initial goals sought in this programme.

Based on this first survey within the eXia programme, it appears that the pedagogy of the PBL structure did promote the transferable skills sought by the employers. Hence, it did permit students to be sufficiently autonomous and adaptable in work situations found within industry. We can assume that the eXia programme may, indeed, adequately prepare students for the professional life; however, these results must be verified through time (Sandel, Allard, & Mauffette, 2006).

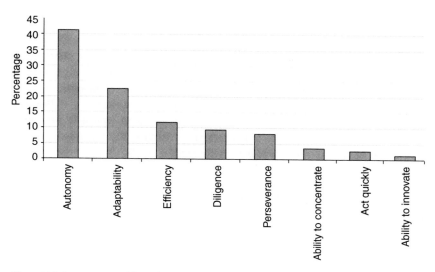

Figure 7.2 Percentage of first choice by supervisors (Allard & Mauffette, 2006b).

Realistic Problem Design

The quality of PBL problems is central to the success of the PBL approach (Duch, 2001). Therefore, increased efforts should be aimed at the development of suitable real-world problems, constructively aligned with the learning outcomes, while also meeting the skills requirements of the professions. Problems used within programmes should be motivating and challenging for the students in order to promote learning (Mauffette, Kandlbinder, & Soucisse, 2004). The challenge faced by a number of PBL practitioners is to consider the issue of problem difficulty within a PBL curriculum in order to meet the effectiveness of the students' learning outcomes (Jonassen & Hung, 2008).

If we take the IT industry as an example, more structured IT problems should be presented to novice PBL students. As the students become increasingly familiar with the PBL process and the subject domain knowledge, the facilitators should gradually reduce the scaffolding supports (Beaumount, Sackville, & Cheng, 2004). Brodie, Zhou, and Gibbons (2008) view the development of the PBL problem as the most arduous aspect of IT curriculum development. In an effort to counteract this difficulty, they have provided three suggestions for developing suitable problems, which could be applied to any discipline. These suggestions are:

1. Use problems obtained directly from the IT industry.
2. Develop new problems from published guidelines.
3. Draw from existing case studies that have been written up within the field.

1. Use Problems Obtained Directly from the IT Industry

Brodie et al.'s (2008) first suggestion involves consulting with the IT industry in order to obtain relevant projects and problems currently in existence in their workplace. In Drohan's (2005) study, it was found that, in general, IT industry problems were highly suitable for the PBL classroom. The IT practitioners rated the extent to which the nine characteristics of the PBL problems (Duch, 2001; Glasgow, 1997) were prevalent in typical IT problems. Table 7.1 illustrates that each characteristic of the PBL problem, except reflection on the solution, was extremely similar to the characteristics of IT problems encountered in industry. Reflection on the solution was not prevalent in industry due to time constraints and the workload of practitioners. However, extra attention to reflection in higher education could enable practitioners to reflect more speedily (see Chapter 12 for strategies for developing students' reflection skills). It is this overall similarity in the characteristics of PBL problems and IT problems in industry that renders IT problems highly suitable for the PBL classroom.

The approach described here, of using typical workplace problems, can be applied to any discipline and is particularly beneficial for PBL students, as they prefer working on authentic real-world problems as opposed to problems bearing little resemblance to those found in industry (McCracken & Waters, 1999). In addition, employers' suggestions for enhancing transferable skills in undergraduate education included using industry-specific case studies and workshops (Curry et al., 2003).

2. Develop New Problems from Published Guidelines

Brodie et al.'s (2008) second suggestion is to construct new problems using published guidelines for developing PBL problems (for an example of such guidelines, refer to chapter 4, Delisle, 1997). A perspective of IT practitioners

Table 7.1 Prevalence of PBL Characteristics in IT Problems in Industry (Drohan, 2005)

PBL Characteristic	Mean	Standard Deviation
Problems have several correct solutions	4.4	0.8
Problems are complete	3.1	0.9
Problems are ill-structured	3.5	1.0
Problems are multidisciplinary in nature	4.4	1.0
Problems require collaboration to solve them	4.0	1.0
Explicitly plan an approach to solve a problem	3.3	1.1
Reference to similar problems as an aid	4.1	0.8
Identification of learning issues	3.5	1.3
Reflection on the solution	2.6	1.0

Note
Key scale: (not at all) 1–5 (very much so).

is that the unrealistic, trivial IT problems used in academia contribute to the shortcomings in the graduates' transferable skills, such as problem-solving skills (Drohan, Stapleton, & Stack, 2006), thus, when developing team-based IT problems, an academia–industry collaboration may produce more realistic real-world problems for students to solve (Gorka, Miller, & Howe, 2007; Sabin, 2008). Academia should endeavour to work closely with industry partners, using published guidelines to develop suitable PBL problems. In Chapter 3, a process for problem design days with academics and professionals from different workplaces is outlined.

It is important to note that frequent industry–academia collaboration is not always feasible owing to the many pressures such as workload, urgency of problem development, unanticipated workplace demands on professionals, and so on. In addition to working with employers, academics can also turn to Figure 7.3 for guidance in which the nine characteristics of PBL problems (as presented in Table 7.1) are accompanied by practitioner suggestions regarding the development of real-world problems for the classroom and the skills that could potentially be developed (Drohan, 2005). These guidelines could be used as a starting point and then amended or extended to support PBL problem development for specific professions.

3. Use Case Studies in Textbooks

The third and final suggestion is to use and manipulate case studies in textbooks in order to ensure that the PBL team can complete the selected project in one semester (Brodie et al., 2008). However, Duch (2001) cautions against selecting a problem that is too trivial, as students may break the work down into independent tasks, assign the tasks to individuals, and then amalgamate the contributions at project submission time. This may result in students learning less instead of more.

Implications for Your PBL Practice

Select or Amend any PBL Model So That the Tutorial Process Is Representative of Your Discipline/Profession

Beyond the nature of the problems, successful learning in PBL lies in the interactivity and function of the tutorial sessions (Virtanen, Kosunen, Holmberg-Marttila, & Virjo, 1999). It is assumed, according to Davis and Harden (1999), that PBL learning is most effective when active and independent students handle problems together, enquire into the beliefs and arguments behind their own thinking and actions, deliberate about theoretical explanations for phenomena, and, thus, construct their personal knowledge and understanding. In addition, it is the structure of the problem-handling process, such as the classic "Seven-jump model" from Maastricht University or the "Tampere Model" described by Holmberg-Marttila, Hakkarainen, Virjo, and Nikkari (2005), that engages the learning process for the students.

PBL problem characteristics	Suggestions for use in PBL scenarios	Potential skills developed
Problems should have more than one right solution.	Students should investigate various possible solutions balancing a multitude of criteria including resourcing, time constraints, costs, adherence to standards, and efficiency. The student should then implement the solution that best satisfies these criteria.	Decision making, appraisal skills, quality control, ability to see bigger picture and stamina.
Problems should be more complex than simple.	As many professional problems are complex, the solution for the problems developed for the classroom should not be obvious.	Flexibility and ability to decompose problems.
Problems should be ill-structured in nature.	As the information gathering phase is considered one of the most crucial steps in professional problem solving, the students should rarely get sufficient requirements in order to tackle the problem. This would require a great deal of investigation, as well as communication between, for example, the person acting as a client and the students in order to tie down the requirements.	Investigative skills, improved communication skills with non-technical users, conversion of business needs to technical requirements, and stamina.
Problems should be multidisciplinary in nature.	Problems should cross boundaries into other disciplines.	Multidisciplinary knowledge in the context of the discipline being studied.
Problems should focus on team work and collaboration.	Each problem should have several students assigned to it. The problems should increase the focus on team work; the more team-based assignments, and the larger the team size, the better.	Collaborative skills, team work, interpersonal skills, and conflict management.

Figure 7.3 PBL characteristics and their potential for use in PBL scenarios (adapted from Drohan, 2005).

PBL problem characteristics	Suggestions for use in PBL scenarios	Potential skills developed
Problems should require planning.	Planning an approach to a problem contributes to the successful, timely completion of the task. Planning is not that important for simple tasks, but is crucial for larger problems, in particular, where team work is required.	Time management, delegation, planning, and organisational skills.
Problems should promote the use of reference tools.	The students should use reference tools such as knowledge bases, the Internet, and prior knowledge arising from exposure to similar problems. If used correctly, these tools could provide necessary information for solving a reoccurrence of a problem or a similar problem situation.	Ability to draw on prior experiences/ reuse of prior work, efficiency, and investigative skills.
Problems should require the identification of learning issues.	The identification of learning issues requires students to list what they do and do not know about the problem. Each learning issue then requires investigation in order to solve the problem.	Self-directed learning, investigative skills, ability to see bigger picture, understanding own knowledge and limitations.
Each student/ group should reflect on the effectiveness of the solution.	Practitioners generally do not reflect on their solutions due to time constraints and work pressures. However, if circumstances allowed, the majority would reflect. Those practitioners that did reflect found it beneficial. As reflection is very important when learning in the PBL environment, it should be performed both individually and as a team-based exercise in the classroom.	Self-appraisal skills, peer review, critical and analytical thinking.

Figure 7.3 Continued.

Thus, it is essential that the model is adapted to its domain and to its actors. See Chapter 1, Figure 1.2 for an example of an adapted PBL process guide.

Therefore, the model must adhere to the principles of PBL and reflect the specific profession/discipline/context. Careful planning must be undertaken to elaborate the steps of the tutorial process in order to represent the nature of the field. For example, formulating hypotheses within the scientific method is a key element in the reasoning process of future scientists; the PBL model and its steps should reflect such consideration (Poliquin & Mauffette, 1997). Hence, the parallel between the PBL steps and the scientific method for future biologists, described in Poliquin and Mauffette (1997), is a key element in the training of any scientist. Similarly, within our PBL practices, the steps required for future IT experts should also reflect the underlying reasoning process of the profession.

Design Realistic Problems

What should PBL practitioners do to design problems that promote transferable skills in the PBL classroom? We suggest that you consider the following checklist.

Realistic Problem Design Meeting Academic Learning Outcomes

Consider realistic problem design and whether you want to source an existing problem from the professions, collaborate with industry to write a problem, or use a case study from a relevant textbook. Ensure the problem is constructively aligned with your learning outcomes.

Realistic Problem Design Meeting the Professions' Transferable Skills Requirements

Consider the transferable skills that are particularly relevant for your profession and your PBL course. When designing or selecting the problem, consider each of the characteristics of PBL problems (see Figure 7.3) and the transferable skills that the students could potentially develop. Ensure the problem is constructively aligned with the transferable skills requirements of your profession.

Select Problem Difficulty

Decide on the problem difficulty, based on your students' novice, intermediate, or advanced level of study and exposure to PBL.

Engage Your Students

Ensure the PBL problem is motivating and will suitably challenge your students. What are your plans for designing problems so that your students experience the nuances and realities of their chosen discipline?

Conclusion

Cowdroy (1994) suggested that PBL has the potential to answer the transferable skills needed by our present society. However, adopting PBL requires a range of elements such as major changes in the curriculum's design and content, the writing of relevant problems (with employers) and adapting PBL models.

An important challenge for our present educational system is to produce graduates with appropriate professional competences. Our traditional pedagogical approaches fail to adequately equip learners to solve problems in their professional practice and become self-directed learners (Poikela & Poikela, 2005). Our future educational system must be able to respond to emerging pedagogical approaches and to the demands from industry, government, and all levels of society. Therefore, our future programmes must provide graduates with sufficient domain-specific technical knowledge and the transferable skills essential to succeed in their future professions. PBL will do that!

References

Allard, J.-L., & Mauffette, Y. (2006a). L'APP pour un grand nombre d'étudiants réparti sur plusieurs sites: Est-ce possible? In M. Frenay, B. Raucent, & P. Wouters (Eds.), *Actes du 4e colloque "Questions de pédagogie dans l'enseignement supérieur: les pédagogies actives: enjeux et conditions"* (pp. 431–437). Belgique: UCL Presses Universitaires de Louvain.

Allard, J.-L., & Mauffette, Y. (2006b). Experience: Did PBL make a difference during student internships? *Proceedings of the 2006 International PBL Conference*, Lima, Peru.

Association for Computing Machinery (ACM) and IEEE Computer Society (IEEE-CS). (2008). *Computer science curriculum 2008: An interim revision of CS 2001.* Retrieved from: www.acm.org//education/curricula/ComputerScience2008.pdf.

Beaumont, C., Sackville, A., & Cheng, C.S. (2004). Identifying good practice in the use of PBL to teach computing. *Innovation in Teaching and Learning in Information and Computer Sciences, 3(1).* Retrieved from: www.ics.heacademy.ac.uk/italics/vol3iss1.htm.

Bennis, W., & O'Toole, J. (2005). How business schools lost their way. *Harvard Business Review, 83(5),* 96–104.

Bentley, J.F., Lowry, G.R., & Sandy, G.A. (1999). Towards the compleat information systems graduate: A problem-based learning approach. In *Proceedings of the Australasian Conference on Information Systems, 10,* 65–75.

Branine, M. (2008). Graduate recruitment and selection in the UK. *Career Development International, 13(6),* 497–513.

Brodie, L., Zhou, H., & Gibbons, A. (2008). Steps in developing an advanced software engineering course using problem-based learning. *Engineering Education: Journal of the Higher Education Academy Engineering Subject Centre, 3(1),* 2–12.

Byrne, D. (1996). *The needs of the software industry and the content of undergraduate education in Ireland: A survey of the views of practitioners, managers and academics.* Unpublished doctoral dissertation, University of Hull.

Cowdroy, R.M. (1994) Concepts, constructs and insights: The essence of problem-based learning. In S.E. Chen, R.M. Cowdroy, A.J. Kingsland, & M.J. Ostwald (Eds.), *Reflections on problem-based learning* (pp. 45–56). Sydney: Australian PBL Network.

Curry, P., Sherry, R., & Tunney, O. (2003). *What transferable skills do employers look for in third-level graduates?* Results of employer survey summary report. Retrieved from: www.skillsproject.ie/skills/reportemployersurvey.html.

Davis, M.H., & Harden, R.M. (1999). Problem-based learning: A practical guide. AMEE Medical Education Guide No. 15. *Medical Teacher, 21(2),* 130–140.

Delisle, R. (1997). *How to use problem-based learning in the classroom.* Alexandria, VA: ASCD.

Drohan, S. (2005). *The use of problem-based learning practicums to effectively teach problem solving skills in the information systems development classroom.* Unpublished master's thesis, Waterford Institute of Technology, Waterford, Ireland.

Drohan, S., Stapleton, L., & Stack, A. (2006). Problem solving skills in information systems development curricula. In *Proceedings of All Ireland Society for Higher Education (AISHE) Conference*, Ireland.

Duch, B. (2001). Writing problems for deeper understanding. In B. Duch, S. Groh, & D. Allen (Eds.), *The power of problem-based learning* (pp. 47–54). Sterling, VA: Stylus.

Duch, B., Groh, S., & Allen, D. (2001). Why problem-based learning? In B. Duch, S. Groh, & D. Allen (Eds.), *The power of problem-based learning* (pp. 3–12). Sterling, VA: Stylus.

Ellis, A., Carswell, L., Bernat, A., Deveaux, D., Frison, P., Meisalo, V., et al. (1998). Resources, tools, and techniques for problem-based learning in computing. In *Working group reports of the 3rd annual SIGCSE/SIGCUE ITiCSE conference on integrating technology into computer science education*, pp. 41–56.

Glasgow, N. (1997). *New curriculum for new times: A guide to student-centred, problem-based learning*. Thousand Oaks, CA: Corwin Press.

Gorka, S., Miller, J.R., & Howe, B.J. (2007). Developing realistic capstone projects in conjunction with industry. In *Proceedings of the SIGITE Conference on Information Technology Education, 8*, 27–32.

Holmberg-Marttila, D., Hakkarainen K., Virjo, I., & Nikkari, S. (2005). A tutorial script in medical education: The PBL-model designed for local needs. In E. Poikela & S. Poikela (Eds.), *PBL in context: Bridging work and education* (pp 135–144). Tampere: Tampere University Press.

Klaus, P. (2008). *The hard truth about soft skills: Workplace lessons smart people wish they'd learned sooner*. New York: HarperCollins.

Knowlton, D. (2003). Preparing students for educated living: Virtues of problem-based learning across the higher education curriculum. *New Directions for Teaching and Learning, 95*, 5–12.

Jonassen, D., & Hung, W. (2008). All problems are not equal: Implications for problem-based learning. *The Interdisciplinary Journal of Problem-based Learning, 2*(2), 6–28.

McCracken, M., & Waters, R. (1999). Why? When an otherwise successful plan fails. In *Proceedings of the SIGCSE/SIGCUE ITiCSE conference on innovation and technology in computer science education, 4*, 9–12.

McMurtrey, M., Downey, J., Zeltmann, S., & Friedman, W. (2008). Critical skill sets of entry-level IT professionals: An empirical examination of perceptions from field personnel. *Journal of Information Technology Education, 7*, 101–120. Retrieved from: http://jite.org/documents/Vol7/JITEv7p101-120McMurtrey312.pdf.

Mauffette, Y., Kandlbinder, P., & Soucisse, A. (2004). The problem in problem-based learning is the problem: But do they motivate students? In M. Savin-Baden & K. Wilkie (Eds.), *Challenging research into problem-based learning* (pp. 11–25). Buckingham: Society for Research into Higher Education and Open University Press.

Poikela, E., & Poikela S. (Eds.). (2005). *PBL in context: Bridging work and education*. Tampere: Tampere University Press.

Poliquin, L., & Mauffette, Y. (1997). PBL vs. integrity of discipline content: The experience of integrated PBL in a B.Sc. in biology. In J. Conway, R. Fisher, L. Sheridan-Burns, & G. Ryan (Eds.), *Research and development in problem-based learning*. Vol. 4, *Integrity, Innovation, Integration* (pp. 519–526). Newcastle, Australia: PROBLARC.

Sabin, M. (2008). A collaborative and experiential learning model powered by real-world projects. In *Proceedings of the ACM SIGITE conference on information technology education, 9*, 157–164.

Sandel, O., Allard, J.-L., & Mauffette, Y. (2006). Effets d'une formation par l'APP sur l'insertion en entreprise: Évaluations et enseignements des stages de l'eXia. In M. Frenay, B. Raucent, & P. Wouters (Eds.), *Actes du 4e colloque "Questions de pédagogie dans l'enseignement supérieur: Les pédagogies actives: enjeux et conditions"* (pp. 219–328). Belgique: UCL Presses Universitaires de Louvain.

Sanson-Fisher, R., & Lynagh, M. (2005). Problem-based learning: A dissemination success story? *The Medical Journal of Australia, 183*(5), 258–260. Retrieved from: www.mja.com.au/public/issues/183_05_050905/san10226_fm.html.

Shuman, L., Besterfield-Sacre, M., & McGourty, J. (2005). The ABET "professional skills": Can they be taught? Can they be assessed? *Journal of Engineering Education, 94*(1), 41–55.

Skilbeck, M. (2001). *The university challenged: A review of international trends and issues with particular reference to Ireland*. Dublin: The Higher Education Authority.

Swanson, D., & Phillips, J. (2004). A follow up: Developing growing need for soft-skills in IT professionals. In *Proceedings of the ASCUE Conference, 37*. Retrieved from: www.ascue.org/proceedings/2004.

Uden, L., & Moran, G. (2007). More than subject-specific skills for students: Towards the development of industrial placement in higher education. In *Proceedings of the EUI-Net Conference on European Models and Best Practice for Practical Placement of Students*. Retrieved from: www.eui-net.org/Project_documents/Rome_2007_05.

United States Department of Commerce. (2003). *Education and training for the information technology workforce: Report to congress*. Washington, DC: Author.

Virtanen, P.J., Kosunen, E.A.-L., Holmberg-Marttila, D.M.H., & Virjo, I.O. (1999). What happens in PBL tutorial sessions? Analysis of medical students' written accounts. *Medical Teacher, 21*(3), 270–276.

Williams, B., & Day, R. (2009). Employer perceptions of knowledge, competency and professionalism of baccalaureate nursing graduates for a problem-based learning program. *International Journal of Nursing Education Scholarship, 6*(1). Retrieved from: www.bepress.com/ijnes/vol6/iss1/art36.

Yen, D.C., Chen, H.-G., Lee, S., & Koh, S. (2003). Differences in perception of IS knowledge and skills between academia and industry: Findings from Taiwan. *International Journal of Information Management, 23*(6), 507–522.

Further Resources

Study guides and strategies, PBL: www.studygs.net/pbl.htm.

Study guides and strategies, transferable skills: www.studygs.net/index.htm.

Transferable skills resources for students and academics: www.skillsproject.ie/useful/index.html.

Videos of employer, student, and staff comments on PBL: http://pbl.tp.edu.sg/PBL-Resources/videos/PBL%20Voices/voices_of_PBL.htm.

Creating PBL problems: http://meds.queensu.ca/pbl/pbl_in_practice/writing_pbl_cases.

Web resources for PBL: www.seda.ac.uk/ed_devs/vol2/web_developments.htm.

8

Evaluating Problem-based Learning Initiatives

Ivan Moore and Sari Poikela

Introduction

This chapter explores the question of:

How can we evaluate problem-based learning initiatives in order to improve and develop them?

It considers some of the key purposes, principles, and practices involved in evaluating innovative or developmental approaches to supporting student learning through problem-based learning (PBL). The purpose of this chapter is to provide some ideas about practical approaches to evaluating PBL practice, some of which can be implemented with a minimum of effort, in order to provide useful and rich information about the effects of the problem-based learning initiative. This chapter will show how evaluation, which is an important element of the professional practice of educators, involves a range of stakeholders who can contribute to and benefit from the outcomes of the evaluation process. The chapter includes an overview of some common approaches to evaluation and some examples of evaluation strategies that will be of interest to the readers.

Chapter Overview

This chapter will discuss three questions:

- What is evaluation?
- What key principles might be applied to evaluating PBL initiatives?
- What methods have been used to evaluate PBL initiatives and how can you explore the use of these methods within your own context?

You will be directed to references for tried-and-tested evaluation instruments and studies that used these instruments in a variety of PBL contexts.

What is Evaluation?

In this book, the term "evaluation" is used to describe the processes of exploring the total value, impact, and effectiveness of a PBL initiative. Evaluation is not to be confused with the term "assessment" which, in this book, refers directly to measuring and confirming individual student learning.

Evaluation may be defined as a process of obtaining and analysing information in order to be able to make judgements about the value of the process or innovation being investigated. Chelimsky (1997) identifies three purposes for evaluation:

1. evaluation for accountability;
2. evaluation for development;
3. evaluation for knowledge.

Each purpose has a different meaning and focus.

The focus of this chapter will be on the second purpose, evaluation for development, which is intended to provide information on which to base improvements in practice and student learning and is fundamental in enhancing the quality of student learning through PBL.

Quality-enhancement processes are designed to consider how the student is *experiencing* the course rather than how *satisfied* they are with the teaching. Thus, evaluation is moved away from teaching in order to consider student learning and to obtain information on which to base improvements in the students' environment.

In teaching and learning, scholarly practice includes gathering feedback from students on how they experience the course, reflecting on this feedback in the context of the relevant literature in order to make sense of it, and using the outcomes of this reflection to adjust the learning environment in order to improve the student learning experience. There are several benefits that arise from promoting this professional, scholarly approach to teaching within the community of PBL practitioners:

	Purpose	Meaning	Focus	In short
1.	Evaluation for accountability	To measure results or efficiency	Quality assurance	Summative evaluation
2.	Evaluation for development	To provide information to help to improve practice	Quality enhancement	Formative evaluation
3.	Evaluation for knowledge	To obtain a deeper understanding of a particular area of practice such as student learning or change management	Knowledge creation	Research

Figure 8.1 The purposes, meaning, and focus of evaluations.

- The individual evaluation helps to improve practice and develop a high-quality PBL environment.
- Meta-analysis of evaluation information can enhance an understanding of PBL as it applies across the disciplines and, thus, supports the central research activity.
- Evaluations can lead to publications which can profile the PBL initiative and help to inform other PBL practitioners.

What Key Principles Might Be Applied to Evaluating PBL Initiatives?

When you are planning the evaluation of your own PBL initiatives, it is useful to apply the following key principles:

1. Evaluation should *facilitate enquiry by and among students*, academic staff, and professional services staff about the nature and practice of effective learning. An important implication here is the involvement of *students* in evaluation. The students should not simply be the target for responding to questions or completing surveys, but they should be *active* in evaluating their own reaction to learning, the skills they are developing, and the effectiveness of their own learning. Clearly, the staff involved in developing and facilitating learning through PBL should take responsibility for evaluating their own practices and any staff involved in supporting and advising the students should evaluate the effectiveness of their support activities.

2. The core skills required to learn effectively are *self-evaluation* and *critical reflection*; therefore, evaluation should aim to model effective learning and incorporate opportunities for PBL practitioners to reflect on and to evaluate their own practice. In reflective practice, many of the more general themes (Brookfield, 1995) show how self-reflection and evaluation can enrich the overall sense of what has happened within specific PBL contexts and what can be learned for the future. To this end evaluation should not be seen as something that is "done to" people or processes, but that there is ownership of the strategies and outcomes of the evaluation. Evaluation should not disempower practitioners.

3. Evaluation should be *participatory* and *inclusive* in engaging all of the stakeholders and involving them in *collaborating* in evaluation activities and in sharing the lessons learned from evaluation. At an early stage, it is important to identify the full range of stakeholders that need to be involved in the evaluation of your PBL initiative (see also Chapters 3, 4, 7, and 17 for more information on working with stakeholders on the development and evaluation of PBL initiatives).

4. Evaluation should distinguish between *formative* and *summative* purposes. Formative evaluation is undertaken for the purpose of improving the learning environment, summative evaluation is undertaken essentially to provide evidence of the effectiveness of the

environment for the benefit of others. One of the powerful dimensions of PBL is that it creates many opportunities for formative evaluation to be seamlessly embedded into the learning process. For example, the natural, conversational dynamics of the PBL tutorials and the explicit existence of a review phase creates the infrastructure for regular, planned evaluation that is formative in the early stages, so that changes can be incorporated as you go along, and summative at the later stages, so that the impact and effectiveness of the PBL initiative can be gauged.

5. Evaluation should be focused on the *outcomes* of the PBL initiative including the effectiveness of the actions in achieving the learning outcomes and on the value of those learning outcomes for students. Evaluation of outcomes should distinguish between the more managerial tasks of monitoring activity, milestones, and deliverables and the pedagogical imperative to review what students have learned and how their PBL experiences have helped them to learn. A focus on outcomes also helps to identify, from the perspective of the learners, the barriers and areas for improvement.

6. Evaluation should be *open* and *honest*. The purpose of evaluation should be to provide information on the effectiveness of any activity so as to inform *development* rather than simply to provide evidence of good practice or to find fault. A dimension that promotes evaluative openness and honesty within a PBL context is that learners in PBL teams make their own ground rules and become accustomed to communicating within the agreed guidelines. Openness and honesty confirms the real strengths of any PBL initiative and identifies areas for improvement.

7. Evaluation should be *ongoing*; it is not an activity that is carried out at the end of an initiative or development activity. Effective evaluation of PBL initiatives provides continuous feedback information in order to inform development, support recommendations, and underpin management decisions. To this end, evaluation should be an embedded and integrated aspect of any PBL activity.

8. The *resource* spent on evaluation should be proportional to the resource spent on the activity.

9. Evaluation should be conducted *ethically* and *respectfully*.

What Methods Have Been Used to Evaluate PBL Initiatives? and How Can You Explore the Use of These Methods Within Your Own Context?

In planning a PBL evaluation it is important to decide on what the focus of the evaluation will be. For example, do you want to focus on evaluating and improving the student experience? Are you interested in evaluating tutor effectiveness in ways that provide feedback to tutors? Do you want to focus on the development of specific key skills? There are numerous rationales, goals, or purposes for which individual educators or teams may wish to introduce PBL. Thus, it is important to articulate these goals clearly and to align them with evaluation in order to keep the development focused on the goals and to provide a framework for evaluation.

Common approaches to evaluation can range from "quick and often" to "comprehensive and periodic". Quick methods include end-of-session student responses to one or two questions, whereas comprehensive methods include questionnaires, surveys, and focus groups. Another model for comparing methods can identify a continuum which ranges from richness to coverage. Rich data can be gained from methods such as structured interviews, reflective logs, and video diaries; it essentially comes from student comments and is illuminative. For example, in a student focus group conducted by a colleague, one student said that he was astounded when his tutor mentioned that he had emerged as the group leader – this student said that he had never thought of himself as a leader and felt "quite chuffed" that he was regarded in this way. This student stated that he would be more confident in taking lead roles in future. Quite often students will provide illuminative comments that point to outcomes that the educator or evaluator had not considered.

Essentially, PBL practitioners need to be free to use many different types and sources of information in order to explore the value and the impact of how their initiatives are working. Reeves (1999) describes an evaluation matrix that allows the user to map a number of evaluation methods to different evaluation purposes. Here are some methods that you might consider using within your own context.

Qualitative Illuminative Data

Qualitative illuminative data and information can be gained from intensive contact with students. The purpose of such qualitative methods is to gain detailed insights into how the students are reacting to the learning environment, how they feel and behave and what they are getting out of the experience. The aim of this qualitative approach is to try to "get into the head of the student" using methods that include structured interviews (one-to-one), video diaries, video-recordings of PBL tutorial focus groups, and maintaining reflective logs. These methods can help to confirm what is working well in the PBL initiative and what specific areas need to be improved together with recommendations for doing so.

Focus Groups

It is often useful to combine the illuminative information that can come from focus groups with the evaluation data acquired from the comprehensive coverage of questionnaires and surveys. For a focus group, the evaluator's first consideration might be to have a representative sample of students. For a PBL initiative involving a small number (15 to 20) of students, it is possible to involve all students in one or two focus group sessions. However, as the student numbers grow, it becomes less practical to involve all students, so representative samples are employed. Although a focus group of fewer than four participants offers the opportunity for each student to give comprehensive feedback, it tends not to afford the benefits of shared (or opposing) views which can result from participants building on the comments of other members of the group. In contrast, focus groups that are larger than 10 participants can result in some students not contributing and may be difficult to manage. If the evaluator wants particular topics/outcomes to be discussed, the topics must be kept to a small number or the discussion on each topic/outcome will be very short. An optimum group size of eight participants in three focus groups would constitute a quarter of a class of 100 students. If focus groups are the only evaluation method employed, then focus groups might not provide sufficient representation. Organising more focus groups may put too much of a burden on the evaluation resource, especially if the evaluations are to be organised during and again at the end of a teaching programme. Chapter 5 describes how student focus groups were used to evaluate issues of conceptual connections in PBL. Below are some aspects that an evaluator might consider when organising and running a focus group.

- Ensure that all of the discussion is recorded in some way. It is useful to use digital voice recording methods, as it is often difficult to simultaneously lead a focus group and record the feedback in writing. Before recording a discussion, it is important to seek and obtain the participant's permission in writing.
- Provide a list of the key aspects of the PBL programme/module on which the feedback is sought. These key aspects might be clustered around a small number of key themes such as organisation, goals, support, information, problems, learning, and assessment.
- Allow time for "free discussion" in which the students are encouraged to follow their own path of discussion. However, it is important not to allow the discussion to become unfocused and irrelevant.
- Try to ensure that all of the students are involved and that everyone makes a contribution. To this end, address some questions to some of the quieter students in the group and provide positive feedback to them after their contributions. Special forms of focus group can be helpful here, for example, normative group technique is a structured approach to gathering feedback from all members of a group.
- When dealing with a very large focus group of 20 or more students, it may be beneficial to subdivide into smaller groups, allocate a

discussion facilitator for or within each group, establish clear topics for discussion and gather feedback from each group. This subdividing into smaller groups is akin to group teaching and learning processes common in PBL environments.

Examples of suggested questions for focus groups in the areas of curriculum design, facilitation, student experience, and assessment and achievements are provided by Marcangelo, Gibbon, and Cage (2009, pp. 24–25). Campion and O'Neill (2005) describe how focus groups have been used in evaluating PBL in veterinary medicine and Morgan (1988) provides a guide to using focus groups in evaluation.

Reflective Logs and Journals

Chapter 11 explores students developing as reflective learners through PBL. A range of strategies for structuring learning from reflective practice and journals, as discussed by Brown, Mathre-Maich, and Royle (2001), could also be used to evaluate the learning of a student group. Key factors to consider in using reflective logs and journals for evaluation are as follows.

- It is important to have a framework for reflections which allows the students to focus their thoughts and facilitates gaining evaluation information in a structured manner.
- If a framework contains suggested headings, it is important to achieve a balance between consistency of themes and avoiding exhaustion of a theme. Headings should be rotated and refreshed periodically and new themes should be introduced from time to time.
- Ensure that the students feel that there is a significant level of confidentiality attached to their reflective thoughts.
- If students are provided with opportunities to share their reflections, they are more likely to maintain reflective records. Therefore, it is helpful to encourage the students to discuss or share their thoughts with others.
- It is helpful to structure the reflection process so that the students can maintain a confidential reflective diary or journal and can also periodically share some of their thoughts with other students and with the tutor and evaluator.

Video-recording as a Means of Evaluation and Development

Another option is to video-record PBL tutorial sessions or other PBL learning activities. Video-recording can provide useful insights into both student and tutor activity, particularly when the tutor is unable to make direct observations of the activity due to being actively engaged in the activity itself. Some PBL tutors have found it very useful to peer-review and evaluate their

PBL tutor facilitation using videotapes as a means of being confirmed in their strengths and in developing and improving their tutoring.

Qualitative approaches can be complemented by quantitative approaches, for example, using quantitative questionnaires as part of an evaluation strategy in order to develop PBL initiatives.

Questionnaires

The methods outlined above are effective at achieving rich data and illuminative feedback from students. Where classes are small or where there are sufficient resources, qualitative illuminative approaches can be used to evaluate the experience of all students. However, when classes are large and resources for large-scale qualitative research are limited, the main limitation is that although these methods rely on representative samples of students, the samples are often very small. For large student cohorts or large-scale development programmes (which may even involve a significant number of staff), the limitations of these qualitative evaluation methods can be overcome by using standardised questionnaires and surveys. It is useful to combine qualitative and quantitative methods in an overall evaluation strategy. Sometimes, it is useful to develop a customised questionnaire in order to gain feedback on a particular teaching and learning development.

At the core of problem-based learning is the aim to provide high-quality learning experiences for students and to stimulate students to develop strategies for deep learning. In PBL contexts, questionnaires that focus on the student experience have often been used to assist in the development of initiatives. A first approach may be to follow a widely accepted methodology such as the Course Experience Questionnaire (CEQ) which was developed by Ramsden (1991) in Australia and is now being used or adapted in many countries. Although the term "questionnaire" is used, the "questions" are presented as "statements" and the students are asked to score the statement on a Likert scale which ranges from one to five, where one represents "definitely disagree" and five represents "definitely agree". There are six sub-scales on the CEQ (Ramsden, 1991), namely: good teaching, appropriate assessment, clear goals and standards, generic skills, appropriate workload, and emphasis on independence. Lyon and Hendry (2002) have discussed the use of the CEQ as a monitoring evaluation tool. The full questionnaire or some sub-scales can be used as appropriate.

Educationalists have designed many other study strategies questionnaires. For example, Meyer and Parsons (1989) describe an inventory developed at Lancaster University and Newstead (1992) compares two "quick and easy" methods. Study strategies questionnaires were designed to help the student to identify their approaches to study, their learning strategies, and their learning styles. The Further Resources section at the end of this chapter provides web addresses of several sites that use and have evaluated some of these study strategy questionnaires.

Learning strategies and approaches to study questionnaires can be used for the purpose of evaluation. The questionnaires should be processed at an early stage in the learning programme and then repeated towards the end of the programme. It is then possible to identify any changes in styles or strategies that have arisen as a result of the PBL initiative. The use of these learning strategy type of questionnaires has several advantages as noted below.

- These questionnaires have been researched, designed, and published, therefore they have public acceptance. This also means that evaluators do not have to design their own questionnaires.
- The students gain useful insights into their approaches to learning, so these questionnaires benefit the student directly.
- Many such questionnaires come with comprehensive analysis and developmental material so the students can read the advice about how to build on and to develop their own approaches to learning.
- Questionnaires can be processed for a whole cohort of students, thus gaining comprehensive coverage for evaluation.

Another popular standardised questionnaire is one that evaluates PBL tutor effectiveness. Dolmans and Ginns (2005) describe and review a short (11-statement) questionnaire that is very useful for evaluating PBL tutors and providing them with feedback to develop their practice.

End of Tutorial/Session Evaluations

At the end of each tutorial/learning session or on a regular basis (once a week or fortnight) it is useful to ask a few questions of the students. The students can write short responses and either leave them on a table as they leave the session or share them in the group. To prevent overload, it is best to focus on only one or two questions that can be recycled periodically from a base of six to eight questions, for example:

1. What was the most useful learning point from the tutorial/session?
2. What did you not understand from this tutorial/session?
3. What did you find most difficult?
4. What would you like me to stop doing, because it hinders your learning?
5. What would you like me to continue doing, because it helps your learning?
6. What would you like me to start doing, because it will help your learning?
7. What do you do that hinders your learning?
8. What can you start to do that will help you to learn more effectively?

Simple questions such as the ones listed above can provide a rich array of useful feedback from students. When using this approach, it is helpful to analyse the responses quickly and to provide feedback to the students on what they have written and what changes have been made as a result of the feedback.

Evaluating the Development of Transferable Skills

A commonly cited strength of PBL initiatives is the capacity that they create to develop transferable skills (e.g. teamwork, communications, information literacy, critical thinking) among learners, in tandem with the development of discipline-specific competences. See Chapter 10 for the development of information literacy in PBL initiatives. Some of the evaluative prompt questions for exploring these transferable skills could include the following:

1. What helps me most to develop my team working skills is…
2. I have been developing information skills by…
3. I have learned about doing research by…
4. I have gained most confidence as a learner through…

Quantitative questionnaires can be used to evaluate specific transferable skills. For example, Yuan, Kunaviktikul, Klunklin, and Williams (2008) used the California Critical Thinking Test to evaluate changes in critical thinking skills in PBL students. What specific transferable skills are you interested in evaluating? What standardised questionnaires are appropriate for you in evaluating these?

Implications for Your PBL Practice: Developing an Evaluation Strategy

It is by linking evaluation methods to the outcomes of PBL initiatives that comprehensive information can be gained to provide evidence of the nature of the PBL environment for the students and on which improvements in the PBL initiative can be based. While, on their own, each method can provide useful information, taken together, they can provide a comprehensive range of rich, illuminative, and numerical data. In addition, each method can provide outputs that will inform improvements in the learning environment and developments in the evaluation system. For example, it may be that student responses to sub-sections of the questionnaire (e.g. teamwork) may inform planned focus group meetings, which can then further unpack the issues around team working. Also, unexpected outcomes from focus group sessions may identify further topics for inclusion in the survey. It is by linking evaluation methods and their outcomes that comprehensive information can be gained to provide evidence of an effective PBL environment for the students and on which improvements in the PBL initiative can be based.

Developing an evaluation strategy involves clarifying the purpose and focus of the evaluation in the context of the goals of the PBL initiative and then selecting appropriate evaluation methods. For example, an evaluation strategy could combine the following three methods.

1. *End of tutorial/session evaluations*: quick, frequent, illuminative, comprehensive coverage.
2. *Focus groups*: periodic, qualitative and illuminative, representative.
3. *Student surveys*: periodic, qualitative and quantitative, comprehensive coverage.

Marcangelo et al. (2009) have edited a *Problem-based Learning Evaluation Toolkit* that is the work of the Problem-based Learning Special Interest Group of the Higher Education Academy in the United Kingdom. This toolkit is available online and is very useful for PBL practitioners.

References

Brookfield, S. (1995). *Becoming a critically reflective teacher.* San Francisco: Jossey-Bass.
Brown, B., Mathre-Maich, N., & Royle, J. (2001). Fostering reflection and reflective practice. In E. Rideout (Ed.), *Transforming nursing education through problem-based learning* (pp. 119–164). Sudbury, MA: Jones and Bartlett Publishers.
Campion, D., & O'Neill, G. (2005). Reviewing PBL together: A case study of a PBL programme in the Faculty of Veterinary Medicine, University College Dublin. In T. Barrett, I. Mac Labhainn, & H. Fallon (Eds.), *Handbook of enquiry and problem-based learning: Irish case studies and international perspectives.* Galway: CELT, National University of Ireland Galway and All Ireland Society for Higher Education. Retrieved from: www.nuigalway.ie/celt/pblbook/chapter19.
Chelimsky, E. (1997). Thoughts for a new evaluation society. *Evaluation, 3*(1), 97–118.
Dolmans, D., & Ginns, P. (2005). A short questionnaire to evaluate the effectiveness of tutors in PBL: Validity and reliability. *Medical Teacher, 27*(6), 534–538.
Lyon, P.M., & Hendry G.D. (2002). The use of the course experience questionnaire as a monitoring evaluation tool in a problem-based medical programme. *Assessment and Evaluation in Higher Education, 27*(4), 339–352.
Marcangelo, C., Gibbon, C., & Cage, M. (2009). *Problem-based learning evaluation toolkit.* Health Science and Practice Subject Centre of the Higher Education Academy UK. Retrieved from: www.health.heacademy.ac.uk/projects/commissionedwork/execsumpbltoolkit.
Meyer, J.H.F., & Parsons, P. (1989). Approaches to studying and course perceptions using the Lancaster inventory: A comparative study. *Studies in Higher Education, 14*(2), 137–153.
Morgan, D.L. (1988). *Focus groups as qualitative research.* London: Sage.
Newstead, S.E. (1992). A study of two 'quick-and-easy' methods of assessing individual differences in student learning. *British Journal of Educational Psychology, 62*(3), 299–312.
Ramsden, P. (1991). A performance indicator of teaching quality in higher education: The course experience questionnaire. *Studies in Higher Education, 16*, 29–150.
Reeves, T.C. (1999). *Evaluation matrix.* Georgia Tech. Retrieved from: www.ceismc.gatech.edu/mm_tools/EM.html.
Yuan, H., Kunaviktikul, W., Klunklin, A., & Williams, B. (2008) Improvement of nursing students' critical thinking skills through problem-based learning in the People's Republic of China: A quasi-experimental study. *Nursing and Health Sciences, 10*, 70–76.

Further Resources

Marcangelo, C., & Ginty, A. (2006). A *literature review table: A review of evaluation studies across disciplines.* http://feedback.bton.ac.uk/pbl/pbldirectory/toolkit/HEAToolkitHome.php. This useful table provides a summary of the evaluation, focus and methods used in PBL evaluation studies together with links to these studies.
Evaluation Cookbook: www.icbl.hw.ac.uk/ltdi/cookbook/contents.html. The Learning Technology Dissemination Initiative was a project funded by the Scottish

Higher Education Funding Council to promote the use of learning technology. This is a really useful website, which provides an outline of a wide range of evaluation methods. Although the initiative focused on learning technologies, the evaluation methods and advice given are not specific to learning technologies.

Course Experience Questionnaire (CEQ) Project: www.teaching.rmit.edu.au/progimprov/ceqdescr.htm.

The CEQ was designed as a performance indicator for higher education. It consists of statements relating to aspects of students' learning experience.

Course Experience Questionnaire (CEQ): www.itl.usyd.edu.au/CEQ.

This website is maintained by the Teaching and Learning Institute of the University of Sydney, Australia. It provides the full Course Experience Questionnaire which was devised by Paul Ramsden and is recognised widely as a useful tool for evaluating the student learning experience.

Course Experience Questionnaire (CEQ) – Oxford: www.learning.ox.ac.uk/oli.php?page=43.

The University of Oxford adapted Ramsden's CEQ for its own purposes. This website provides Oxford University's customised version of CEQ.

Approaches to Study and Study Strategies Questionnaires. The Approaches to Study Inventory (ASI): www.ucd.ie/vetphysio/approches_to_study_inventory.htm; www.sesdl.scotcit.ac.uk:8082/resources/pv_rasi.doc.

This is a 52-item questionnaire that measures deep, strategic, and surface learning.

VARK Guide to Learning Styles: www.vark-learn.com/english/index.asp.

The questionnaire indicates the variety of different approaches to learning. Teachers who would like to reach more students can also benefit from using VARK. Although VARK can be used with a group, a class or with one-to-one counselling, it does require some explanation to avoid leaping to inappropriate conclusions.

Learning and Study Strategies Inventory (LASSI): www.hhpublishing.com/_assessments/LASSI.

The LASSI is a 10-scale, 80-item assessment of the students' awareness about and use of learning and study strategies related to the skill, will, and self-regulation components of strategic learning.

Part II

Students Using Problem-based Learning to Enhance Capabilities

Students Maximising the Potential of the Problem-based Learning Tutorial

Generating Dialogic Knowing

Terry Barrett and Sarah Moore

Introduction

This chapter explores the concept of "dialogic knowing" and introduces practice principles for students and tutors facilitating the deep learning that dialogue can foster.

Dialogic knowing is a concept that is at the heart of problem-based learning and a key idea underpinning all good learning. This kind of knowing is generated when people create and re-create knowledge together. We argue that students and tutors can maximise the potential for the emergence of dialogic knowledge in the context of the PBL tutorial settings by talking and listening to each other, by sharing ideas, by confronting divergent views, and by approaching problems in interactive, collaborative, communicative ways.

This chapter is based on what we have learned about dialogic knowing from listening to how students talked about PBL tutorials. We draw on a study that involved video- and audio-recording all of the PBL tutorials of two teams of students undertaking a PBL module (Barrett, 2008). These students, who are given pseudonyms, were lecturers in higher education and became PBL students for the module. The module was part of a Diploma in Teaching and Learning in Higher Education and both the content and the process of the module was problem-based learning.

A critical discourse analysis (Fairclough, 2003) of this data was conducted in order to understand what we, as PBL practitioners, can learn about PBL from how students talked about it in tutorials (Barrett, 2008). Student talk in PBL tutorials is at the heart of this student-centred methodology and we argue that a critical discourse analysis (CDA) study is a fruitful way to understand more about such talk (Barrett, 2004). Clouston (2007, p. 183) suggests that discourse analysis methods, including CDA, "could enable an understanding of how effective problem-based learning is constructed". We share with you the practice principles for constructing effective PBL in tutorials that emerged from this study (Barrett, 2008).

This chapter simply looks at how PBL students talked about the tutorial in the naturally occurring talk of the tutorials (Barrett, 2008) in order to explore three student practice principles in PBL tutorials. Although PBL curricula are designed to create interactive, engaged, and collaborative dynamics among students, PBL curriculum design does not guarantee any of these dynamics. Facilitating active interaction among students and generating dialogic knowing are not necessarily straightforward.

Dialogic knowing can be constructed by students in the following ways: by creating more democratic social relations, by co-constructing knowledge through co-elaboration, and by the relinquishing of individual control and the embracing of shared control of PBL tutorials and the products produced. We share education development strategies from our practice experience of PBL in different contexts. We argue that students equipped with an understanding of the dimensions of dialogic knowing are in a strong position to maximise the tutorial for learning. If students develop their abilities to construct knowledge together in PBL tutorials, they will bring this ability to other learning and work situations.

Chapter Overview

In this chapter, we discuss how the PBL tutorial can be a particularly fruitful context for students to enhance their learning and knowledge through active discussion. We also elaborate on this process by focusing on three practice principles for making the best use of PBL tutorials:

1. creating more democratic social relations;
2. co-constructing knowledge through co-elaboration; and
3. adopting the principle of shared control.

Understanding these three interdependent principles facilitates the use of the tutorial as a discursive site for realising dialogic knowing. We share ideas about practice strategies that can be used by tutors and students in the PBL tutorial itself to promote dialogic knowing. On the basis of these principles, we also make recommendations about tutor and student development, both within and outside of the PBL tutorial, in order to ensure that the potential benefits of PBL tutorials are realised as fully as possible.

This chapter focuses on students and tutors maximising the PBL tutorial as a site for generating dialogic knowledge. An overview of the PBL tutorial process, together with tutor and student roles, was provided in Chapter 1; readers who are new to PBL may want to read that chapter first.

The PBL Tutorial as a Potential Site for Dialogic Knowing

The word dialogic comes from the ancient Greek:

> **dia** meaning in two or apart and logos, which has a cluster of meanings including account, ratio reason, argument, discourse, saying and word. The Greek compound word **dialogos** means conversation between two

people, and is associated with the pursuit of knowledge (reason, argument, discourse). It also has a connotation of **difference** (**dia** as apart): the two or more who partake in dialogue are separate and distinct as individual beings, as speakers and as thinkers, but the conversation brings them together and fashions a unity of process through their joint engagement. Dialogue is an unfolding process, a search or quest for knowledge and understanding.

(Rule, 2004, p. 320)

Treating knowledge as dialogic means more than just treating knowledge as an exchange of ideas and viewpoints; it is an epistemological position that views knowledge as something that is constructed together, socially. In PBL settings, dialogic knowledge is created, reinforced, elaborated, and developed during conversations that take place within tutorials:

What is dialogue in this way of knowing? Precisely this connection, this epistemological relationship, the object to be known in one place links the cognitive subjects leading them to reflect together on the object.

(Shor & Freire, 1987, p. 100)

In PBL, the purpose of the dialogue is to work through the problem and to proceed to a conclusion by reason and argument. The concept of the PBL tutorial, as a potential site for dialogic knowing, acknowledges that whether

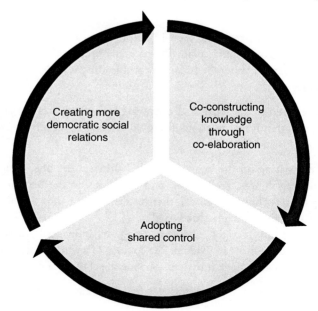

Figure 9.1 The PBL tutorial as a potential site for dialogic knowing: Three key principles (adapted from Barrett, 2008, p. 181).

or not this potential is realised depends, very heavily, on the nature of the student talk in the PBL tutorials.

We focus on three important principles as fertile ways to develop dialogic knowing:

1. creating more democratic social relations;
2. co-constructing knowledge through co-elaboration; and
3. adopting shared control.

Creating More Democratic Social Relations

If PBL tutorials are to fulfil the purposes for which they are designed, students need to move towards democratic learning dynamics than might, otherwise, prevail in more conventional learning contexts. In PBL tutorials, the active engagement and empowerment of students and their capacity to influence what happens in tutorial settings provides an essential basis for dialogic knowing.

The values of democracy and of ensuring that students all have the opportunity to provide input and influence are not always easy to instil.

The students that we observed and listened to (no doubt due to their academic experiences of operating in a relatively conventional organisational environment) often referred to PBL tutorials as quite different from many of the other group contexts, within which they were used to operating. They regularly cited the difference between a traditional committee meeting and a PBL tutorial process:

SUE: One of the different things [about the PBL tutorial] was there were group decisions and the group action plan. It was just bringing the group in, rather than, *one* person being the hierarchy and leading it and everybody sharing together.

The participants referred to the sense that operating as a group was not easy, that it took time, and that it was not something that happens overnight, even if the conditions for PBL are good:

JULIE: We were all writing on the board. ... And I think at the beginning it was, unfortunately it was, really slow, and you Kate, at the beginning, were finding it pretty hard [laughter], then, at the end, we were all taking up a pen and actually writing on the board.
KATE: I think your point is right, about it being an individual, minutes and agenda tends to be more individual. The concept of a white board being a shared learning environment, it took us too long to get that concept.

In the students' talk, we can find strong evidence that they charted a movement in the PBL tutorial from one person's agenda to the more democratic social relations of a shared learning environment and a group action plan. Two dimensions, in particular, seem relevant in terms of the changes that we have often observed as PBL processes unfold over time: "power" and "solidarity" (Brown & Gilman, 1960) or "social hierarchy" and "distance" (Fairclough, 2003). In changing their genre, from a traditional committee meeting to a PBL tutorial, the individuals in the team quoted above moved from hierarchical, distant social relations to less hierarchical, less distant, more democratic social relations with greater solidarity among the PBL students.

It is striking that the issues of social hierarchy and distance emerged both at the micro level of the PBL tutorial and at the macro level of institutions. The students' comments suggest that they perceived the PBL tutorials to be more democratic than the traditional committee meetings. They chose traditional committee meetings as their comparator, that is, they used their experiences at traditional meetings as a contrast to their group experiences in the PBL tutorial settings.

We argue that the principle of creating more democratic social relations is a fundamental prerequisite to dialogic knowing. Democratic social relations mean that there is a level of respect, openness, reciprocity, and equality that facilitates students to actively listen to other students' ideas and to express their own ideas freely. Democratic social relations is the basis on which the other two principles of dialogic knowing (co-constructing knowledge through co-elaboration and adopting shared control) can develop. Without some level of democratic social relations, it is impossible to have dialogic knowing.

A barrier to dialogic knowing is authoritarianism, where one person dominates, sets the agenda, and makes the decisions. Problem-based learning clearly moves tutors away from a dominant stance within the tutorial and moves students away from the passivity and disempowerment to which such a power imbalance can give rise. The PBL tutorials are expressly designed to shift the balance of power and the onus of participation from teachers to students. Although this shift is not without its challenges, we argue that the pedagogical and motivational benefits can be extraordinary.

Teachers are often looking for ways to enhance student engagement. The PBL tutorial process is structured in a way that creates specific strategies, processes, and roles for interaction; it is a process that is aligned with the view of many teachers, that is, that students should be doing more, talking more, and engaging more during the contact time with tutors and with each other.

Strategies for Moving Towards Democratic Social Relations

There are strategies and tools, particularly suited to PBL, which we have found can assist students in teams that sometimes struggle in their attempts to move towards democratic learning dynamics.

Making and Reviewing Ground Rules

At the start of the PBL tutorials, it is important that students make their own ground rules for the team. The making of ground rules is particularly good for maximising the participation of all team members as they engage in the process of constructing knowledge together. Tutors introduce the importance of writing ground rules, the student chair facilitates this discussion and the recorder writes down the ground rules. The students can review the ground rules to confirm or amend them. Periodically, at the review part of the tutorial, students can engage in self- and peer-formative assessment of the chairperson's performance generally and specifically in relation to encouraging the team to work in ways that are compatible with their ground rules. This formative assessment process can be a way of helping students to develop their abilities of being a facilitative and inclusive chairperson.

Using the Whiteboard as a Shared Learning Environment

One of the essential PBL tools is the use of a whiteboard (electronic or physical) to articulate the ideas and inputs of all team members, to record team decisions about the learning issues to be researched, to display the action plan that the group has constructed together, and to share, review, and summarise their learning. The tutor and students can ensure that the whiteboard represents a shared learning environment where everyone's contributions are represented. For example, if a tutor notices that the recorder has been busy recording the views of the other students, she/he can invite the recorder to make a contribution and record it on the whiteboard. Tutors can encourage students to work with visuals as well as words to construct knowledge together and benefit from the strengths of all of the students. At the start of a PBL initiative, the tutor can explain that, although the scribe has the responsibility for recording on the whiteboard, other team members are also welcome to take markers in hand and add to the whiteboard.

Co-constructing Knowledge through Co-elaboration

Students need to construct knowledge together in order to maximise the tutorial for learning. In the transmission model, knowledge is characterised as unidirectional from the person who knows to those who do not know. In dialogic knowing, knowledge is multidirectional, going both to and from many or all of the people on the team. It is in this process of multidirectional co-elaboration that knowledge is co-constructed.

The PBL students talked about building their knowledge together (group knowledge) through elaborating their own ideas, listening to new ideas from other students, linking what one student said to what other students said, and "editing" their work together. One student distinguished between the two perspectives of working individually and in a PBL group as follows:

PHILIP: Well, my opinion of PBL, working in groups, if I was working independently I couldn't have been as creative as the group has been. And the number of ideas that were thrown around and developed by the group creates a whole new dynamic.

This co-construction of knowledge meant that there was a greater number of ideas being considered by the team compared to when someone works individually to construct knowledge. The participants referred to this co-construction of knowledge as more productive and the team members felt it gave rise to more creative fluency among the group than might have been possible otherwise.

PBL tutorial structures and processes are designed to ensure that many ideas are considered and explored; even the participants' use of language relating to ideas being "thrown around" and "bouncing off" one another suggests dynamism and animation that contribute to the essence of what is good about PBL.

In the PBL tutorials, the group discussions created "a whole new dynamic compared to working independently". Students described the PBL tutorial as being characterised by collective ownership; they referred to *our* knowledge and *our* control. This team talked about the co-construction of knowledge in the PBL tutorials in terms of shared ownership. They contrasted the PBL tutorial with the transmission model of knowledge creation where knowledge was given in formal lectures. It was clear that the learners saw and talked about their PBL experiences in positive ways and derived benefits from the processes involved. However, it was not all positive; the students often struggled with the PBL processes, especially when they faced these processes for the first time. Some students were critical of the PBL tutorial, they were concerned about a lack of structure, sometimes they felt that the PBL tutorials were wasting time, and they worried that the PBL process was "all over the place". At other times, the students valued co-constructing knowledge together in the PBL tutorials:

MICHAEL: I think the group gives a value to this; it's almost like an editing process. Like, when you get an idea, you can go off on a tangent and develop it yourself, so you are in a situation where you hand up a thesis to the tutor, they mark it, correct it, it becomes very, very closed system almost. And often you get a tutor who likes what your approach is, this is brilliant, maybe the research isn't that great. But then maybe you get a tutor who hates what you are doing and then you can get a worse mark or you get a roasting over it because he doesn't like what you are saying or she doesn't like what you are saying and doesn't like your research methods. Whereas, in a group like this you can feel, like sometimes you put in something and it's rubbish and the group will tell you pretty quickly. You feel okay, that idea didn't work, or that was a crazy idea and then you think about that, and then maybe that is a good idea, so it helps if a lot of people are thinking the same way, it validates your idea better. I think that is the strength of the group work.

The students talked about the PBL tutorial being like an "editing process", where the group, rather than the individual, decides which ideas to run with and which not to pursue. It is through the co-elaboration of ideas that the PBL students, as a group, validate some ideas as the most appropriate to develop in order to work on the problem and to further their knowledge.

Myers Kelson and Distlehorst (2000, p. 176) summarise the reasons why work on PBL problems is collaborative in the PBL tutorials rather than individual:

> Put simply for most of us acting individually, problem complexity triggers a tendency to come to simplistic resolutions out of our present state of ignorance. The more novice the problem-solver, the greater the tendency. The collaborative problem-solving group however provides the ideal situation for remedying this, while developing expertise in problem-solving through the interaction between reasoning and attuning to problem affordances.

It is by socially constructing new knowledge together in thought-language that PBL students can move from their current zone of development (CZD), where they can acquire new knowledge unaided, to a wider zone, where they can attain greater knowledge through discussions with others in PBL tutorials. Vygotsky (1978, p. 86) said that the Zone of Proximal Development (ZPD) is the "distance between the actual developmental level as determined by independent problem solving and the level of potential development as determined through problem solving under adult guidance or in collaboration with more capable peers". As problem-based learning makes use of the students' diverse level of prior knowledge on various topics, it has possibilities to exploit the potential for co-elaboration and co-construction of new knowledge. In Schmidt's (1993, p. 428) words, in PBL, the "elaboration on prior knowledge through small group discussion both before and after new knowledge has been acquired, has a cognitive effect on student learning".

Strategies for Promoting the Co-construction of Knowledge through Co-elaboration

Two main strategies for promoting the co-construction of knowledge are:

1. encouraging student behaviours that foster co-elaboration;
2. tutors and students asking questions that facilitate learning together.

Encouraging Behaviours that Stimulate the Co-construction of Knowledge

To construct knowledge together, it is important that students:

- benefit from one another's prior learning;
- brainstorm ideas without initial censoring;
- engage in high-quality independent study;

- evaluate information sources critically;
- justify arguments with evidence;
- challenge one another;
- confirm one another;
- build on one another's ideas;
- review their learning;
- move from their current position based on evidence and ideas;
- make links between different concepts;
- work in a range of media; and
- compare the depth and breadth of their own knowledge with that of other students.

Stop and Think

Within your own context, reflect on:

- current ways you encourage these activities
- new strategies you could add to your facilitation style to promote these student behaviours.

We argue that it is useful for us, as PBL practitioners, to think about the co-construction of knowledge as having three dimensions and to consider tutor and student questions for stimulating all three dimensions.

Asking Questions that Prompt Students Co-constructing Knowledge

Many tutors new to PBL often ask us, as education developers, about what type of questions they should ask their students in PBL tutorials in order to promote critical thinking and knowledge acquisition. In our conceptualisation, the co-construction of knowledge has three dimensions: depth of knowledge, breadth of knowledge, and span of knowledge application.

Tutors can model effective questions for promoting the co-construction of knowledge in PBL tutorials. The role of the tutor in encouraging student learning has been summarised by Halela (2008, p. 65):

Challenge your team to explore
To dig deeper for more

We argue that students, themselves, play an important role in asking stimulating questions to promote learning together.

We have also found five other strategies for developing dialogic knowing: the use of independent study templates, team annotated bibliographies, constructing team concept maps, introducing students to design thinking processes, and summarising learning in the review phase of tutorials.

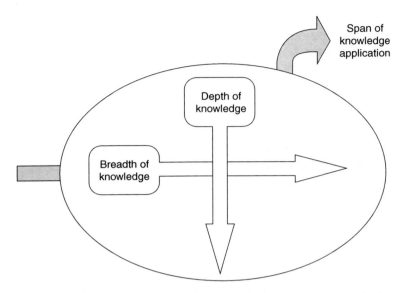

Figure 9.2 Three dimensions of co-constructing knowledge through co-elaboration in PBL tutorials.

A sample of an "Independent Study Summary and Additional Insights from Group" is presented in Chapter 5, Figure 5.2, and in Chapter 12, introducing students to design thinking processes is explored.

Teams Constructing Concept Maps

Novak and Cañas (2008, p. 1) define concept maps as:

> tools for organizing and representing knowledge. They include concepts usually enclosed in circles or boxes of some type, and relationships between concepts indicated by a connecting line linking two concepts. Words on the line, referred to as linking words or linking phrases, specify the relationship between the two concepts.

Figure 9.4 presents a team concept map created by PBL students, who were lecturers, working on a problem as part of a PBL in Higher Education module. They had decided to design a PBL module for early-stage doctorate students, entitled *Great Thinkers, Great Ideas to Great Research*, and drawing a concept map helped them to clarify the relationships between the concepts.

Summarising Learning in the Review Phase of the Tutorial

In the review section of the tutorial, students can sometimes individually review the main things that they learned, how they learned them, and discuss how their understanding has developed from the specific contributions of other students. The tutor can help the students take stock by giving them

Aspect of knowledge	Sample tutor/student questions
Depth (how robust, accurate, and precise the knowledge is)	• Why do you think that? • What is your evidence for that argument? • How do you evaluate your sources of evidence? • What is the counterargument? • What are the important ethical issues here? • How has your understanding of key concepts developed from working on this problem? • Will you draw that and explain it more?
Breadth (how interconnected and networked the knowledge is)	• What other factors are important? • How do all of those issues connect? • What are the social, cultural and political issues that it is important to consider? • What is the practice in other countries? • How has your understanding of the problem broadened and advanced from other students' contributions? • Will you represent how all of your knowledge of this problem interconnects by drawing a team concept map?
Span (how applicable and transferable the knowledge is)	• Have you seen anything like this before? • How would you do that in practice? • What is the most important thing to do? • What would you find the most difficult to do? • What did you learn from your errors/mistakes that is relevant to practice? • Will you demonstrate how that would work in practice?

Figure 9.3 Sample tutor/student questions to facilitate the co-construction of knowledge through co-elaboration.

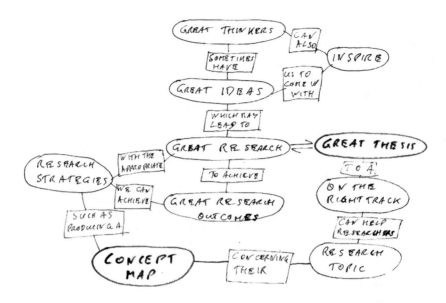

Figure 9.4 A concept map of the module (Kador, 2009).

feedback on how far they have come, noting how baffled they may have been about tackling the problem initially, and how they have learned to address ambiguity, to build on different students' strengths, and to gain insights from research, mistakes, and discussion.

Adopting the Principle of Shared Control

There is no real dialogic knowing without some degree of shared control. A third principle of the PBL tutorial, as a potential site for dialogic knowing, is adopting shared control. A PBL student contrasted shared control with individual control as follows:

BETTY: As an individual you have control over the start and finish of a product, whereas, you need to give this up as this is group knowledge and it's a group process, you don't have control over it, what the finished product is. That is different, it's different.

The student distinguished between the individual control that is experienced in some situations and relinquishing this individual control in PBL tutorials, where the final product is a result of "group knowledge" and a "group process". Individual control is about directing something oneself.

In the co-construction of knowledge through co-elaboration, it is a question of co-directing the tutorials and the product, rather than directing them. If there are democratic social relations and the co-construction of knowledge through co-elaboration, then it is possible for some degree of shared control to follow.

Some students viewed shared control negatively, as having to give up control while preferring to be in control:

PHILIP: I feel the whole process is very messy and a lot of time was wasted at our group meetings. I would much prefer to be in control of a learning and discussion or decision making myself.

Other students viewed shared control positively, as a sharing of ideas and ownership:

MAURA: No, I don't really agree, I enjoyed the whole process of discussion and sharing of ideas, workload, and presentation. I feel a form of shared ownership in the solution of the problem.

One student highlighted the fact that:

BEATRICE: …context, students and tutors are all variables and that is why dialogue and conversation are important. They are not static. That is why we are saying we don't have control. We have lack of control. We really don't know what the end product is, we are less afraid. We are helping colleagues not to be afraid and concerned about not being in control.

Strategies for Encouraging Students to Adopt the Principle of Shared Control

In the review session of the tutorials, the students can, from time to time, self- and peer-assess their individual contribution to the team, both in terms of their current contributions and their plan for developing their teamwork. They can also review what they have learned about teamwork through the experience of working in a PBL team and reflect on the issues of power and control that emerged in the team. Outside of the tutorial, there are education development strategies that can also contribute to the students maximising the tutorial for learning. These strategies will be discussed in the next section.

Education Development Strategies to Enhance Dialogic Knowing

Student induction and tutor development are two key strategies for enhancing dialogic knowing in PBL tutorials and programme teams can design these strategies with an education developer.

Student Induction

During student induction, students can be introduced to the PBL tutorial roles of chairperson, scribe, recorder, observer, and timekeeper. In particular, the students can engage in activities that will help them to reflect on their experience of chairpersons in other contexts and the role of the chair in the

PBL tutorial context. In each tutorial team, the importance of making ground rules can be explored and the teams can be given specific time to engage in this exploration. Reviewing critical incidents from DVD clips (De Grave, 1998) is one way that students can be facilitated in exploring how they would deal with critical incidents that affect dialogic knowing, e.g. one student dominating the tutorial, some students failing to do any independent study, or students reviewing the PBL tutorial superficially. A very effective way to help students to realise the potential of the tutorial to construct knowledge together, and specific enhancers and inhibitors of this process, is to organise a panel of previous students to share their experiences of the PBL tutorial and to take questions. In addition to preparing students on *how* to maximise dialogic knowing in tutorials, it is important to explore with students *what* dialogic knowing is and *why* the aim of the PBL tutorial is to facilitate this process. Student induction should consist of a series of sessions in the first semester/term rather than one session in the first week.

Tutor Development

Tutor development programmes can focus on the tutor's role as a facilitator of the PBL tutorial. It is important that tutors realise that it is through student talk that dialogic knowing emerges for the students, and that tutors themselves should not talk much in tutorials. The role of the tutor is better achieved through active listening in order to decide when and how to make process interventions rather than content interventions. This orientation can be vital in facilitating student learning. Thus, tutor development should provide a range of opportunities including: tutor development workshops, role-play and video-work, reading research papers on PBL tutoring, observing other tutors in action and being observed as a tutor. In addition, it is important to create spaces for tutors to think philosophically about *what dialogic knowing is* and what ideas energise us intellectually in order to understand how students construct knowledge together and what our role as tutor is in this process (Barnett, 2000, 2004; Barrett, 2001; Buber, 1964; Shor & Freire, 1987; Silén, 2006).

We argue that conceiving of the PBL tutorial as a site for maximising dialogical knowing highlights PBL as one way of addressing learning for a "supercomplex world" (Barnett, 2000, p. 257). Pedagogies are needed that fit the purpose of living and working with supercomplexity, uncertainty, and constant change. Barnett (2000, p. 257) elaborates on his understanding of supercomplexity as follows:

> Supercomplexity denotes a fragile world but it is a fragility brought on not merely by social and technological change: it is a fragility in the way that we understand the world, in the way in which we understand ourselves and in the ways in which we feel secure about acting in the world.

Barnett (2004, p. 257) also argues that an essential element in a curriculum for a supercomplex world "will be an exposure to dilemmas and uncertainties. These may be from the complexities within a field of knowledge ... but, here will widen such that the human being itself is implicated". It is crucial to maximising the fit of PBL for a supercomplex world that we continually develop our understanding of dialogic knowing and give tutor development the attention that it deserves. Please note that a more detailed exploration of strategies for the continuous professional development of tutors can be found in Chapter 16.

References

Barnett, R. (2000). Supercomplexity and the curriculum. *Studies in Higher Education, 25*(3), 255–388.

Barnett, R. (2004). Learning for an unknown future. *Higher Education Research and Development, 23*(3), 247–260.

Barrett, T. (2001). Philosophical principles for problem-based learning: Freire's concepts of personal development and social empowerment. In P. Little & P. Kandlbinder (Eds.), *Refereed proceedings of the 3rd Asia Pacific Conference on PBL, The Power of Problem Based Learning* (pp. 9–18). Newcastle, Australia: PROBLARC.

Barrett T. (2004). Researching the dialogue of PBL tutorials: A critical discourse analysis approach. In M. Savin-Baden & K. Wilkie (Eds.), *Challenging research into problem-based learning* (pp. 93–102). Buckingham: Open University Press.

Barrett, T. (2008). *Students' talk about problem-based learning in liminal spaces.* Unpublished doctoral dissertation, Coventry University.

Brown, R., & Gilman, A. (1960). The pronouns of power and solidarity. In T.A. Sebeok (Ed.), *Style in language* (pp. 253–276). Cambridge, MA: MIT Press.

Buber, M. (1964). *Between man and man.* London: Collins.

Clouston, T. (2007). Exploring methods of analysing talk in problem-based learning tutorials. *Journal of Further and Higher Education, 31*, 183–193.

De Grave, W. (1998). *Improving tutoring: How to deal with critical incidents* [DVD]. Retrieved from: www.unimaas.nl/PBL.

Halela, M. (2008). *Tracing the roles of the PBL tutor: A journey of learning.* Helsinki: Haaga-Helia University of Applied Science.

Kador, T. (2009) *A concept map of the module.* Presented as part of a PBL team oral presentation during a module on PBL in Higher Education at University College Dublin.

Myers Kelson, A., & Distlehorst, L. (2000) Groups in problem-based learning: Essential elements in theory and practice. In D. Evenson & C. Hmelo (Eds.), *Problem-based learning: A research perspective on learning interactions* (pp. 167–184). London: Lawrence Erlbaum Associates.

Rule, P. (2004). Dialogic spaces, adult education projects and social engagement. *International Journal of Lifelong Education, 23*(4), 319–334.

Schmidt, H. (1993) Foundations of problem-based learning: Some explanatory notes. *Medical Education, 27*, 422–432.

Shor, I., & Freire, P. (1987). *A pedagogy for liberation.* London: Bergin and Garvey.

Silén, C. (2006). The tutors' approach in base groups (PBL). *Higher Education, 51*, 373–385.

Vygotsky, L.S. (1978). *Mind in society: The development of higher psychological processes.* Cambridge, MA: Harvard University Press.

Further Resources

Alanko-Turunen, M. (2005). *Negotiating interdiscursivity in a problem-based learning tutorial site.* Doctorate thesis, Tampere: Faculty of Education, Tampere University. Retrieved from: http://acta.uta.fi/pdf/951-44-6305-6.pdf.

Curzon-Hobson, A. (2002). Higher education in a world of radical unknowability: An extension of the challenge of Ronald Barnett. *Teaching in Higher Education, 7*(2), 179–191.
An overview of the contributions of Buber, Freire, and Barnett to our understanding of the concept of dialogue in higher education.

10

Shining a Spotlight on Students' Information Literacy in the PBL Process

Lorna Dodd, Eeva-Liisa Eskola, and Charlotte Silén

Introduction

In this chapter we argue that the power and potential of PBL is significantly strengthened when it goes hand-in-hand with a clear focus on the development of information literacy skills. We also show that, by engaging with a PBL programme, higher education institutions can build stronger, more collaborative links between academic teachers and librarians than might otherwise be possible. We suggest that when students are encouraged to engage in PBL, their levels of engagement increase both within and beyond the classroom, and this engagement becomes a lever that helps educational systems to reorient themselves in more integrated ways, in particular, when it comes to the development of information literacy.

For many years, commentators have been calling for stronger alignment between teachers and librarians in higher education (e.g. Kotter, 1999; Peacock, 2001). It has long been lamented that highly skilled librarians, who can enhance learning environments in a range of ways, often find themselves somewhat dislocated from the main business of teaching and learning at college and university (see, for example, Moore & Murphy, 2005).

Our own research suggests that the development of information literacy is likely to be of a significantly higher quality when teachers, librarians, and students work together in a collaborative way. In this chapter, we reorient the traditional focus on building information literacy skills among students by moving beyond a focus on the independent study phases of learning and by shining the spotlight on all aspects of the PBL process from the point of view of the students.

By summarising the practical implications of key research, and by providing practice examples, this chapter also presents practitioners with transferable principles in designing, facilitating, and assessing the development of information literacy in PBL. It draws on the authors' experiences as PBL tutors and librarians in conjunction with three recent research studies. The first of these studies examined the impact of PBL on the information literacy of undergraduate veterinary medicine students in Ireland (Dodd, 2007); the second was a research project comparing the information-related behaviour of medical students studying in a PBL curriculum and a traditional curriculum in Finland (Eskola, 2005, 2006, 2007); and the third study examined the relationships between the tutorial process, self-directed learning, and information literacy in Sweden (Silén & Uhlin, 2008).

Based on our analysis of information literacy in the PBL process, we present a reconceptualisation of the key competences that are required when learning to access and use information. Our conceptual map offers readers an integrated way of thinking about information literacy and of understanding problem-based learning by showing how both of these domains of activity link together and provide crucial supports to each other.

Our discussion, therefore, challenges much of the discourse on information literacy development in a PBL context in higher education. Most research carried out in the area of problem-based learning, libraries, and information literacy tends to focus on how librarians and information resources are affected by the introduction of PBL rather than on student competences (Elredge, 1993, 2004; Friden, 1996; Oker-Blom & Martensson, 1996). Our focus suggests that the starting point should always be the student; that by motivating the learners' own information literacy development and by designing authentic problems for them to tackle, we help them to generate their own energy for learning. It is this energy that, in turn, helps organisations to provide more integrated support to students' learning. Sometimes this PBL approach to information literacy can manifest itself in the simple difference between a student who says to a librarian, "I'm looking for a book", and one who says "I'm trying to solve a problem".

In PBL, the student is more likely to say the latter. The problem is a starting point that can mobilise the curiosity and energy of learners and learner supports in a range of different ways, especially when there has been strong involvement from librarians in the design of PBL curricula from the outset.

Chapter Overview

This chapter begins by reconceptualising information literacy as an integral part of the PBL process. It then uses this framework to discuss practice strategies for:

- designing PBL for the development of information literacy;
- facilitating learning in PBL to develop information literacy;
- assessing students' information literacy.

Reconceptualising Information Literacy as an Integral Part of the PBL Process

In order to conceptualise "competence with information" as a part of the PBL process, we have been guided by the American College of Research Libraries

(ACRL), which defined information literacy as the ability to "recognise when information is needed and … to locate, evaluate, and use the information effectively" (ACRL, 2000). Our own research projects, along with a review of the literature, have helped us to show how the development of information literacy within PBL can be defined in six iterative steps (see Figure 10.1, below), which occur both during and outside of the tutorial process. These steps are:

1. the inquiry process which leads to identifying a learning issue or information need for working on "problems";
2. identifying the most appropriate resources for working on learning issues;
3. searching for information effectively;
4. identifying, evaluating, and retrieving information;
5. integrating information into existing knowledge and applying it to the problem;
6. further enquiry triggered by the new information.

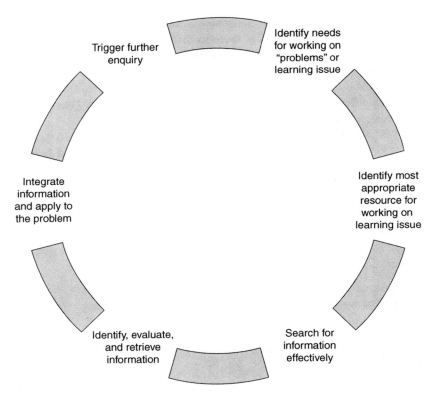

Figure 10.1 Information literacy requirements for PBL.

One of the principles of PBL is its deliberate stimulation of self-directed learning. By engaging in the processes associated with tackling and solving problems, students learn more quickly to take responsibility for their learning and to develop skills and insights about their learning processes. There is an important and strong link between development of self-directed learning and the enhancement of the students' information literacy. Taking responsibility for and developing independence in learning is enhanced by the capacity to search for, find, and use information effectively. Becoming information literate is not an automatic process and it does not just happen, not even in environments where information is freely available and easy to access; to develop information literacy students need challenges, support, and feedback.

In this essential dimension of students' self-directed learning, the specific skills of librarianship are very important. Librarians can align their practice with any PBL process by using the same facilitating approach that PBL tutors employ in small-group tutorials. In turn, lecturers and other experts can align their practices in ways that support the students' development of information literacy. Together then, teachers, librarians, and learner support staff can challenge the students' views on the information needed and support them by initiating reflections and modelling their own choices (Silén & Uhlin, 2008).

We argue that, if librarians commit to adopting a PBL orientation within their own practice, the relationships between the learning that happens inside the classroom and that which occurs beyond the classroom setting becomes more seamless and more supported at every stage of a PBL process. Such an orientation could help to reconceptualise how we might develop information literacy in higher education and could revitalise the thinking about how PBL can become a "joined- up" process, served by teachers and librarians together. Reconceptualising information literacy as an integral part of the PBL process has implications for all aspects of the PBL curriculum including design, practice, and assessment. The next section explains what implications our own research has suggested about how information literacy can be integrated into the design of any PBL process.

Designing PBL for the Development of Information Literacy

In order to design PBL in a way that supports the development of information literacy, it is necessary to identify the key information literacy requirements that relate directly to the activities that are part of the PBL process. As these requirements may be most easily identified by librarians (who come face-to-face with information literacy needs among students in the course of their daily professional practice), it is imperative that they are involved in the design process. Involving librarians will be more likely to enable the successful integration of appropriate and timely information literacy instruction and the design of relevant "problems".

Identifying the Information Literacy Requirements of PBL to Inform Curriculum Design

Our review of the literature and our analysis of primary data in three different learning contexts has highlighted the key skills and competences that can be used to build a framework for the development of information literacy within a PBL context. Previous studies have found that PBL students choose information sources that are typical of independent learners such as online journals and databases. Compared to their traditional curriculum counterparts, students involved in PBL acquire information literacy skills earlier, use the library for longer periods of time, ask more complex questions at the reference desk, display greater ease in locating information, use a wider variety of resources to support their learning, and challenge learner support staff to provide additional instruction in information literacy skills (Oker-Blom, 1998; Rankin, 1996).

PBL's Effects on the Learner Experience of Information Literacy

Qualitative studies were conducted on the students' experiences of PBL in two different cultural contexts, comparing these students with the experiences of students of more conventionally delivered programmes. In the first of these studies, the impact of PBL on the information literacy of undergraduate veterinary medicine students in Ireland was examined by comparing data relating to PBL and non-PBL activities (Dodd, 2007). The second study was a research project that compared the information behaviour of medical students studying in a PBL curriculum and a traditional curriculum in Finland (Eskola, 2005, 2006, 2007). The third study examined the relationship between the tutorial process and self-directed learning information literacy in Sweden (Silén & Uhlin, 2008).

Our analysis of the responses from each study suggest that, when it comes to the development of information literacy, PBL contexts present both challenges and opportunities.

PBL Challenges Related to Information Literacy

Students who encounter problem-based learning often report that they experience at least some difficulties when seeking information. In our studies, the student responses suggest that, compared to their counterparts on more conventional learning programmes, PBL students encounter challenges when it comes to:

- understanding how information is structured;
- determining the most appropriate sources of information for their needs;
- navigating their way through the multiple informational choices available to them;

- finding the "right" information;
- accessing information efficiently.

PBL as a process is often described by students as being both more engaging and more difficult than conventionally delivered programmes. Barrett (2005) conceptualises student learning in PBL as "hard fun", that is, both difficult and engaging at the same time. Our own research echoes Barrett's description, and the "hard fun" concept also permeates the information literacy dimensions of problem-based learning.

It makes sense that students engaging in problem-based learning struggle to find the "right" information, feel the need to build time efficiencies into their information search, and encounter challenges when it comes to choosing and using information to apply to the problems they grapple with on their programmes of study (Silén, 2001). However, they also enjoy the excitement and curiosity of naming their own learning issues and becoming more information literate as they find relevant up-to-date information and relate this information to the problem.

PBL Opportunities Related to Information Literacy

Similarly, our findings show that while working in a PBL context, observable benefits are associated with the development of students' information literacy skills. These benefits include:

- a stronger understanding of the importance of different types of information sources in choosing information;
- the stronger likelihood that they will access a wider number of information sources;
- the intrinsically motivating nature of the problem-based tasks that encourage autonomous, self-directed searching and finding of information;
- the more elaborate and conscious use of information and sources;
- a greater awareness of the topical relevance of information and of how information can be applied to real problems and challenges within their disciplines;
- the development of greater levels of skill in evaluating information.

All of these benefits or opportunities relating to PBL information literacy development reflect some of the key aims of PBL and endorse the use of PBL as a powerful learning process.

Overall, we found, in both of the studies which examined the impact of PBL on information literacy, that the self-direction and critical evaluation associated with PBL were typical for students. The implication of this finding is that, within the PBL setting, students require a higher level of information literacy skills than within a traditional setting.

All of these experiences, reported by PBL students themselves, simply underline how important it is to provide students with the opportunity to develop skills that will enable them to locate, retrieve, evaluate, and absorb information in an efficient and effective manner. In addition, these findings suggest that the PBL environment, while presenting challenges, may also provide one of the most appropriate contexts for the effective development of information literacy skills.

Taking the student experiences into consideration, in order to ensure that the development of information literacy skills is fully supported, it is useful to track and assist students in navigating a series of steps, some of which occur during contact time with tutors, some of which occur when they meet librarians, and some are encountered as part of the "self-study" phase of the PBL process. Silén and Uhlin (2008) provide a series of phases that are well placed to reflect the challenges and opportunities that we have identified as part of information literacy in PBL.

Session 1 – Enquiry before study (in the PBL tutorial)

Identify information needs for working on "problems", name "learning issues"

Identify the most appropriate resource for working on learning issues

Session 2 – Independent study (between PBL tutorials)

Search for information effectively

Identify, evaluate, and retrieve relevant information

Review information as it relates to the problem

Session 3 – Enquiry after independent study (in the PBL tutorial)

Integrate the information into their existing knowledge

Apply it to the problem

Co-construct knowledge by discussing independent study

Trigger further enquiry

Figure 10.2 Phases of information literacy development for PBL (adapted from Silén & Uhlin, 2008).

We propose that, within a PBL setting, this process of information literacy development should assume a cyclical nature and be integrated into the process of learning (as illustrated in Figure 10.2). Once new information is integrated into the students' existing knowledge and applied to the problem, it should then trigger further enquiry that leads to the identification of a new information need.

Involving Librarians Early in PBL Curriculum Design

The literature suggests, and our own investigations confirm, that librarians can offer another vital element in the successful design of PBL programmes, particularly when it comes to the development of information literacy. Once key competences are identified, information literacy skills can be more effectively facilitated by librarians and, in collaboration with teachers, these skills can be linked to PBL "problems". Moreover, the identification of key information literacy competences at the earliest stages in curriculum development also means that these competences can be considered when "problems" are being designed.

Integration of Information Literacy Instruction (ILI)

So, while even the most conventional curricula tend to offer some type of library instruction, PBL presents the opportunity to develop a more integrated approach to ILI. The introduction of PBL can often present a "window of opportunity" for librarians and academics to create a dynamic, learner supportive partnership. For example, in the University of Manchester, the introduction of PBL led to the first ever formal library skills programme which was planned by the librarian in conjunction with teaching staff (Ferguson, 1996). For librarians in Linkoping University in Sweden, becoming involved in the curriculum planning process was "much easier in the PBL setting than in a traditional educational system" (Friden, 1996, p. 4). In fact, PBL provides an opportunity to go further than embedding information literacy instruction into the curriculum.

Throughout the literature, a key element in PBL curricula is that ILI should fit into the main educational philosophy. Rankin's (1996, p. 38) review of the literature discusses how "the integration of instructional activities into the curriculum proper is quite readily achieved at PBL schools". As collaborative partners in a PBL process, librarians are well positioned to "demonstrate effective information-gathering procedures" and, when learning objectives are clear, link library skills with PBL cases (Rankin, 1996, p. 38). Oker-Blom (1998, pp. 4–5) maintains that "to work most successfully, information skills must be taught as part of the curriculum and be embedded in the learning process" and that the challenge lies in identifying the skills required by students (Oker-Blom, 1998, p. 5). Examples of this type of integration are well documented. For example, at the University of New Mexico, PBL cases are specifically created to encourage the development of information literacy skills. This process begins with a problem-based case study that encourages students to learn how to use resources in a PBL context (Elredge, 1993). In addition, in the University of Pittsburgh, the involvement of librarians in curriculum development, from design to implementation and evaluation, resulted in librarians providing training to students prior to the PBL sequence and acting as resource guides throughout the PBL block (Rankin, 1996).

In analysing the data that we collected from students, it became clear that they also saw information literacy as an integral part of the PBL process. The interviews with the librarian and academic staff in University College Dublin (UCD) demonstrated the importance of information literacy within the PBL setting (Dodd, 2007). Information literacy was considered to be "the core of it [PBL]" and students were expected to have the ability to "learn what kinds of resources are available". Indeed, we have found that it was precisely the consultation between faculty and librarian that resulted in the decision to integrate ILI into a PBL course. Furthermore, in analysis of the process at UCD, it was the librarian's role as a PBL tutor that made it possible to engage in an effective observation of students' needs and to understand the ways in which they used information resources (Dodd, 2007). Our observations and those that have been articulated by other authors in the field suggest that the librarians' involvement in the development and design of PBL programmes allow for more appropriate and effective information literacy interventions to be developed.

If librarians are involved in the early stages of curriculum design, they can contribute to the creation of more meaningful learning environments for PBL that will enable students to develop better information literacy skills. When information literacy is considered in the design stage, it facilitates development and support for students. To illustrate this, in UCD, the librarian was involved at the design stage and was, therefore, able to adapt ILI to better suit the requirements of each problem. This meant that students were presented with greater opportunities to develop their information literary skills.

Facilitating Learning in PBL to Develop Information Literacy

The nature of the learning process, within a PBL tutorial, plays a significant role in the development of the students' information literacy skills; this process includes the vital role of the tutor and the collaborative process that occurs within the tutorial setting.

Role of the PBL Tutor

Within the tutorial setting, the tutor can play a significant role in enabling the students to develop the six information literacy competences that we have outlined above. One of the most effective ways of beginning to facilitate these competences is through the use of tutorial-based questions that address key issues associated with information-seeking as illustrated in Figure 10.3. It is useful to ask students these types of questions at the beginning of a PBL process in order to initiate reflective and critical thought regarding their information-seeking orientations. As the curriculum progresses, the students should be able to ask themselves and each other these questions both during and outside of the tutorial.

Recognise their information need	The tutor can encourage students to turn their learning issues into information queries	**Questions:** What keywords from your learning issue will you use for your search? Are there any other keywords that could be used to retrieve useful information? How will your learning issue turn into a search strategy?
Identify the most appropriate resource	Tutors can ensure students understand what kind of information they require and stimulate critical thinking and reflection regarding their choices	What kind of information are you looking for? Why are you looking for that kind of information? Which resources are most appropriate for that kind of information? Why is that resource appropriate?
Search for information effectively	Tutors can enable students to critically evaluate and improve their information literacy skills	Where did you find that information? What other sources did you use? What is your critical overview of that paper and its source? How would you verify that information?
Identify, evaluate, and retrieve relevant information		
Integrate information into existing knowledge and apply to the problem	Tutors can stimulate students to think about the information they find and place it in context with their own knowledge, experience and the "problem"	How do you know this is a suitable resource? How does the paper relate to what you already know? How does that point relate to the problem?

Figure 10.3 Facilitating information literacy in the PBL tutorial.

Collaboration

The development of students' information literacy skills can also be facilitated through the collaborative process of PBL. Collaboration and cooperative learning in groups can influence learning by extending the available knowledge and supporting various approaches to problems. When learners get to know alternative points of view, their own initial understandings are challenged. When monitoring individual thinking, group members can clarify difficult or complex ideas. Thus, in collaborative groups, tutors can support and enhance learning without the unwanted effects of oversimplifying the learning task (Glaser, 1991).

In each study, the analysis of student feedback indicated that the students in the PBL groups shared not only the content of the information that they gathered for the learning issues, but also information on how the relevant documents were accessed, gathered, and evaluated (Eskola, 2006). It is important to note that this kind of social information sharing, defined by Talja (2002) as a relationship- or community-building activity, did not appear among the traditional students. So, collaboration, an essential element in PBL, benefits not only knowledge sharing but also the learning of effective processes.

Assessing Students' Information Literacy

Once the required information literacy competences are identified, they can be included in assessment criteria as illustrated in Figure 10.4 below. Useful assessment tools can include annotated bibliographies, a critical review of journal papers, independent study summaries with references and self-assessment of information literacy in tutorials. Furthermore, responses to the questions presented in Figure 10.4 will provide guidelines that can be used to formatively assess students' information literacy through self-, peer, and tutor-assessment.

Conclusion

This chapter has identified some of the central requirements and processes associated with information literacy within a PBL process. It suggests that PBL creates an ideal arena in which to sharpen and focus such skills, and provides authentic challenges for students in a way that is unlikely to be achieved via more conventionally delivered curricula.

In order to provide students with the opportunity to develop the skills required for participating in PBL, it is essential to reconceptualise information literacy as an integral part of the entire PBL process rather than merely something belonging to independent study. Because information literacy is a prerequisite for the development of self-directed learning and, as such, an essential part of all aspects of PBL, there is enormous scope for maximising the expertise and contribution that both librarians and PBL tutors can bring

Recognise their information need	Assessments should require students to outline clearly their information need at the beginning of the assignment. Ability to identify an information need correctly will influence the success of the entire assignment. If students do not identify the correct need, they will not retrieve relevant information
Identify the most appropriate resource	Assessments should require students to state clearly which resources were used to retrieve information. Students could be asked to give reasons for selecting each resource used
Search for information effectively	Assessments could require students to include their search strategy. This will illustrate whether students have used the most appropriate keywords and limiters for their search. If students have not used an appropriate search strategy, they may not retrieve relevant information
Identify, evaluate, and retrieve relevant information	Assessments should require students to critically evaluate the information source used. Students could also be asked to compare the resource to other relevant resources. Content of assignments will also demonstrate whether students have used a sufficient range of resources
Integrate information into existing knowledge and apply to the problem	Assessments should require students to demonstrate their understanding of the information they found by relating it to their existing knowledge and applying it to the problem

Figure 10.4 Assessing information literacy in PBL.

to the information literacy acquisition process. Adopting a collaborative, co-ordinated approach to design, facilitation, and assessment has the potential to unlock the power and potential of PBL in a range of important ways that, in particular, can serve to build the lifelong transferable skills associated with information literacy.

By shining the spotlight on the students' information literacy, the ideas in this chapter support the call for the creation and maintenance of collaborative and creative partnerships between librarians, tutors, teachers, and students in PBL settings. In fact, it is students who shine this spotlight on themselves, by recognising information literacy as a vital component in PBL.

References

Association of College Research Libraries (2000). *Information literacy competency standards for higher education*. Retrieved 20 June 2007, from: www.ala.org/ala/acrl/acrlstandards/informationliteracycompetency.htm.

Barrett, T. (2005). "Lecturers" experience as problem-based learners: Learning as hard fun. In T. Barrett, I. Mac Labhrainn, & H. Fallon (Eds.), *Handbook of enquiry and problem-based learning: Irish case studies and international perspectives*. Galway: CELT, National University of Ireland Galway and All Ireland Society for Higher Education.

Dodd, L. (2007). The impact of problem-based learning on the information seeking behaviour and information literacy of veterinary medicine students at University College Dublin. *Journal of Academic Librarianship, 33*(2), 206–216.

Elredge, J.D. (1993). A problem-based learning curriculum in transition: The emerging role of the librarian. *Bulletin of the Medical Library Association, 81*(3), 310–315.

Elredge, J.D. (2004). The librarian as tutor/facilitator in a problem-based learning (PBL) curriculum. *Reference Services Review, 32*(1), 54–59.

Eskola, E.-L. (2005). Information literacy of medical students studying in the problem-based and traditional curriculum. *Information Research, 10*(2). Retrieved from: http://informationr.net/ir/10-2/paper221.html.

Eskola, E.-L. (2006). Information literacy and collaborative information behaviour of medical students studying in the problem-based and traditional curriculum. In *Information Use in Information Society. Proceedings of the International Conference* (pp. 155–163). Bratislava: Centrum vedecko-technických informácii SR.

Eskola, E.-L. (2007). Information literacy in medical education: Relationships with conceptions of learning and learning methods. *Advances in Library Administration and Organization, 25*, 203–238.

Ferguson, V. (1996). Planning and providing a course of problem-based library skills for medical and dental undergraduates: The first year. *Health Libraries Review, 13*, 43–47.

Friden, K. (1996). The librarian as a teacher: Experiences from a problem-based setting. *Health Libraries Review, 13*, 3–7.

Glaser, R. (1991). The maturing of the relationship between the science of learning and cognition and educational practice. *Learning and Instruction, 1*, 129–144.

Kotter, W.R. (1999). Bridging the great divide: Improving relations between librarians and classroom faculty. *Journal of Academic Librarianship, 25*(4), 294–303.

Moore, S., & Murphy, M. (2005). *How to be a student: 100 great ideas and practical habits for students everywhere*. Maidenhead: Open University Press.

Oker-Blom, T. (1998). Integration of information skills in problem based curricula. *64th IFLA General Conference*, 16–21 August 1994, Amsterdam, pp. 1–8, IFLA.

Oker-Blom, T., & Martensson, D. (1996). Editorial: Problem-based learning and the librarian's role. *Health Libraries Review, 13*, 1–2.

Peacock, J. (2001). Teaching skills for teaching librarians: Postcards from the edge of the educational paradigm. *Australian Academic and Research Libraries, 3*(5), 343–359.

Rankin, J.A. (1992). Problem-based medical education: Effect on library use. *Bulletin of the Medical Library Association, 80*(1), 36–43.

Rankin, J.A. (1996). Problem-based learning and libraries: A survey of the literature. *Health Libraries Review, 13*, 33–42.

Silén, C. (2001). Between chaos and cosmos: A driving force for responsibility and independence in learning. In P. Little & P. Kandlbinder (Eds.), *Refereed proceedings of the 3rd Asia Pacific Conference on PBL: The power of problem-based learning*. Newcastle, Australia: PROBLARC.

Silén, C., & Uhlin, L. (2008). Self-directed learning: A learning issue for students and faculty! *Teaching in Higher Education, 13*(4), 461–475.

Talja, S. (2002). Information sharing in academic communities: Types and levels of collaboration in information seeking and use. *New Review of Information Behaviour Research, 3*, 143–160.

Further Resources

American College of Research Libraries: www.ala.org/ala/acrl/acrlissues/acrlinfolit/information-literacy.cfm.

Blake, J. (1994). Library resources for problem-based learning: The programme perspective. *Computer Methods and Programs in Biomedicine, 44,* 167–173.

Brock Enger, K., Brenenson, S., Lenn, K., MacMillan, M., Meisart, M.F., Meserve, H., & Vella, S.A. (2002). Problem-based learning: Evolving strategies and conversations for library instruction. *Reference Services Review, 30*(4), 335–358.

Friden, K. (1996). The librarian as a teacher: Experiences from a problem-based setting. *Health Libraries Review, 13,* 3–7.

Snavely, L. (2004). Making problem-based learning work: Institutional challenges. *Libraries and the Academy, 4*(4), 521–531.

Society of College, National and University Libraries: www.sconul.ac.uk/topics_issues/info_literacy.

11

Developing Reflective Practitioners through PBL in Academic and Practice Environments

Marja-Leena Lähteenmäki and Lars Uhlin

Introduction

Self-directed learning (SDL) is an important approach for professionals. However, the problem is how to develop SDL and how to address SDL as a learning issue in itself. Learning can be seen as a problem-solving process, where the learner has to analyse the situation, find the possible solutions, and be able to select the most suitable one for each situation (Dewey, 1960). New learning is based on prior learning and, for new learning, the learner needs to reflect on this prior learning. Without reflection, which simply means the ability to think in order to learn something new, learning does not happen.

We argue that reflection must be viewed as an integral part of daily learning processes. Reflection must be seen as transformational, and focus on personal and professional development. We offer you a holistic view of reflection addressing curriculum design issues, practical guidelines, and specific strategies for supporting reflective activities.

Problem-based learning supports the development of reflection, as the learner is actively involved in enquiry into real world problems and, observing, analysing, and clarifying her/his learning needs. In this chapter, our main interest is to emphasise the important strategies that guide the learner to become a reflective practitioner. We draw on the experience gained from the journeys we have travelled as PBL tutors, education developers, and researchers both in Finland and Sweden.

Chapter Overview

This chapter begins by reconceptualising learning as a reflective knowledge-creation process. We will discuss how students can use reflection to make connections in their learning and how to enhance reflective practices within a PBL curriculum. We outline ways of maximising the potential of tutorials to make links between different parts and activities within academic and professional settings through different modes and tools for reflection. Building on these ideas, we discuss reflection in relation to three areas of activity in PBL practice:

1. supporting critical enquiry and reflection in PBL tutorials;
2. developing reflexivity in practical settings; and
3. using portfolios to support the students' journey through education.

Throughout the chapter we provide reflective spaces for you as a reader.

Knowledge and Learning

Traditionally, knowledge has two dimensions: theory and practice. Burnard (1987) defines knowledge for the experiential professions as having three dimensions: theory, praxis, and experience. Theory is abstract; it can be obtained, for instance, from books and research reports. With praxis, we understand the knowledge, which is concrete and it is connected to practical situations and techniques specific to each profession. In the learning process, the learner actively integrates theory and praxis in a meaningful way, creating the learner's own individual theory, the experiential knowledge (see Figure 11.1). In this three-dimensional, reflective knowledge-creating process, the individual develops his/her personal knowledge.

In Broberg et al.'s (2003) framework for curriculum design, presented in Figure 11.2, the individual knowledge-creating process can be seen as an ongoing process of professional developmental (spiral arrow 2). The professional content is in the centre of the process (middle arrow); during formal education the student is aiming to learn a profession's (a) core concepts, (b) practices, (c) working areas, and (d) research area. It is important to remember that learning always happens in a social, cultural, and political context (layer 3).

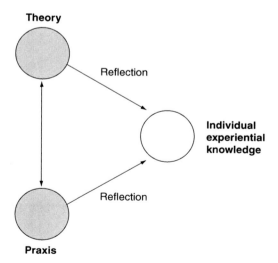

Figure 11.1 Learning as a reflective knowledge creating process (adapted from Poikela, 2006).

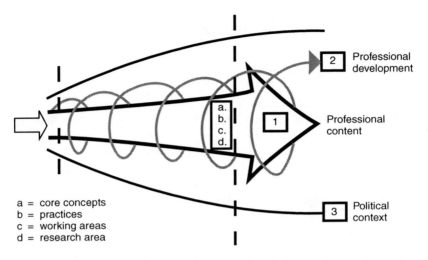

a = core concepts
b = practices
c = working areas
d = research area

Figure 11.2 A conceptual framework for curriculum design (Broberg et al., 2003).

Everyday learning (e.g. hobbies, work) is an important part of the context and plays a central role in the students' learning alongside organised formal education. In this framework of curriculum design, the learner builds new knowledge on the foundation of all of the knowledge she/he possessed before the education began (left arrow). The learning process supports SDL during the education programme to ensure that lifelong learning and professional development continues after the education (the right dotted vertical line).

Reflective Space

Think about learning in your own professional area:

- What is the theory that is important for your students?
- What is the praxis, the learning from professional practice situations, for your students?
- How are your students supported in integrating theory and praxis?
- How does your educational system support students' individual learning process over time?

Reflection, Critical Reflection, and Self-reflection

Reflection is an essential part of good practice. Every practitioner should learn the skills of reflection and critical reflection in order to act in a professional way and to develop as an expert practitioner.

Although reflection has been defined as reviewing one's own actions (Johns, 2000), a more target-oriented view defines reflection as thinking for learning something new (Dewey, 1960). Reflection can also be defined as a metacognitive process that occurs before, during, and after situations in order to develop a greater understanding of the self and the situation so that future encounters with the situation are informed by previous encounters (Sandars, 2009). In this chapter, we define reflection as active thinking that is essential for learning. As such, reflection requires learners to be involved in observing, analysing, and clarifying their actions. It is only after reflection that new learning can emerge (Boud, Keogh, & Walker, 1985; Kolb, 1984; Mezirow, 1991). In contrast, one does not use or even need reflection in reproducing given models (Schön, 1987).

Reflective practice requires the practitioner to be willing to accept knowledge that may be against his or her prejudices, preconceptions, and interests. This willingness to accept this knowledge is critical reflection; it involves questioning and actively adjusting previously learned practices (Mezirow, 1991). The practitioner needs to compare his or her previous knowledge to the new knowledge and be ready to change his or her prior viewpoints when new knowledge gives adequate reasons to do so. Reflective practice can be seen as an active observation of actions and as the clarification of reasoning which leads to new and, if necessary, changed understanding.

Self-reflection involves the ability of a practitioner to simultaneously observe him-/herself and the world outside; it involves three dimensions: knowledge, feelings, and actions. For example:

1. Knowledge – you are willing to take into account the new knowledge that you have received in order to be able to make more healthy food for your family.
2. Feelings – you select nice-looking soup bowls, put flowers on the table, or put on enjoyable music.
3. Actions – you listen to your own body (pains, tiredness, and so on) and choose working positions and utensils that are more ergonomic for yourself.

Reflective Space

- Stop reading for a few minutes and think about these definitions of reflection. Think of some examples of reflection, first of all from your own professional area and, second, from your own private life.
- In your own teaching, how do you support students' reflection in different learning situations?

Making the Most of PBL through Different Modes of Reflection

Building on the theoretical frameworks presented previously, in PBL, we regard reflection as an essential, intrinsic aspect of student learning processes. Like Brown, Matthew-Maich, and Royle (2001), we suggest that reflection must permeate the whole PBL process; it is through the core activity in PBL, the enquiry into reality-based situations in groups, that students develop understanding and skills. For learning to occur, students must engage in a thorough enquiry in which their assumptions and conceptions are challenged. This process of enquiry opens up a process of critical reflection on what the students think they understand already and what they need to learn. Within the format of the tutorial group, facilitated by a tutor, a safe space can be created for critical reflection and enquiry into the thoughts, feelings, and actions that occur in the group work (Silén & Uhlin, 2008).

From our experiences of PBL, we argue that the potential of PBL lies in how well, within a PBL curriculum, the tutorial work is acknowledged as a space for critical enquiry and reflection. The PBL tutorial must be regarded as a place where students are challenged and supported and can monitor their journey of development as self-directed learners and professionals.

In combining the theoretical frameworks presented in Figures 11.1 and 11.2 and applying these frameworks to the general structure of a PBL curriculum, we want to show the potential of PBL for reflection. In Figure 11.3, we outline a general structure of a PBL curriculum that consists of three parts (represented by dotted vertical lines), which could be modules, courses, semesters, or years within a whole curriculum. For students, the curriculum consists of activities within both an academic environment and a practical/ professional environment. The academic and the practical/professional environments can be seen as two discourses that students enter and become part of. Within the academic setting, teachers design and organise formal teaching and learning activities such as seminars, lectures, labs, skills training, and tasks. Between the organised activities there are informal activities. The students choose the informal activities that they will engage in during their independent study, within and outside of the academic environment. In the practical/professional setting, the students' learning is usually organised as field studies and placements of different length and timings within the curriculum.

In the centre of the programme, there is PBL tutorial work that operates like a linking chain during education. The PBL tutorial work functions as the heart or the hub of the educational programme, in mediating between the academic and the practical/professional aspects of the education process. During the education process, tutorial work must become increasingly authentic, progressing from being an academic activity to professional action.

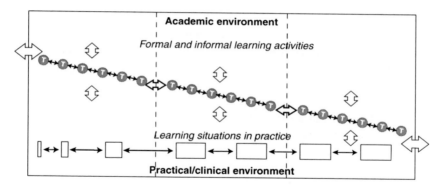

Figure 11.3 Maximising the potential of tutorials as a reflective space in a PBL curriculum.

In designing and organising a PBL curriculum, there are many issues and challenges for teachers concerning logistics and constructive alignment. Although Biggs and Tang (2007) regard PBL as an aligned system, is this always the case from a student's perspective? We argue it is the students' own alignment (connecting different parts and phases of the curriculum) that is the most important and that reflection becomes the means by which the students make connections every day. In this chapter, our main interest is to focus on how students, through reflection, can make the most out of a curriculum, no matter how well we, as teachers, have designed it.

The arrows in Figure 11.3 show potential connections to be addressed for critical reflection by students. The vertical arrows symbolise the challenge of connecting the academic and theoretical knowledge with practical and professional knowledge in real-world praxis. In the tutorial group (during the series of tutorials (marked T) the enquiry processes serve as a means for students to develop understanding and individual experiential knowledge.

The horizontal arrows show important connections to be made, over time, addressing issues of progression and development. The small arrows are related to progression in the processes of tutorial work and how students develop as professionals in practice placements during education. We also believe that moving from one module, course, semester, or year to the next calls for student reflection on development.

We argue that, in a PBL curriculum, the students' own alignment, connecting the different parts and phases of a curriculum, is vital for the success of student learning. It is a challenging task for teachers to design and to support students in making connections and transferring knowledge between the parts. It is not unusual that modules and courses become isolated parts on the student's journey through education and that tutorial work, placements in practice, and other teaching and learning activities become separate strands.

In the next section, we will discuss how reflection can be enhanced in tutorial work and in the practical/professional setting, and how the use of portfolios can become a powerful tool for students and teachers in PBL.

Reflective Space

- How do the structures and the working methods of your educational programme support students' reflection?

Tutorial Work as Space and a Hub for Reflection

One consequence of using PBL is that students become more aware of what is being studied. In PBL, the students have an opportunity to combine theory with practice and to improve their ability to learn and memorise information and may see the importance of different subjects, lectures, and other learning activities. In a study of the experiences of 1st-year PBL students' experiences (Lähteenmäki, 2001, p. 80), one student wrote the following comment:

> So I felt it would be a very good idea if physiotherapy lessons and anatomy would go hand in hand. ... And when you really do something then you think of the way that you are doing it, with what muscles and so on. I wish it could work that way.

When asked to describe problem-based learning as his/her way of learning, another student (Lähteenmäki, 2001, p. 79) wrote the following comment about tutorials:

> It is really funny to notice that learning can be fun and encouraging. In tutorial meetings students give such different and interesting views on subjects. I, myself, would never have thought about subjects from so many points of view. When you are thinking aloud with the group, it's like you, by chance, understand what it is about. When the topic is thrown backwards and forwards during the discussion it also stays more alive in your mind than if you just read it in a book and try to learn it that way. There is so much less thinking when you read it from a book.

In Lähteenmäki's (2001) study, most of the students were enthusiastic about their way of learning and believed that the way of dealing with the subject matter in PBL served to reinforce learning. Independent study and the need to take responsibility for one's own learning were seen as essential. By the second semester, the students had noticed that their skills in acquiring information had advanced considerably and that their approach to independent study was becoming more effective. The analysis of knowledge, during the second part of the tutorial, was viewed as the most interesting and beneficial stage of the learning process (Lähteenmäki, 2001). This suggests that reflection for constructing new knowledge was seen as the most fruitful part of the studies.

Silén and Uhlin (2008) describe four major processes in tutorial work: enquiry into the situation, enquiry into the learning process, working together, and enquiry into thoughts, feelings, and actions. They stress that, in PBL, these processes must be regarded as both means and goals. The core of tutorial work is the authentic enquiry into real-life situations. In medical education for example, using real patient encounters as the starting point for learning has been shown to be powerful for learning and in enhancing integration of theory and practice (Diemers et al., 2007). Enquiry into the learning process involves capturing the space between tutorials in order to address students' development as self-directed learners and their information literacy (Silén & Uhlin, 2008).

Reflection on the group process can address issues like roles, communication, decision-making, effectiveness, and learning climate. For working with these issues, tools and strategies are needed that help students in making norms and patterns visible. This reflection can be achieved by having different roles such as chairperson, recorder, critical thinker, challenger, elaborator, and supporter. Also, using students as observers or using audio- or video-recording can help in making things visible. At the end of each tutorial, the processes are evaluated with the aim of developing the students' self-reflection abilities.

Even if the students have been given guidance about the different roles at the beginning of the course, it is essential that the tutor provides guidance, whenever needed, throughout the education process. We have often heard tutors mention, for instance, that, "in that group only some students take part in discussion" or "that group stays too much at a surface level". From our perspective, in the tutorials, the tutor plays a key role in how the students work and learn to reflect, how they learn to enquire deeply into an issue, or how they participate. Thus, the tutors have to reflect, be active listeners, and facilitate the students in these processes. The tutors' best tool, in our experience, is to ask questions. Questions help the students to, for instance, define concepts, notice the appropriate level of knowledge, and make connections between different concepts. In addition, questions help the students to concentrate on their roles, to take other students' input into account, and to help each other to create new and shared experiential knowledge in the group.

Next, we will offer some examples of the questions that can be posed during the tutorials.

Questions for the first half of the tutorial cycle:

- What do you already know about this?
- What does this concept mean?

- How do the concepts/items mentioned connect to each other?
- What do you need to know more about in order to be able to understand this?
- How did you understand what Lisa just said?
- Pete, you seem to have something on your mind about this. Could you please tell us what you are thinking?
- What kind of experiences do you have of this?
- How do you understand the learning task?
- Where/how can you find appropriate knowledge for this learning task?

Questions for the second half of the tutorial cycle:

- What references did you use? How valid are they?
- How can you argue for what you just said?
- How does your point connect with Maija's?
- What knowledge did you get from the lectures, practical lessons, or clinical visits for this?
- How could you, Mark, as a chairperson, encourage everybody to participate in the discussion?
- What is your common understanding now about what you have learned?
- How could you visualise your common understanding?
- What other good questions would you add to these?

Reflective Space

Think about the last few tutorials you participated in:

- What were the best moments for student reflection? Why do you think so?
- How can you, as a tutor, support the dialogue in the tutorials to be even more reflective?

If you have not been a tutor, you can think about the following question:

- How would you act as a PBL tutor to promote reflection in tutorials?

Developing Reflexivity in the Practical Setting

Drawing on conclusions from a longitudinal study (Lähteenmäki, 2005), a transformative model of practical supervision was created in which reflection begins from the experiences gained by actively observing or taking part in practical situations of working life. The student recalls past experiences and, when necessary, the supervisor or teacher helps to clarify them. The student reflects on past events (reflection-on-action; Schön, 1987). The supervisor helps the students to reflect by asking questions (see Figure 11.4) but avoids giving direct answers. In this way, the students are supported to make connections between theory and practice and, in the process, they become aware of the need for new knowledge.

Next the student thinks about future events (reflection-for-action; McAlpine, Weston, Beauchamp, Wiseman, & Beauchamp, 1999). The supervisor's role is to encourage and support the student in finding relevant information, in making conclusions, and in producing written plans. When the student is in action, it is important that the supervisor creates a positive atmosphere and gives only the most essential advice and instruction (see Figure 11.4). This limitation on the supervisor's role is because the less experienced student needs more time than the supervisor to be able to reflect in action (reflection-in-action; Schön, 1987).

Reflective Space

Think about the process in Figure 11.4 in connection to your own professional area:

- Specify one or two questions or points of advice to the student in each of the four phases.

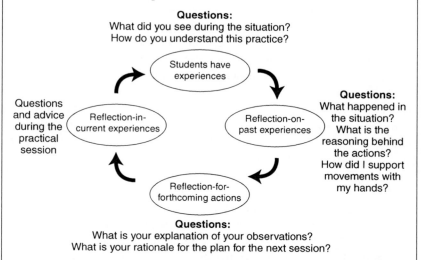

Figure 11.4 Supportive questions and advice for the students' reflection in different phases of the professional developmental process.

Using Portfolios to Support Student's Reflective Journey through Education

We have argued that reflection is an inherent or natural part of PBL. Even though we have seen many good examples of approaches to reflection in specific teaching and learning activities, we have also seen a strong need to develop a more systematic approach for reflection that helps students and teachers monitor learning and professional development on a continuous and coherent basis. We have seen that a portfolio can be a powerful tool for students to align and communicate their own learning.

The use of portfolios is widely recognised, especially within professional education, as a powerful tool for reflection and for monitoring personal and professional development (van Tartwijk & Driessen, 2009). By using a portfolio, the learning process can be supported by making development visible and by empowering students' independence, responsibility, and awareness. Portfolios, combined with PBL, have also been shown to increase the students' self-direction and motivation (Stockhausen, 2004). The use of information technology tools, such as blogs and e-portfolios, offers new ways to enhance and support reflection. Riedinger (2006, p. 93) suggests that an e-portfolio "opens wide the possibilities for reflections of all types: in action, before action, after action, in solitude, in consultation with peers, in consultation with instructors, coaches, and advisers, written, spoken, videotaped, or graphically represented". Students bring images of their chosen profession and conceptions about learning and expectations, as well as a great variety of competences. The encounter between students and academia has mostly been looked at from an academic perspective with a view to assimilating the students into the academic environment. We argue for the importance of paying attention to the identity and experiences that students bring with them and to make use of the added value of diversity (McInnis, 2001).

We have often heard from teachers that, for students, the shift to PBL is so difficult that it must be introduced gradually and that a blended approach is needed. In contrast, we argue that it is easier for students to handle an immediate shift to the demands of PBL. We believe that most students can handle this challenge if the tutorial group is used as a supportive and reflective space; however, this requirement demands experienced tutors who can handle the students' frustration and are able to facilitate reflection.

An example of supporting reflection is an educational development project which has implemented reflective writing and the idea of the portfolio (Uhlin, Johanneson, & Silén, 2007; Uhlin, 2009). In the first semester of the educational development project, the students were asked to keep a collective reflective journal. In addition, they reflected individually at specific points: the 1st week, the 3rd week, the end of the first course after 8 weeks, and at the end of the semester. The first reflection involved writing a letter to themselves about their choice of education and images of the profession, useful experiences, and the knowledge they brought with them and expectations about the education and PBL. The following reflective tasks were made as contributions in the tutorial group's own web-based discussion forum. Each time, students looked back on what they had written before and reflected on what had been important and difficult in their studies, their development as learners and as professionals, and what they thought would be important in the continuation of their studies. These written reflections formed the basis for their portfolio together with other items including a learning style inventory, approaches-to-learning questionnaire, documentation of stereotypes of different professions, and learning from early encounters with patients and professionals.

It is through the early introduction of reflective writing and documentation in a portfolio that the students' thoughts, feelings, and beliefs about learning and professional roles can be made visible, challenged, and made available for further reflection. The collection of this information in a portfolio allows the students the opportunity to look back and see their development.

Writing reflective summaries at specific points in time, looking back and forward, for example reflecting on moving from one module, course, or semester to the next (see Figure 11.3), are ways to keep the students' portfolio alive. Here, again, we suggest that the tutorial group is used as a reflective space for students to acquire new perspectives and obtain feedback from their peers and the tutor. The use of an e-portfolio will facilitate this communication.

The idea of problem-based learning is that students will enter working life well prepared to meet the demands of the profession and handle challenging situations. We expect the students to become reflective practitioners with the desire and the skills for continuous professional development. We believe that the portfolio has the potential to become a powerful tool for the development of professional identity and the transition into working life.

Reflective Space

- What are/would be the benefits of using portfolios in your context?
- How could you start or develop portfolio work?

Concluding Reflections

Reflecting on our own experiences of reflection in PBL and on the process of writing this chapter has resulted in a deepened understanding of the essentials in PBL. We have broadened our perspectives on reflection and discovered that, within a PBL curriculum, there are plenty of possibilities to maximise the students' engagement in reflective practice. We have also experienced that critical reflection is neither an easy nor a straightforward activity. We have identified a few areas which we regard as prerequisites for making the most of reflection in problem-based learning.

We want to offer some important issues for further discussion:

- We must continue to take a student perspective that includes learning from and making better use of the previous experiences and competences that the students bring with them into education. As reflection is triggered by challenges in encountering and enquiring into the new and unknown, we must find ways to make diversity explicit and make good use of this diversity in professional and interprofessional learning.
- During education, it is important to use and develop a variety of tools and approaches in order to stimulate and support students to reflect *before*, *in*, and *on* action, and to make the most of different learning situations, both formal and informal. This approach can include using tools for individual and group documentation and reflection, varying the focus and form of writing, and using different kinds of documentation such as audio, video, pictures and drawings. The students' documentation also has to be used and asked for in different ways. We believe that the tutorial group has a potential to provide a reflective space for feedback to students on their own development.
- The use of portfolios can be an important part of developing a more systematic approach to reflection that helps students and teachers to monitor learning and professional development on a continuous and coherent basis. Using information technology allows one to use many new tools, offering new opportunities for facilitating collection, sharing, feedback, and presentation. In this technological field students are the experts. How do we make use of their competences? Chapter 18 explores technology and PBL.

This chapter focused on developing students' reflective capabilities and explored the role of the PBL tutor in this development. Developing effective PBL tutors is discussed further in Chapter 16.

References

Biggs, J., & Tang, C. (2007). *Teaching for quality learning at university* (3rd ed.). Maidenhead: Open University Press.

Boud, D., Keogh, R., & Walker, D. (1985). What is reflection in learning? In D. Boud, R. Keogh, & D. Walker (Eds.), *Reflection: Turning experience into learning* (pp. 7–17). Worcester: Billing & Sons Limited.

Broberg, C., Aars, M., Beckmann, K., Vandenberghe, R., Emaus, N., Lehto, P., Lähteenmäki, M.-L., & Thys, W.A. (2003). Conceptual framework for curriculum design in physiotherapy education: An international perspective. *Advances in Physiotherapy*, 5(5), 161–168.

Brown, B., Matthew-Maich, N., & Royle, J. (2001). Fostering reflection and reflective practice. In E. Rideout (Ed.), *Transforming nursing education through problem-based learning* (pp. 119–163). Sudbury, MA: Jones and Barlett.

Burnard, P. (1987). Towards an epistemological basis for experiential learning in nurse education. *Journal of Advanced Nursing, 12*(2), 189–193.

Dewey, J. (1960). *How we think? A restatement of the relation of reflective thinking to the educative process.* Lexington, MA: D.C. Heath and Company.

Diemers, A., Dolmans, D., van Santen, M., van Luijk, S., Janssen-Noordman, A., & Scherpbier, A. (2007). Students' perceptions of early patient encounters in a PBL curriculum: A first evaluation of the Maastricht experience. *Medical Teacher, 29*(2–3), 135–142.

Johns, C. (2000). *Becoming a reflective practitioner: A reflective and holistic approach to clinical nursing, practice development and clinical supervision.* Iowa: Blackwell.

Kolb, D. (1984). *Experiential learning: Experience as the source of learning and development.* London: Prentice-Hall.

Lähteenmäki, M.-L. (2001). Problem based learning during the first academic year. In P. Little & P. Kandlbinder (Eds.), *The power of problem-based learning: Experience, empowerment, evidence* (pp. 73–84). Newcastle, Australia: Australian PBL Network and University of Newcastle.

Lähteenmäki, M.-L. (2005). Reflectivity in supervised practice: Conventional and transformative approaches to physiotherapy. *Learning in Health and Social Care, 4*(1), 18–28.

McAlpine, L., Weston, C., Beauchamp, J., Wiseman, C., & Beauchamp, C. (1999). Building a meatacognitive model of reflection. *Higher Education, 37*, 105–131.

McInnis, C. (2001). Researching the first year experience: Where do we go from here? *Higher Education Research & Development, 20*(2), 105–114.

Mezirow, J. (1991). *Transformative dimensions of adult learning.* San Francisco, CA: Jossey-Bass.

Poikela, E. (2006). *Knowledge, knowing and problem-based learning.* In E. Poikela & A.R. Nummenmaa (Eds.), Understanding problem-based learning (pp. 15–31). Tampere: University Press.

Riedinger, B. (2006). Mining for meaning. In A. Jafari & C. Kaufman (Eds.), *Handbook of research on ePortfolios* (pp. 90–101). Hershey, PA: Idea Group.

Sandars, J. (2009). The use of reflection in medical education: AMEE Guide No. 44. *Medical Teacher, 31*(8), 685–695.

Schön, D.A. (1987). *Educating the reflective practitioner.* San Francisco, CA: Jossey-Bass.

Silén, C., & Uhlin, L. (2008). Self-directed learning: A learning issue for students and faculty. *Teaching in Higher Education, 13*(4), 461–475.

Stockhausen, L.J. (2004). The clinical portfolio. *The Australian Electronic Journal of Nursing Education, 2*(2), 1–12.

Uhlin, L. (2009). Supporting transition into higher education using a portfolio. In A. Sonesson & M. Hedberg (Eds.), *Proceedings NU2008* (pp. 61–74). Lund, Sweden: Lund University, Centre for Educational Development.

Uhlin, L., Johannesson, E., & Silén, C. (2007). *To challenge students' beliefs to support transition into higher education.* Final report of a project financed by the Council of Renewal of Higher Education. Linköping, Sweden: Linköping University, Centre for Educational Development and Research, Faculty of Health Sciences.

van Tartwijk, J., & Driessen, E. (2009). Portfolios for assessment and learning: AMEE Guide No. 45. *Medical Teacher, 31*(9), 790–801.

Further Resources

Jisc InfoNet – What are e-Portfolios? www.jiscinfonet.ac.uk/infokits/e-portfolios/index_html.

12

Enriching Problem-based Learning through Design Thinking

Norman Jackson and Fred Buining

Introduction

This chapter explores the question:

> How can we enrich problem-based learning (PBL) using the creative thinking techniques used by designers when they are trying to innovate?

One of the most exciting qualities of the PBL learning environment is that it actively and explicitly encourages you and your students to draw from many different disciplines in the interests of solving a problem. The design discipline contains a range of concepts, techniques, and ideas that can be used, to good effect, to create engaging learning environments and activities. This chapter explores these possibilities and shows why and how the principles of Design Thinking are particularly suited to PBL processes.

Solving problems is a central process in work and engaging students to learn through problem solving is preparing them for work. Most complex problems in work are solved by teams of people working together, so engaging students in group problem solving prepares them for the social problem solving that they will encounter in the workplace. Really challenging problems require people to use their creative as well as their analytical abilities, thus, if we are to prepare students for the complexities of the world of work, teaching that enables students to develop and to use their imaginations is essential.

PBL provides an excellent learning environment for students to use both their imaginative and analytical abilities. To engage fully in the PBL process, students need to draw on their creative reserves and to think in inventive, and sometimes ingenious ways, but they also need to be critical about their ideas and solutions. Part of your job, as a teacher, is to encourage and stimulate innovative, creative thinking, in order to help your students learn the dynamics of collaborative processes that are aimed at harnessing the collective creativity of the members of the group as they apply their energies to the tasks and problems that have been set. So, how can you help your students to think in innovative, creative ways?

How do you create conditions that are more likely to lead to innovative solutions to problems? How do you create problems and challenges that require students to use their creative as well as their analytical abilities? This chapter outlines some of the techniques, tools, and ideas for encouraging and facilitating creative thinking in your students and in yourself. It begins by providing a rationale for incorporating design thinking into PBL processes and goes on to describe how we share these techniques in our Creative Academy, which is a 1-day workshop for teachers and others involved in student development. At the end of the chapter, in the list of resources, we include the URL of our Creative Academy wiki that provides film clips, PowerPoint slides, and background papers to illustrate the techniques that are described in this chapter.

Chapter Overview

This chapter will explore the following design-based practice principles:

- using Design Thinking in PBL and collaborative problem solving;
- developing and exploring problem statements;
- facilitating collaborative thinking and idea generation;
- evaluating innovative ideas and discovering inspiring solutions;
- involving higher education teachers in designing their own learning and teaching scenarios to incorporate the techniques and principles of Design Thinking into their own PBL practices.

Principles of Design Thinking

In the professional work environment, learning is a by-product of problem-focused working compared to the educational environment, where learning is the main product of work. When people solve problems in the work environment, they draw on generic and discipline/field-specific knowledge and skills which they adapt according to their work situations; they often apply the benefits of other experiences of problem working that they have had in similar contexts – their experiential knowing (Cook & Brown, 1999). Figure 12.1, adapted from Marsick and Watkins (1990, 1997) and Cseh, Watkins, and Marsick (2000), provides a conceptual framework for describing what happens when people learn through problem working situations at work.

When confronted with a work problem, people engage in a range of different problem-focused activities:

- They frame the problem and the situation.
- They use their judgement based on their knowledge and previous experience of similar problems.
- They diagnose the problem based on their previous experience of diagnosing similar problems.
- They identify or invent solutions using approaches that have worked for them in the past.

This process may be very rapid, e.g. a doctor consulting with a patient, or may require a significant period of time, e.g. a teacher designing a new course. This approach works well when working with a routine/familiar problem and works less well when a complex and unfamiliar challenge is encountered or a radical change in approach is desired. It is in the complex type of situation that the techniques of Design Thinking can be usefully applied to provide more potential solutions to the problem (see Figure 12.1).

Design Thinking (Brown 2008a, 2008b) is a creative process based on the generation of many ideas and the selection of really good ideas from the many generated. In order to engage in Design Thinking it is necessary to think generatively and to postpone judgements on the ideas that emerge. In Design Thinking, problem framing and diagnosis are replaced by a process of exploration that is facilitated through extensive questioning.

Through this thinking process, designers or design teams come to understand the complexities that are often embedded in a problem and they may see more easily a multitude of problems from different perspectives. This exploratory stage provides the basis for a generative stage in which numerous potential solutions to the explored problem(s) are identified before an evaluative stage occurs that leads to the selection of the best ideas.

Design Thinking does not follow a linear or logically reasoned pathway; it is fundamentally different from the scientific, analytical, rational, linear, and convergent processes that tend to be encouraged in academic, higher education environments. Academics' cognitive styles are significantly more likely to be analytical as opposed to intuitive. Analytical thinking involves breaking problems into smaller parts in order to study them. Rational

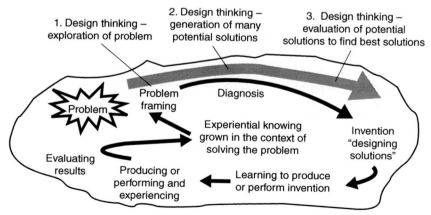

Design thinking opens up the problem through the: (1) exploration of the problem; (2) generation of possible solutions; (3) evaluation of potential solutions.

1. Design thinking – exploration of problem

2. Design thinking – generation of many potential solutions

3. Design thinking – evaluation of potential solutions to find best solutions

Problem

Problem framing

Diagnosis

Experiential knowing grown in the context of solving the problem

Invention "designing solutions"

Evaluating results

Producing or performing and experiencing

Learning to produce or perform invention

Figure 12.1 Conceptualisation of learning as part of problem-based working in the workplace (adapted from Marsick & Watkins, 1990 and Cseh et al., 2000).

thinking requires a detached, balanced, objective approach. Linear thinking evolves in a particular direction and convergent thinking involves starting with available choices and issues and working towards a single best solution.

Design Thinking is a different sort of process which, at times, can feel chaotic and uncomfortable and may require people to suspend their disbelief and/or to "turn off" logic in order to participate in the process. Some teachers find that Design Thinking is difficult to do as formal educational environments tend to favour problem-solving modes that are linear and algorithmic. However, real-world problems, particularly if they have a strong social dimension, tend to be less amenable to linear ways of thinking.

We need to learn to look at problems from many different perspectives. Designers have developed routines and techniques that can really help us to do this. In response to being confronted with the problem of innovation, designers have developed ways of thinking about the problem that enhances their ability to imagine a number of possibilities from which they can choose the best solutions. A consequence of the way that designers think about problems is that they are particularly good at creating novel solutions to their problems.

Design thinking involves a series of divergent and convergent steps (Brown, 2008a, 2008b). During divergence, we are creating choices and during convergence we are making choices. Divergent thinking can feel frustrating, as it demands a high tolerance for ambiguity and uncertainty, and, at least for a time, feels directionless; it almost feels like you are going backwards and getting further away from the answer. In the early stages of a PBL experience, the students often struggle with a feeling that they are unproductive, "going nowhere" and are "all over the place" (see student insights outlined in Chapter 9). Designers will tell you that divergence is often the place where really creative/innovative ideas are born.

Divergence needs to feel optimistic, exploratory, and experimental, but often feels confusing to people who are more comfortable with a scientific approach to solving a problem. Design Thinking relies on an interplay between analysis (breaking problems apart) and synthesis (putting ideas together). The uncertainty of divergence and the integrative, head-hurting complexity of synthesis are the characteristics of Design Thinking; they are the very experiences that make this type of creative thinking both challenging and liberating at the same time. This creative thinking process resonates with Barrett's (2005) description of PBL as "hard fun"; difficult, challenging, puzzling, even baffling, on the one hand, and empowering, exciting, fun, and full of creative potential on the other. This concept of "hard fun" has been discussed further in Chapter 2.

Designers have evolved visual ways to synthesise ideas, and that is another one of the obstacles for those new to Design Thinking: a discomfort with visual thinking. A sketch of a new product is a piece of synthesis and so is a scenario that tells a story about an experience. Design thinkers create visual frameworks for synthesis that, in themselves, describe spaces for further creative thinking.

Creative Academy: A Process for Developing Design Thinking Skills

So, how can we help students develop and practise their inventive thinking skills in order to solve complex unfamiliar problems? And, how can we facilitate the process of learners pooling their creative ideas and inspiring each other in the process? Figure 12.2 shows the process that we have designed to help teachers develop facilitation skills that will enable students to think like a designer faced with the problem of having to invent a new design solution. In the professional development process teachers take the part of the learners and so experience the techniques for themselves. The context or challenge for problem solving in our Creative Academy was defined as: "designing courses or teaching/learning situations to improve students' creativity". However, you can substitute any design challenge, for example, we could have used "designing problem-based learning situations where learners are required to invent an original solution". In the rest of this chapter, we take you through the process of design thinking to enable you to see how you might adapt our model to your own PBL contexts.

Exercise 12.1 Reflections on Teaching for Creativity

Think about an occasion when you tried to encourage your students to be creative. Write brief notes to yourself about this experience. You will draw on these experiences during the process.

- What was the context?
- What did you do?
- What did students do?
- What did you learn about facilitating students' creativity through the experience?

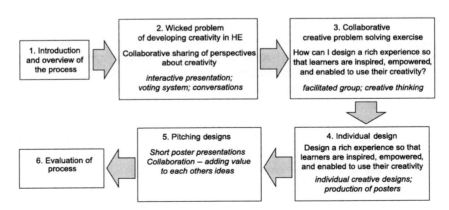

Figure 12.2 The sequence of activities in our Creative Academy professional development process.

Exercise 12.2 Getting Started: An Exercise to Start Students Thinking about Their Views and Perspectives on Creativity (or Any Other Topic)

Have your students form a circle and introduce themselves and say what they hope to get out of the experience. The whole group engages in a short "warm-up" exercise. The one we used involved: (1) writing on a piece of paper three things you associate with being creative; (2) screwing the paper into a ball and throwing it to another participant on the other side of the circle; (3) reading what was on the paper; (4) adding your own three points and repeating the exercise. After repeating the process three times students are invited to call out the words written on their sheet; after a dozen shout-outs, the facilitator might ask a question like "how many of you agree that these things are associated with being creative?"

This activity is a good way of showing students that there are many widely held beliefs about creativity.

The same or a similar exercise can be used to encourage people to start sharing their thinking and beliefs about other topics, e.g. student-capabilities topics, such as teamwork, or discipline-specific topics.

Exercise 12.3 Sharing Understandings about Creativity (or Another Topic)

We have found that it is fruitful to help learners to make their beliefs about creativity public. We use an electronic voting system to reveal patterns of beliefs but you can use coloured cards if you do not have a voting system. The main purpose of the exercise is to develop trust within the group – as soon as students start to share their beliefs about creativity, they begin to get a stronger sense of themselves and of each other, and to explore some of the opinions and ideas that they have in common and those on which they disagree. This type of dialogue creates fertile ground for interaction and subsequent collaboration.

When we do this sharing exercise with faculty groups, we put propositions about creativity on a PowerPoint slide, and invite particip-ants to vote on the proposition (typically a five-point scale ranging from strongly agree to strongly disagree is used). If you do not have a voting system, you can give each participant three or five pieces of coloured card to represent the scale you use and invite them to raise the appropriate colour when they vote. We also invite whole group or paired discussions using the perspectives that emerge from the voting.

> Negotiation here involves participants taking the discussions in whatever direction they feel it needs to go in order to resolve their questions or to elaborate on their beliefs. The propositions we use and typical patterns of voting for a group of higher education teachers can be found on the Creative Academy wiki.

The same or a similar exercise can be used to encourage people to start sharing their thinking about problem-based learning topics, for example, problem-solving or discipline-specific topics.

Design Thinking Techniques

Following the initial exploration of the idea of creativity, we move into the collaborative problem solving part of the process (Figure 12.2) which comprises a series of exercises that you could use with students at an early stage in a PBL module or programme in order to help them to share their notions of creativity (or any other subject) and to gain greater insights about how they might work best together.

Thinking Like a Designer

The process of this exercise takes about 75 to 90 minutes to complete. You will need a large wall or expanse of windows for this process and the wall or windows need to be systematically covered with sheets of flipchart paper. Participants sit in a semi-circle facing the papered wall. The optimum size for

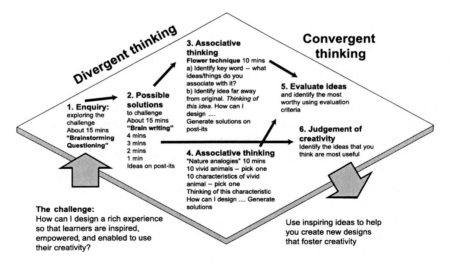

Figure 12.3 A process map showing the techniques used to stimulate Design Thinking for creative enquiry and problem solving.

a group is 10–12 but this process can be undertaken with smaller or larger groups. If the group is larger than 15, it should be split into two groups, each with its own facilitator. Participants will need half a pad of Post-its® and a felt-tip pen or biro to write on the Post-its.

Framing the Challenge: Creating a Problem Statement

At the start of the process, the participants are told that they are going to work as a team to engage in a creative problem solving exercise; they are provided with a map of the process (Figure 12.3) and told that this process will help them generate many new ideas, some of which might be highly innovative. The process is explained in terms of a series of techniques for facilitating divergent (opening-up) and convergent (narrowing down) thinking – the sort of strategy that a design team trying to come up with an innovative idea might engage in. The map acts as a navigational aid and the facilitator draws attention to the map as each new technique is introduced in order to reinforce understanding of the process and how the techniques are connected.

Participants are invited to formulate a powerful question that will be the focus for creative enquiry. This is a negotiated process in the sense that participants are encouraged to form a "How can I?" question, to address the problem of "designing courses or teaching/learning situations to improve students' creativity". The question is written across a wall of flip-chart paper. In our Creative Academy, we used the question: "How can I design a rich experience so that learners are inspired, empowered and enabled to use their creativity?" The emphasis on "I" is important as this is all about individuals being able to change something in the teaching and learning situations that they have control over.

Having created a problem statement, the next stage is to reveal some of the complexity in the problem by posing many supplementary "How can I?" questions that are triggered by the main question. Participants are instructed to write down their supplementary questions on a Post-it – *one question per Post-it*. After a few minutes, participants are invited to read out their question to the rest of the group to trigger further ideas and the facilitator then posts the question on the wall under the heading "Questions".

Examples of these questions include:

- How can I create the space within a module to provide a rich experience?
- How can I secure the necessary resources?
- How can I find out what sorts of experiences/problems would inspire and motivate learners?

In our experience, a group of 10 people can generate up to 100 supplementary questions in 10 minutes. After a lot of questions have been generated, you can invite a pair of participants to cluster the questions into themes and then label the theme, while other participants continue to pose questions. Typically, the following kinds of themes will be revealed: resources; people; training; organisational structures; barriers; and leadership.

Once the themes have been identified, the group can be invited to identify any obvious gaps in the themes and pose further questions to fill the gaps. This process is negotiated, in the sense that the facilitator is merely helping the group to explore their understandings of the problem and what emerges from this questioning process is the product of their collective minds, not the knowledge of the facilitator.

Generating Potential Solutions

Having explored the problem statement (principal question) and thought about the complexity within the problem through the many supplementary questions, the group can now start to generate potential solutions.

Brainstorming Techniques

You could use traditional "brainstorming", but we use a quieter and more introverted collaborative process called *brain writing*, in which participants write down their ideas in silence. You explain that there will be four rounds of brain writing, with each round declining in length: 4 minutes, 3 minutes, 2 minutes, and 1 minute. You introduce the first round of 4 minutes and invite the participants to write down, in silence, as many possible solutions to the question that forms the problem statement – one solution per Post-it. In doing this, they can draw on all the supplementary questions that have been posed, since they also relate to the problem. So, rather than offering solutions to one question, the students are being asked to offer potential solutions to more than 100 questions relating to the problem. During the process of the 4 minutes, you repeat the problem statement three times and encourage the students to make their solutions as concrete and practical as possible.

At the end of the 4 minutes, you ask the group members to stick their Post-its together in a long list, put their name at the top of the list, and pass the list of Post-its to the person sitting on their right. The person receiving the Post-its looks quickly at the list and uses the ideas to trigger new ideas and add further Post-its (one idea per Post-it) to the bottom of the list, but this time only 3 minutes are given to idea-generation. The process is then repeated with 2 minutes and 1 minute being given to generate ideas. After the final round, the lists of Post-its are given back to the person whose name is at the top of the list. Typically, each person might have between 20 and 30 ideas. The participants are then invited to post their ideas on the papered wall in a nice, orderly fashion under the heading "Possible solutions". With over 200 ideas on the wall, you can draw attention to the wealth of ideas grown in just a few minutes from the creative minds of the participants.

You can adapt this technique to any PBL context where you want students to think imaginatively about a problem; it can be a very effective trigger for helping learners to find creative solutions.

Associative Thinking Techniques

The next stage in the challenge of "Thinking Like a Designer" is to utilise associative thinking techniques (see Figure 12.3). In Creative Academy, we use the techniques to generate solutions to our problem of "How can I design a rich experience so that learners are inspired, empowered, and enabled to use their creativity?" But here, we will modify this exercise to the sort of PBL context that you may encounter using a problem that you could pose for a group of students in your PBL sessions like, "How can I contribute to my PBL group in ways that will enable us to harness our collective imaginations to create novel solutions?"

Start the exercise by explaining that you are going to try to encourage learners to seek more unusual or novel solutions to a problem by encouraging them to think differently. There are many associative thinking techniques that can be used to encourage learners to generate ideas that have the potential for creating novel solutions to a problem. All work on the principle of picking a word/idea within the problem statement, and then encouraging, through an associative thinking process, the generation of ideas that seem to be far removed from the original idea. In introducing the idea of associative thinking, you might point to a student and say "if I say bicycle you say ..." (student may respond with "ride"). You repeat, pointing at the next student ... "if I say bicycle you say ..." (student may respond with "wheel"). The students quickly get the idea.

Flower Association Technique

Before you begin this exercise, it is a good idea to draw the shape of a flower with its petals on the wall (see Creative Academy wiki for the facilitation process). Pick a word from your problem statement that is likely to generate some interesting ideas – words like "contribute", "enable", "harness", "imagination", "novel", and "solution" – and put the word at the centre of the flower. You then ask the students, "What do you associate with the WORD in the centre of the flower?" As words are shouted out, the facilitator writes them in the petals, one word per petal. The inner petals are quickly filled up. But this is only the brain dump of obvious associations. What the facilitator is really interested in are ideas that are far removed from the starting point. Therefore, the facilitator should try to nudge the participants further away with remarks like "think of another context in which [WORD] happens". Eventually, some unusual words start appearing, for example, "ballroom dancing" might emerge. Using the unusual word as an illustrative example, you then say, thinking of ballroom dancing, how can I contribute to my PBL group in ways that will enable us to harness our collective imaginations to create novel solutions?

Write your new ideas down, one per Post-it, and, after a few minutes, ask the students to call out their ideas and post the written ideas on the wall. Students will be surprised at some of the novel ideas that emerge.

Analogies Technique

In this associative thinking technique you invite students to name ten animals that are bright and vivid or interesting. You list the names of the animals on the wall as they are called out and then invite the participants to identify one of the animals and ask them to name 10 things about the animal. These 10 things are also listed. You then ask the participants to identify one of these characteristics. For example, a distinctive characteristic of an "anteater" might be "a long sticky tongue". Using the words that describe the characteristic as an illustrative example, you then say, "thinking of a long sticky tongue, how can I contribute to my PBL group in ways that will enable us to harness our collective imaginations to create novel solutions?" Write your new ideas down, one per Post-it. After a few minutes, ask the students to call out their ideas and post the written ideas on the wall. The act of calling out the idea triggers further ideas in the group. You and your students will be amazed at the way such bizarre associations stimulate imaginations.

Generating More Ideas from Ideas Already Generated

To encourage deeper exploration of interesting and novel ideas, you might draw attention to an idea on a Post-it, and then invite participants to use the idea as inspiration to generate further ideas, for example: thinking of this [novel idea] … how can I contribute to my PBL group in ways that will enable us to harness our collective imaginations to create novel solutions? This process helps students to make sense of and be stimulated by someone else's idea.

In all of these techniques, your role as facilitator is to encourage divergent, associative thinking that is connected, albeit tangentially and remotely, to the problem statement. Design thinking is not a process that has right or wrong answers, nor is it a process where one knowledgeable person is imposing his or her thinking on others. In that sense, all of these activities involve negotiation and the movement to democratic social relations among groups of learners and teachers (see Chapter 9 for more on the importance of democratic social relations in PBL teams).

Evaluating Potential Ideas

Having generated hundreds of ideas and possible solutions, the next stage of the process is to engage the participants in a process of evaluation and decision-making. Out of all of these ideas, which ideas are just ordinary and which ideas are truly inspiring? Which ideas are great ideas and can be implemented now, and which ideas are great, but are just not feasible at the moment? With a group of 8–10 people, over 200 ideas/possible solutions should have been generated on Post-its by this stage of the process. Referring to the map of the process (Figure 12.3), you explain to the students that they have now completed the divergent thinking part of the Design Thinking process and that they are now going to embark on a more convergent, analytical, and judgemental thinking process. You explain that the students are going to use a simple tool to help them to evaluate the ideas (see Figure 12.4) and go through the criteria. You invite participants to spend about 5 minutes looking at all of the ideas and, during this time, they must select three ideas that they feel are particularly good/inspiring/useful. Using the criteria shown in Figure 12.4, the participants are invited to place the ideas that they have selected in one of three boxes (three sheets of flip-chart paper stuck on the wall, labelled BLUE, RED, and YELLOW).

If there are many ideas, it is useful to number the ideas to help with the next stage of the process. When the ideas have been numbered, invite the participants to spend 5 minutes looking at all of the ideas and to make a selection in their minds. The students are given three circular stickers which represent three chances to vote for the ideas that they believe, if they could be implemented, would make a real difference, i.e. it is their individual evaluation of the best potential solutions to the problem that they think can be implemented.

After 5 minutes, you instruct the participants to get ready to vote and when you give the signal they vote together. After voting, you can ask the students to organise the ideas so that those with the most stickers are at the top and those with fewer or no stickers are underneath. You can then review and discuss the ideas considered to be most useful by the participants.

Discussion

The exercises that we have outlined above are all designed to contribute to the creation of a safe and supportive, but demanding and challenging environment for sharing beliefs and trying out new techniques. The purpose

Blue ideas	Red ideas	Yellow ideas
• Few risks • High acceptability • Examples already exist that can be copied • Would be easy to implement in this university	• Innovative ideas • Breakthrough ideas • Exciting ideas • Risky ideas that will need selling • Could be implemented in this university	• Ideas for the future • They are not feasible or would be impossible to implement in this university • Would need a radical change in organisational thinking and behaviour

Figure 12.4 A simple framework for evaluating ideas and possible solutions to the problem.

of the exercises is to introduce the thinking and facilitation skills used by designers to promote thinking that will lead to imaginative and innovative designs; these ways of thinking and behaving are rarely encountered in disciplinary problem working. These exercises also create reaffirming spaces for teachers who care about their students' creative development and who want to be creative themselves.

We argue that PBL tutors, teachers, and students can benefit from being able to utilise Design Thinking skills when confronted with problems that require innovation. Teachers who want to create innovative curricular designs provide a good example of a professional problem situation, where the use of Design Thinking skills would be useful. And students facing the challenges of PBL can benefit from learning creative, divergent dynamics associated with design-type thinking.

PBL practitioners will find it useful to have these types of thinking and facilitation techniques in their toolbox and, by extension, student learners will also benefit from being able to facilitate collaborative problem working processes using these techniques. Other practical examples of the use of thinking and facilitation techniques are described by Feathers (2003).

References

Barrett, T. (2005). Who said learning couldn't be enjoyable, playful and fun? The voices of PBL students. In E. Poikela and S. Poikela (Eds.), *PBL in context: Bridging work and education. Refereed papers* (pp. 159–176). Tampere: Tampere University Press.

Brown, T. (2008a, June). Design thinking. *Harvard Business Review.* Retrieved from: http://web.me.com/deatkins/CIC/Seminar_Schedule_files/HBR-Timbrown.pdf.

Brown, T. (2008b). Design thinking thoughts. Tim Brown's blog. Retrieved from: http://design-thinking.ideo.com.

Cook, S.D.N., & Brown, J.S. (1999). Bridging epistemologies: The generative dance between organizational knowledge and organizational knowing. *Organizational Science, 10*(4), 381–400.

Cseh, M., Watkins, K.E., & Marsick, V.J. (2000). Informal and incidental learning in the workplace. In G.A. Straka (Ed.), *Conceptions of self-directed learning, theoretical and conceptual considerations* (pp. 59–74). New York: Waxman.

Feathers, J. (2003). Creative problem solving with product design staff and students. In N.J. Jackson (Ed.) (2008) *Tackling the wicked problem of creativity in higher education.* SCEPTrE Scholarly Paper. http://surreycreativeacademy.pbwiki.com.

Marsick, V.J., & Watkins, K.E. (1990). *Informal and incidental learning in the workplace.* London: Routledge.

Marsick, V.J., & Watkins, K.E. (1997). Lessons from informal and incidental learning. In J. Burgoyne & M. Reynolds (Eds.), *Management learning: Integrating perspectives in theory and practice* (pp. 295–311). London: Sage.

Further Resources

Baillie, C. (Ed.). (2003). *The travelling case: Creativity in art, science and engineering. How to foster creative thinking in higher education.* York: Centre for Materials Education.

Eraut, M. (2007). Learning from other people in the workplace. *Oxford Review of Education, 33*(4), 403–422.

Design Thinking wiki: http://en.wikipedia.org/wiki/Design_thinking.

Creative Academy Wiki contains film clips and other resources to support the process described above: http://surreycreativeacademy.pbwiki.com.

13

Using Assessment to Promote Student Capabilities

Catharine Pettigrew, Ingrid Scholten, and Emma Gleeson

Introduction

This chapter explores the following question:

How do we maximise the development of student capabilities with effective and innovate assessment strategies?

The assessment of student capabilities within problem-based learning (PBL) remains a hot topic, and is understandably one of the primary concerns for PBL practitioners (Savin-Baden, 2004). The choice of assessment(s) implemented within a PBL curriculum has a powerful impact on student learning – when used effectively, assessment can promote and optimise student capabilities; when used unsuccessfully it can disempower students, undervaluing them and their work. In this chapter, we argue that assessment in PBL can be used as a *strategic fulcrum* for designing curricula that promote student capabilities. That is, the choice and design of PBL assessments can form the pivotal point for PBL practitioners in their creation of a curriculum that facilitates students' achievement of learning outcomes and professional competence.

To describe how this can be done, we will first focus our discussion on a *conceptual framework* for the design and implementation of PBL assessment, namely, the "alignment" of PBL assessments, teaching activities, and curriculum objectives, to promote student capabilities (Biggs, 1999). To further illustrate the concept of alignment we will present two contrasting case studies from different sides of the world that demonstrate how this can be achieved through the integration of PBL and professional education in assessment activities. Furthermore, we will discuss some recent innovations in PBL assessment that may be new to many readers, which support the concept of alignment and are easily adapted for any discipline. The overall aim of this chapter is, thus, to revitalise PBL practitioners as they review curriculum design and develop PBL assessments that will maximise the promotion of student capabilities in their field of study.

Chapter Overview

This chapter will explore:

- foundational principles of PBL assessment;
- types of PBL assessment and ways they can be combined;
- alignment in PBL practice – case study examples and practice models from University College Cork, Ireland, and Flinders University, Australia;
- recent innovations in PBL assessment;
- issues to consider when revitalising assessments in PBL practice.

Aligning Assessment, Activities, and Curriculum Objectives

Foundational Principles of PBL Assessment

It is well established that assessment drives learning (Macdonald, 2005), and this is particularly true for assessment in PBL curricula. PBL is both a curriculum *and* a process. That is, learning outcomes include not only acquisition of critical knowledge (i.e. curriculum content), but also more generic skills, such as problem-solving proficiency, self-directed learning skills, and team participation skills. Therefore, assessments must be compatible with both the learning outcomes *and* the learning process and must include assessment of the generic skills and attitudes developed through PBL (Macdonald, 2005; Wood, 2003).

To achieve this, PBL promotes learning *through* assessment, rather than *for* assessment. For example, many types of PBL assessments are based on the PBL "teaching" activities themselves, providing further opportunities to learn, while determining whether learning outcomes have been achieved.

The principles of PBL assessment are well established, and are summarised effectively by Macdonald and Savin-Baden (2004). Assessments should:

- be based in a practice context (i.e. be "authentic");
- assess process-based professional activity;
- reflect learners' development from novice to expert practitioner;
- provide students with an experience of being "assessed" as they would in a professional capacity (e.g. in professional encounters with colleagues, users, professional bodies);
- include student self-assessment and reflection as a basis for future self-directed learning and continual professional development;
- be aligned with course/module objectives/outcomes.

Further recommendations are that assessment methods be inclusive (i.e. they facilitate and recognise different types of learners) and incorporate a variety of approaches for which all students (and staff) are adequately prepared. Thus, the challenge facing PBL practitioners is the development of assessment activities that cover *all* of these principles effectively, in ways that are fair to all students (and staff) and encourage students in the skills that are crucial for meaningful learning (e.g. self-awareness, reflection, development of new perspectives, or changes in behaviour). So how can these challenges be met? We argue that the key lies in the concept of "alignment".

The Concept of Alignment

John Biggs described a blueprint for curriculum design, whereby desired learning outcomes, appropriate learning activities, and strategic assessment tasks provide a cohesive structure to the teaching and learning context as "constructive alignment" (Biggs, 1999) (see Figure 13.1). In this deceptively simple concept, the teacher's role is to design and encourage students to engage in learning activities that are likely to result in achievement of those outcomes, and the assessment tasks not only inform us how well the objectives have been met, but also inform students about what is required of them. As mentioned above, the importance of constructive alignment to problem-based learning has been acknowledged by Macdonald and Savin-Baden (2004) in their description of key principles of assessment. But the pivotal role of assessment for curriculum design in PBL programmes has not been fully exploited for its potential in developing student capabilities.

Students often work backwards through the curriculum, focusing first and foremost on how they will be assessed and what they will be required to demonstrate they have learned (James, McInnis, & Devlin, 2002, p. 7).

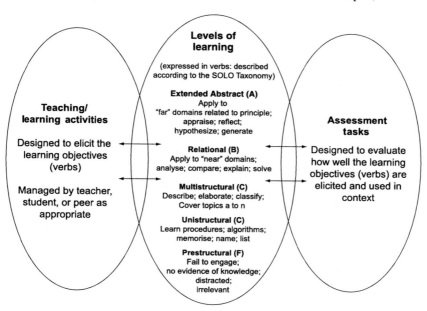

Figure 13.1 Model of alignment across teaching activities, levels of learning, and assessment tasks (adapted from Biggs, 1999).

The choice of the most suitable assessment type is crucial (Carrillo-de-la-Pena et al., 2009). For example, if lecturers coming from a traditional approach attempt to retain their traditional assessment methods for a new PBL curriculum, misalignment between learning outcomes, the teaching and learning methods, and assessment of student learning can result (Macdonald, 2005). "Assessment requirements and the clarity of assessment criteria significantly influence the effectiveness of student learning. Carefully designed assessment contributes directly to the way students approach their study and therefore contributes indirectly, but powerfully, to the quality of their learning" (James et al., 2002, p. 7). Well-designed assessment:

- sets clear expectations;
- establishes a reasonable workload;
- promotes deep approaches to learning;
- provides opportunities for students to spend time on task;
- encourages students to reflect on their learning; and
- facilitates feedback to enhance student competencies.

Types of PBL Assessments

Some examples of PBL assessments that can be implemented within a curriculum to help measure learning outcomes are provided in Figure 13.2. See Macdonald (2005) and Azer (2008) for further details on what some of these assessments may entail, except for Script Concordance Tests, see Charlin, Roy, Brailovsky, Goulet, and van der Vleuten (2000) and Fournier, Demeester, and Charlin (2008).

This list of types of PBL assessments is by no means exhaustive; it simply represents different ways in which learning outcomes in PBL may be measured. For example, concept maps help students to organise their acquired knowledge in a meaningful way, to aid their understanding and conceptualisation of the relationship between pieces of information (Novak, 1990; Novak & Canãs, 2006). The use of information technology in the form of an online chat forum (e.g. communication and collaboration software, free for education: for example, "Google Apps" – see Further Resources) allows for the assessment of teamwork through the analysis and evaluation of online chats between students. Furthermore, these elements could easily be incorporated into an assignment centred on a problem trigger or case scenario.

Variables of PBL Assessment

Depending on the discipline, some of the assessment types outlined in Figure 13.2 can be easily designed to be "authentic", that is, to reflect workplace activity (e.g. role-plays/simulations; group seminars; team meetings; group projects; reports on literature searches for evidence-based practice; presentations on a case study). Furthermore, there are several associated variables still to be considered,

Skill/learning outcome	Assessment
Acquisition/application of critical knowledge	Case-based essays Written examinations Concept maps
Problem-solving and critical reasoning skills	Triple Jump (see Chapter 14) Written examinations/assignments *Viva voce* Script concordance tests
Communication/Teamwork skills	Participation in tutorials Written reports Role plays Online "chat" forum
Self-directed learning skills	Independent study report Reports of search strategies Reference lists (e.g. within assignments) Oral presentations/written reports
Reflection	Reflective journals Oral presentation Portfolio

Figure 13.2 Ideas for assessment of skills developed through PBL.

enabling PBL practitioners to tailor the assessments to the needs and developmental abilities of their students and their discipline (see Figure 13.3). For example, assessments can involve "online" or "offline" activities – students may be required to create their own websites, or communicate and collaborate through online chat fora, as mentioned previously (see also Further Resources). In addition, the formative/summative nature of an

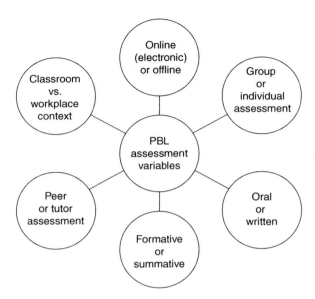

Figure 13.3 Variables of PBL assessment that can be manipulated to create a wide variety of assessments and tailored to the needs and developmental abilities of the students, appropriate to the discipline.

assessment can be used specifically to help students integrate their knowledge effectively (see also Chapter 5).

With careful planning, and clear alignment with learning outcomes and teaching activities, students and staff will be well prepared for the assessment process. Clear rubrics (marking criteria) for each assessment are also essential for transparency and adequate preparation for staff and students alike. As Hildebrand and Edwards (2005, p. 4) state so simply, "you get what you assess, so assess what you value". What we value must be reflected in our learning outcomes, those statements that express what we want students to achieve.

Frameworks for Aligning Assessment Activities, Learning Outcomes, and Professional Competences

Teachers from the professions are often well placed to develop clear learning outcomes. For example, professional organisations often have explicit guidelines about the knowledge, skills, and behaviours that are required. Using such inventories as a basis, it is possible to construct comprehensive learning outcomes reflecting developmental progression to serve as the assessment framework (Mentkowski & Associates, 2000). No matter what the scale of the exercise, whether for individual subjects or at the programme level, the learning outcomes should be embedded in the assessment tasks. Curriculum developers may ensure that all assignments use this language for the assessment criteria or to let students know where they should be at different levels of their progression (e.g. beginning, intermediate, and advanced within a developmental hierarchy). "Any curriculum that has learners at different stages ... requires some explicitly developmental aspect" (Pangaro, 2006, p. 421). This notion is supported by one of the foundational principles of PBL assessment expressed by Macdonald and Savin-Baden (2004): PBL assessment should reflect the learner's development from novice to expert practitioner. In addition to profession-specific competences, there are numerous frameworks that have been developed to support teachers' understanding of the hierarchical development of learning associated with educational programmes, including developmental frameworks and analytical models that address knowledge, skills, and attitudes. Some frameworks are well known, such as Bloom's Taxonomy (Anderson & Krathwohl, 2001; Bloom, 1956) that focuses on the cognitive and affective domains and others, such as Simpson's Taxonomy (1972) which addresses the third, psychomotor, domain, are less familiar. In clinical fields, such as nursing or medicine, educators are well aware of the progression from novice to advanced beginner, competent performance, proficient performance, intuitive expert, and, finally, master clinician, as expressed by Dreyfus and Dreyfus (1986), and Miller's Triangle (Miller, 1990) that describes the levels of competence from "knows" to "knows how" to "shows how" and finally to "does". Pangaro (2006) has described a simple "synthetic" model (RIME: (Observer) Reporter, Interpreter, Manager, Educator) that can be used as a descriptive tool to help teachers make their observations of complex tasks, requiring multiple attributes, more structured and consistent. Furthermore, it can facilitate the provision of feedback that helps students progress to the next developmental step. The SOLO Taxonomy (Structure of Observed Learning Outcomes) (Biggs & Collis, 1982) describes the levels of learning that can be observed in students' work and can be used to provide a hierarchical framework to underpin the curriculum.

Developing and Revitalising PBL Assessment

Case Studies

The following two case studies demonstrate how the concept of aligning PBL assessment, teaching activities, and learning outcomes can be applied using the different frameworks outlined above. Both of these case studies involve speech and language therapy departments, from two different universities from across the world, which apply these frameworks in diverse ways within their PBL curricula. The main ideas in these assessment strategies are transferable to other professions and disciplines.

Case Study One – University College Cork: Implementing Bloom's Taxonomy in Speech and Language Therapy

This case study will outline how the PBL assessment structure at University College Cork (UCC) incorporates Bloom's framework in modules on

Communication Disorders in order to allow for the creation of transferable theory to practise learning outcomes and to bridge the gap between novice learners and competent practitioners. As students make their way through the course, Bloom's Taxonomy is employed when we consider desired learning outcomes, together with PBL process skills, to provide the stepping stones students need to take to gain and understand knowledge, apply, investigate, and critically evaluate relevant information. This approach allows the students to progress, through assessment, towards competence in the field of speech and language therapy. Figure 13.4 indicates a clear developmental progression through 1st, 2nd, and 3rd year, with examples of learning outcomes for each module of communication disorders. Assessment exemplars are provided for evaluating skills based on Bloom's Taxonomy.

At UCC, in keeping with the foundational principles of PBL, we assess students on their PBL *process* skills, rather than merely the content of the PBL curriculum, using a variety of methods in order to be inclusive of all students (Fourie, 2008). The methods of assessment used include:

1. tutor evaluation of student participation/performance in PBL tutorials;
2. products/concept maps (concept maps used mostly in first year);
3. reading forms (individual case-based short essays);

Year	Example learning outcomes	Relationship to Bloom's taxonomy	Examples of assessments
First Year	– Describe the short- and long term impact a communication disorder has on the individual; – Identify causative factors relevant to communication disorders.	These early learning outcomes reflect the basis of Bloom's Taxonomy – gaining and understanding information.	– Short essay – Participation in tutorial – Concept maps
Second Year	– Evaluate risk factors for various speech and voice impairments in children; – Analyse speech samples to identify processes which may result in communication difficulties in children; – Evaluate the reliability of the perceptual ratings as opposed to acoustic measurements of speech with reference to values for typical development.	A clear progression can be seen here in levels of Bloom's Taxonomy. Students are now expected not only to gain an understanding of key areas of knowledge, but also to analyse and evaluate the potential impacts of communication difficulties on the person. A progression from learning information to application of information has occurred.	– Question on Written PBL Examination – Product (written/visual material generated by student – see Recent Innovations) – PBL assignment – Product
Third Year	– Generate informal screening assessments of speech and swallowing function; – Design and develop educational tools aimed at a variety of stake-holders.	These learning outcomes for third-year students show that a further progression is made by students to the development of more sophisticated skills – in the context of Bloom's Taxonomy, skills involving the creation of client-suitable assessment and information tools.	– Product

Figure 13.4 PBL learning outcomes and assessments related to Bloom's Taxonomy in UCC.

4. reflective journals (individual);
5. PBL assignment/written PBL examination.

The learning outcomes within the PBL modules reflect both Bloom's Taxonomy and the criteria for achieving learning outcomes in the Practice Education modules at UCC. These modules are practical and competence-based and, due to the strong connection between the learning outcomes in PBL and the design of the Practice Education modules, students gain the necessary insights required for the development of strong theory to practice links. The students' theoretical knowledge is constantly reinforced through the alignment of learning outcomes in PBL and in Practice Education, as demonstrated in Figure 13.5.

The model shown in Figure 13.5 is readily transferable to various disciplines and professional programmes, demonstrating how students gain skills in PBL that complement those of professional education in any discipline as they progress through their programme.

Case Study Two – Flinders University, South Australia: Aligning Assessment Activities and Curriculum Objectives

The use of assessment as the focal point for course and programme development allows the structuring of content delivery (Toohey & Kumar, 2003). The Graduate Entry Speech Pathology (GESP) programme at Flinders University, in South Australia, has been developed as an alternate entry point for graduates of any primary degree to a postgraduate professional qualification in speech pathology.

To ensure that learning goals are met, we first defined the desired capabilities of graduates (four extensively elaborated skill sets that we call the Academic Abilities) and developed an appropriately aligned assessment scheme (Biggs, 1999). In doing this work we were inspired by, and drew

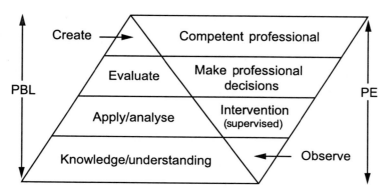

Figure 13.5 Learning outcomes integration model for Problem-based Learning (PBL) and Professional Education (PE).

heavily on, the work carried out at Alverno College, a small independent American college renowned for its work in assessment and curriculum development (Mentkowski & Associates, 2000). In order to provide consistency for the students, the four Academic Abilities that infuse the curriculum mirror the professional generic competences of the tool used throughout Australia and New Zealand for assessment of clinical competence in speech pathology, the COMPASS© (McAllister, Lincoln, Ferguson, & McAllister, 2006); these are: reasoning; professional communication; lifelong learning; and professional role. The conceptual underpinning of both the Academic Abilities and the COMPASS© is that they represent a developmental continuum, although the terminology differs to reflect the environment in which they are used (academic and clinical). Students demonstrate their achievement in each of these four areas through multiple assessment tasks and at three levels of ability (beginning, intermediate, and developed) via a proprietary electronic learning portfolio (PebblePad – see Further Resources) that is submitted at regular points across the course, offering students a means to assemble and evaluate the work that they have completed throughout the programme, as well as to assess their progress towards their development of meta skills.

Multiple criterion measures are needed to assess performance sensitively. We employ a range of assessment tasks that enable the students to demonstrate their application of knowledge and skills across all clinical and academic areas, including critical reviews, simulations, case presentations, written exams, research reports, concept maps, and oral examinations. The tasks allow for creativity, initiative, and independence, and demonstrate the value placed on encouraging students to direct their own learning while also providing necessary structure and support.

Clear learning outcomes and lucid criteria for assessment ensure that students know what it is they must learn and how they should demonstrate that they have met desired goals. In order to encourage a focus on formative learning, students are provided with feedback based on the Structure of Observed Learning Outcomes (SOLO) Taxonomy (Biggs & Collis, 1982). A rubric based on this taxonomy is created for each assignment, with clear documentation of the assessment criteria using the language of the Academic Abilities.

A wonderful way to begin to develop skills in ability-based assessment is to join educators from Alverno College as they share their considerable experience in 1-day seminars each semester and 3-day and week-long summer workshops annually. There is even greater benefit in sharing this experience with colleagues from your own programme, as the energy of the workshops can live on within your workplace.

Recent Innovations in PBL Assessment

The PBL approach is empowering by being dynamic and innovative, yet these same characteristics also render it vulnerable to small- and large-scale changes to its desired implementation (e.g. focus on content at the expense of process, misguided attempts by practitioners to make the approach "more efficient"). Such changes, even subtle ones, can result in the gradual erosion of the original ideas underlying PBL (Moust, Van Berkel, & Schmidt, 2005). According to Moust et al. (2005), the adoption of new forms of assessment and the development of computer-supported PBL environments are two ways in which this erosion can be counteracted. The following innovative methods of PBL assessment have been developed by PBL practitioners in order to better promote student capabilities, in line with the learning outcomes of the modules and the programmes. These examples can be easily adapted to any professional field/area of study.

1. Online template for case delivery

Instructional multimedia can create realistic environments that deliver standardised curricular objectives, motivate students, enhance their learning experience, promote critical thinking and self-directed learning, and reduce the tutor's presence, consequently raising flexibility and reducing costs. Together with international developers of interactive software designed to teach and evaluate reasoning skills with medical students (DxR Development Group – see Further Resources), we created a template for delivering and assessing problem-based learning cases in speech pathology (Scholten & Brebner, 2009; Scholten, Russell, & McCormack, 2006). The template has three major components – the main "face" being what the student interacts with, a "backend" stencil where instructors can provide instructions for scoring students' submissions, including text matching, weighting from within a range of response options and grading of multiple-choice responses, and an administrator's section where cases can be created, shared among teaching staff, edited, and released to students. Unique cases can be created by instructors who upload all the necessary information into the template, including the narrative, tests, and procedures, all the related media and any associated questions to be posed.

Each case opens with a simple scenario. Working either individually or in groups, and for either learning or assessment purposes, students are free to follow their own path of enquiry through the investigation (see Figure 13.6).

The students delve into the available case information, emulating typical client interactions, by investigating such areas as history, psychosocial factors, lifestyle, and the client's perspective of the situation. The diagnostic process in speech–language pathology is highly reliant on direct observation of visual and auditory cues and the template is able to present media links to audiovisual material, completed test forms, and case records. Students "observe" the client via text and/or audiovisual material related to the client's presenting problems. Additional features of the template include a notes section into which students can paste and edit the client data compiled to date and links to resources such as search facilities, establishing the basis for

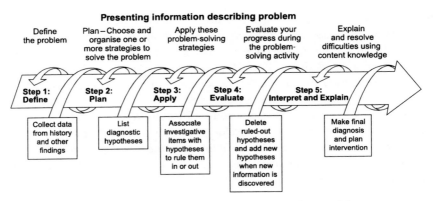

Figure 13.6 Steps of student enquiry using online template for case delivery.

desirable evidence-based practice. At any stage of the programme the student can save data and exit in order to conduct further learning.

Once the student has committed to a final diagnosis, there are a number of management options from which the student can select, including discharging the client, monitoring progress, or conducting an intervention plan, justifying decisions made. If ongoing intervention is chosen, the student is prompted to document a detailed plan.

The software not only presents the necessary case information, it also collates the students' performance for formative or summative assessment. The investigative process is valued, not merely the final diagnosis. The computer record depicts the student's enquiry strategy and organises and presents it according to specifications determined by the case-writer, such as those associated with expert problem solvers. The teacher reviews computer records and can provide critical feedback relating to individual and/or collective problem-solving skills.

The template can be used in a variety of contexts. Not only does it provide an alternative to paper-based case delivery for learning purposes, including for dispersed students who are external to the university, it also offers efficient and cost-effective assessment opportunities. For example, cases can be created for examination purposes, mirroring the process of problem-based learning, covering examination of both content and skills; the template can be used to deliver a "hurdle" task for borderline students on placement; and students can use the template to create their own PBL cases. Additionally, the template can be used to create formative "practice" cases for independent content coverage by students in anticipation of clinical or theoretical exams.

2. Reflective Essay

The evolution of reflective skills should be explicitly linked to professional development in order for students to gain a better understanding of the link between the PBL approach and their own future self-directed learning skills (Williams, 2001). In 2005, the staff of the Department of Speech and Hearing Sciences, UCC, developed a short reflective essay assignment for students nearing the end of their PBL curriculum experience, whereby students are required to actively reflect on and critically evaluate the importance of the PBL approach to their learning and development as competent speech and language therapists (Pettigrew, 2008). The aim of the reflective essay is to maximise meaningful learning and the continuation of self-directed learning in professional practice, as the students move into their final year of study (professional studies, work experience, and research projects).

The students complete a 1,000-word essay on the following topic: "From Theory to Practice: Applications of the Problem-Based Learning Style to the Professional Practice of Speech and Language Therapy." The students are instructed to respond to the essay topic provided by discussing their own experience and reflections of the PBL process, objectively collecting evidence from the literature about the PBL process, collating their personal experiences and the literature evidence in an informative and unbiased way, and describing the applications of the PBL style to the professional practice of a speech and language therapist (i.e. advantages/disadvantages, preparation for being a qualified professional). Thus, the students carry out their own computer-supported searches, critically evaluate the literature and, most importantly, engage in *deep learning* (the search for personal meaning and understanding, active participation in seeking the whole picture, engagement in reflection and exploration in order to make sense of new ideas and experiences within the learning process). According to Mattick, Dennis, and Bligh (2004), these processes are associated with the development of lifelong self-directed learning skills beyond tertiary education.

This reflective essay assessment can be easily transferred to any professional discipline simply by replacing "Speech and Language Therapy" in the title. It thus forms another alternative for PBL coursework assessment, providing PBL practitioners in a wide variety of professions with a constructive and valuable tool for assessing and encouraging self-directed learning through reflection, thereby, optimising the professional competence of their graduates.

3. Products

Student products encourage application of acquired knowledge to a particular context (e.g. research/clinical/workplace) (O'Toole, 2008). Students could be required to develop a wide range of materials, such as information leaflets, clinical assessment tools, and/or analysis of a data sample. They could be asked to create a model for a client (e.g. architecture, computing, business), or problem-solve (e.g. solve a tax issue for a hypothetical client accountant/business). Alternatively, they could be asked to write a report/letter to another professional (e.g. write a short letter to an IT professional detailing issues in relation to a new software product), create a play for the group to perform (Performance Arts), – whatever is deemed appropriate or facilitates students in fulfilling learning outcomes in their professional discipline. Students can be asked to work collaboratively or individually, and may be evaluated on the effort and value of what they create. This method allows for the assessment of practical skills within an educational environment, thus encouraging a further bridging of theory and practice, in a controlled setting.

Where Do You Start?

Now that we have provided you with some practical ideas for assessment in PBL, and conceptual frameworks on which to base your assessments and align them with teaching activities and curriculum learning outcomes, it may be an opportune time to think about how you might see yourself adapting and applying these ideas in your discipline. Below, we have provided you with a list of further resources that we hope will help you on your way to revitalising your PBL assessment practice.

References

Anderson, L.W., & Krathwohl, D.R. (Eds.). (2001). *A taxonomy for learning, teaching and assessing: A revision of Bloom's Taxonomy of Educational Objectives.* New York: Longman.

Azer, S. (2008). *Navigating problem-based learning.* Sydney: Churchill Livingstone Elsevier.

Biggs, J. (1999). What the student does: Teaching for enhancing learning. *Higher Education Research and Development, 18*(1), 57–75.

Biggs, J., & Collis, K. (1982). *Evaluating the quality of learning: The SOLO Taxonomy.* New York: Academic Press.

Bloom, B.S. (1956). *Taxonomy of educational objectives, Handbook I: The cognitive domain.* New York: David McKay.

Carrillo-de-la-Pena, M.T., Bailles, E., Caseras, X., Martinez, A., Ortet, G., & Perez, J. (2009). Formative assessment and academic achievement in pre-graduate students of health science. *Advances in Health Science Education, 14*(1), 61–67.

Charlin, B., Roy, L., Brailovsky, C., Goulet, F., & van der Vleuten, C. (2000). The Script Concordance Test: A tool to assess the reflective clinician. *Teaching and Learning in Medicine, 12*(4), 189–195.

Dreyfus, H.L., & Dreyfus, S.E. (1986). *Mind over machine: The power of human intuition and expertise in the era of the computer.* New York: Free Press.

Fourie, R. (2008). Problem based learning and the construction of an SLP curriculum. *The South African Journal of Communication Disorders, 55*, 110–131.

Fournier, J.P., Demeester, A., & Charlin, B. (2008). Script concordance tests: Guidelines for construction. *BMC Medical Informatics and Decision Making, 8*, 18. Retrieved from: www.ncbi.nlm.nih.gov/pmc/articles/PMC2427021.

Hildebrand, G., & Edwards, S. (2005). *Effective assessment practices: Problem-based learning, peer assessment and rubrics.* Retrieved from: www.monash.edu.au/teaching/vcshowcase/2005program/Presentation/HildebrandEdwardsShowcase.pdf.

James, R., McInnis, C., & Devlin, M. (2002). *Assessing learning in Australian universities.* Melbourne: Centre for the Study of Higher Education, University of Melbourne and the Australian Universities Teaching Committee.

McAllister, S., Lincoln, M., Ferguson, A., & McAllister, L. (2006). *COMPASS®: Competency assessment in speech pathology.* Melbourne: Speech Pathology Association of Australia.

Macdonald, R. (2005). Assessment strategies for enquiry and problem-based learning. In T. Barrett, I. Mac Labhrainn, & H. Fallon (Eds.), *Handbook of enquiry and problem-based learning: Irish case studies and international perspectives* (pp. 85–93). Galway: CELT, National University of Ireland, Galway and All Ireland Society for Higher Education (AISHE). (Available for free download from the AISHE website at: www.aishe.org/readings/2005-2/contents.html).

Macdonald, R.F., & Savin-Baden, M. (2004). A briefing on assessment in problem-based learning, *LTSN Generic Centre Assessment Series*. Retrieved from: http://www.heacademy.ac.uk/assets/York/documents/resources/resourcedatabase/id349_A_Briefing_on_Assessment_in_Problembased_Learning.pdf.

Mattick, K., Dennis, I., & Bligh, J. (2004). Approaches to learning and studying in medical students: Validation of a revised inventory and its relation to student characteristics and performance. *Medical Education, 38*, 535–543.

Mentkowski, M., & Associates. (2000). *Learning that lasts: Integrating learning, development, and performance in college and beyond.* San Francisco, CA: Jossey-Bass.

Miller, G.E. (1990). The assessment of clinical skills/competence. *Academic Medicine, 65*(Suppl.), S63–S67.

Moust, J.H.C., van Berkel, H.J.M., & Schmidt, H.G. (2005). Signs of erosion: Reflections on three decades of problem-based learning at Maastricht University. *Higher Education, 50*(4), 665–683.

Novak, J.D. (1990). Concept maps and Vee diagrams: Two metacognitive tools for science and mathematics education. *Instructional Science, 19*, 29–52.

Novak, J.D., & Canãs, A.J. (2006). *The theory underlying concept maps and how to construct them.* Technical Report IHMC Cmap Tools 2006–01, Florida Institute for Human and Machine Cognition. Retrieved from: http://cmap.ihmc.us/Publications/ResearchPapers/TheoryCmaps/TheoryUnderlyingConceptMaps.htm.

O'Toole, C. (2008). Concept maps and products in a problem-based learning curriculum. In *Proceedings of the 1st Annual Conference of the National Academy of Integrating Research Teaching and Learning (NAIRTL)* (pp. 124–125). Cork: NAIRTL, University College Cork.

Pangaro, L.N. (2006). A shared professional framework for anatomy and clinical clerkships. *Clinical Anatomy, 19*(5), 419–428.

Pettigrew, C.M. (2008, November). *Learning by doing…: Can we assume that successful completion of a Problem-based Learning curriculum provides the student with a good enough understanding of their own learning to maximize continuation of self-directed learning skills in professional practice?* Paper presented at the 2nd Annual Conference of the National Academy for Integrating Research Teaching and Learning, Waterford, Ireland.

Savin-Baden, M. (2004). Understanding the impact of assessment on students in problem-based learning. *Innovations and Education in Teaching International, 14*(2), 221–233.

Scholten, I., & Brebner, C. (2009, July). *Online template for interactive case-based learning in speech-language pathology.* Paper presented at the 34th International Conference of Improving University Teaching (IUT) Vancouver, Canada.

Scholten, I., Russell, A., & McCormack, P. (2006, May). *Template for online interactive PBL in the speech pathology curriculum.* Paper presented at the Inaugural Conference for Problem Based Learning in Speech-Language Pathology, Linkoping, Sweden.

Simpson, E.J. (1972). *The classification of educational objectives in the psychomotor domain.* Washington, DC: Gryphon House.

Toohey, S., & Kumar, R.K. (2003). A new program of assessment for a new medical program. *Focus on Health Professional Education, 5*(2), 23–33.

Williams, B. (2001). Developing critical reflection for professional practice through problem-based learning. *Journal of Advanced Nursing, 34*, 27–34.

Wood, D. (2003). ABC of learning and teaching in medicine: Problem-based learning. *British Medical Journal, 326*, 328–330.

Further Resources

Alverno College – information for educators on assessment and curriculum development: www.alverno.edu/for_educators/index.html.

Central Queensland University – links to PBL online resources: http://pbl.cqu.edu.au/content/online_resources.htm.

CMapTools – free downloadable software for creating concept maps on the computer: http://cmap.ihmc.us/conceptmap.html.

DxR Development Group – producers of interactive software for clinical reasoning in health professions: www.dxrgroup.com.

Innovation in the use of IT for education and research: www.jisc.ac.uk.

eportfolio – PebblePad: www.pebblelearning.co.uk.

Google Apps – communication and collaboration software useful for online assessment of student capabilities – free for education: www.google.com/apps/intl/en-GB/business/index.html.

Solo Taxonomy: www.learningandteaching.info/learning/solo.htm.

14

The Triple Jump Assessment

Aligning Learning and Assessment

Ntombifikile Gloria Mtshali and Lyn Middleton

Introduction

This chapter explores the question:

> Is triple jump an appropriate method of assessment in problem-based learning?

Guided by the principle that assessment should be in line with the teaching methodology used, triple jump is one assessment strategy that is appropriate in problem-based learning (PBL). Triple jump assessment shares similar principles with those observed in problem-based learning. In this chapter, we argue that problem-based learning facilitates development of key professional capabilities and process learning skills in addition to specialist knowledge. Triple jump assessment is an effective way of assessing these three elements of learning. The triple jump assessment exercise is a unique and comprehensive method of measuring the aims of problem-based learning, as well as the specific learning outcomes set forth for students in a particular problem. In this chapter we use nursing and health as the curricular context for exploring this form of attachment.

Triple jump assessment is a three-stage assessment process. Stage one assesses the students' ability to explore the person–health-context–nursing dimensions of a clinical situation and to develop tentative hypotheses and plans of action. Stage two assesses the students' ability to seek and to use appropriate evidence-based knowledge in refining the initial hypotheses and in developing multidimensional, theoretically sound nursing responses and anticipated health outcomes. Stage three assesses the students' ability to present stage two data and to reason the connections between the original hypotheses and nursing responses, the refined hypothesis, and nursing responses and the anticipated health outcomes.

We will provide you with one model of triple jump assessment, strategies for implementing this form of assessment, and examples from our PBL practice. As PBL practitioners, you can adapt these assessments strategies for your own contexts.

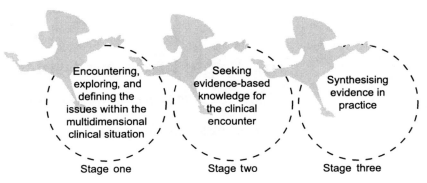

Stage one	Stage two	Stage three
Encountering, exploring, and defining the issues within the multidimensional clinical situation	Seeking evidence-based knowledge for the clinical encounter	Synthesising evidence in practice

Figure 14.1 Triple jump assessment.

Chapter Overview

This chapter:

- begins by highlighting the compatibility of PBL with the development of key professional capabilities and process learning skills;
- explores the tensions associated with implementing PBL curricula;
- in the context of these tensions, explores issues about assessment in PBL;
- explores the practical implementation of two models of triple jump assessment which address some of these issues.

The Compatibility of PBL with the Development of Key Professional Capabilities and Process Learning Skills

Knowledge produced from problem-based learning is context-driven, fluid, and open to change. The outcome of learning is broader than just knowledge acquisition. It culminates with the cessation of the fragmented and compartmentalised nature of learning (Gwele, 1987); the students also acquire learning process competences, which are referred to as transferable skills or graduate attributes. These learning process competences include problem solving, critical thinking, decision making, metacognition, communication, effective team skills, and lifelong learning (Murray-Harvey, Curtis, Cattley, & Phillip, 2005).

In the South African learning process, competences are similar to National Critical Cross-field Outcomes (South African Qualifications Authority [SAQA], 1995) that have to be achieved across all educational programmes. These outcomes include identifying and solving problems in which responses demonstrate that responsible decisions using critical and creative thinking have been made.

1. Working effectively with others as a member of a team, group, organisation, or community.

2. Organising and managing oneself and one's activities responsibly and effectively.
3. Collecting, analysing, and critically evaluating information.
4. Communicating effectively using visual, mathematical, and/or language skills in the modes of oral and/or written persuasion.
5. Using science and technology effectively and critically showing responsibility towards the environment and health of others.
6. Demonstrating an understanding of the world as a set of related systems by recognising that the problem-solving contexts do not exist in isolation.
7. Contributing to the full personal development of each learner and the social and economic development of society at large, by making it the underlying intention of any programme of learning to make an individual aware of the importance of:

   - reflecting on and exploring a variety of strategies to learn more effectively;
   - participating as responsible citizens in local, national, and global contexts;
   - being culturally and aesthetically sensitive across a range of social contexts;
   - exploring education and career opportunities; and
   - developing entrepreneurial opportunities (SAQA, 1995).

According to Veldman, de Wet, Mokhele, and Bouwer (2008), problem-based learning is one mechanism for achieving these learning outcomes.

Application of Problem-based Learning in Nursing Programmes in South Africa

In South Africa, the history of adopting problem-based learning formally in nursing education institutions dates back to 1994 (Gwele, 1997). The analysis of the PBL programmes in a number of nursing schools (Mtshali, 2009) indicates that most of these schools adopted problem-based learning as an instructional pedagogy within community-based or community-oriented programmes. These nursing schools use different types of problem-based learning, ranging from lecture-based case studies to a whole course, where the course is presented in an integrated manner, using a series of problems (reiterative problem-based learning).

Commonly, the nursing education institutions that adopted reiterative problem-based learning use authentic paper-based cases. Other institutions use different types of problem-based learning (as outlined by Barrows, 1986) at different points in their nursing degree programmes. For example, one school of nursing uses lecture-based case studies in 1st year, authentic problems for clinical settings in the 2nd and 3rd years, and a hybrid of these types in the 4th and final year of their degree programme. Hybrid problem-based learning uses a combination of problems and lectures that promote active learning and assessment and also includes traditional forms of assessment.

In general, many schools of nursing in South Africa use either structured paper cases or authentic problems identified from real-life clinical settings. The rationale for using paper cases as well as hybrid problem-based learning is to ensure adequate coverage of content so as to meet the requirements of the regulatory bodies.

The variations in the types of problem-based learning used are as a result of a number of challenges, mainly the availability of resources: both human and material resources and the nature and academic preparedness of the students accepted to the programme. In Africa, especially in South Africa, making higher education accessible to all is crucial; this is primarily due to the political disparities that existed in the past. The new dispensation aims to equalise opportunities and, thus, the number of students from disadvantaged educational backgrounds accessing higher education is increasing.

Problem-based learning has been identified as an important solution for addressing the academic challenges experienced by students from disadvantaged backgrounds (Iputo & Kwizera, 2005); these authors identified poor academic preparation and difficulties in coping with academic demands as the primary challenge of these students in negotiating and succeeding in higher education. Their study revealed that adopting problem-based learning made the teachers realise that teaching the process of learning is as essential as the subject content. This realisation was reinforced by a number of measurable positive outcomes, including reduction in attrition rates and improvement in throughput rates. These outcomes suggest that learning which emphasises the process of learning, as well as the content, and occurs within a supportive, dialogical student–teacher learning environment is critical to student empowerment.

Supporting Students from Diverse Backgrounds

For effective learning to occur, systems are put in place to support students throughout the process of the learning encounter. Supporting students is a collaborative, institutional effort; the school works with the university library, the student counselling unit, the mentorship office, and the academic development office. Support mechanisms include:

- in-depth orientation to problem-based learning and expectations during the teaching and learning process;
- a mentorship programme with senior students (paid by the university) serving as mentors to new students;
- a team-building workshop, which is run by an external organisation, outside the university, to prepare the students for working in groups;

- a librarian dedicated to attend to nursing students in their search for reading materials;
- intensive library orientation, by the librarian, to the library, nursing resources, different search engines, and access the library off-campus to reduce the cost of coming to the university;
- an academic development officer appointed by the university to attend to the academic and psychosocial needs of undergraduate nursing students;
- assessment at the end of each session to monitor the development of all of the students (self, peer, and facilitator evaluations);
- the university quality promotion unit, which assists in evaluating the students' overall experience of each module and the extent to which learning has occurred in a positive, supportive, and mutually respectful environment;
- the students also working on their own individualised learning contracts with their facilitators monitoring their progress on their personal and academic development learning needs;
- training students in the assessment strategies used, including the triple jump assessment.

Tensions Associated with Problem-based Learning

A report on staff's concerns by Gwele (1997), regarding the adoption of problem-based learning in one of the nursing schools in South Africa, highlighted concerns related to the inadequacy of staff support, the stress related to work overload, and the lack of time to do research. Other tensions associated with the adoption of problem-based learning include:

- paradigm shift from passive to active learning: students who are used to a passive and surface style of learning are expected to actively engage in an unfamiliar pattern of active knowledge construction (World Bank, 2002);
- limited availability of resources that directly address the problems in multicultural local contexts. The limited availability of culture-specific intervention and outcome evidence has the potential to compromise how problems are theoretically understood within a specific local context and, in the worst case scenario, to decontextualise content. Although problem-based learning aids in counterbalancing this tension, tutors need to assist students to rigorously scrutinise evidence for transferability;
- high turnover of highly prepared nurse educators: a "brain drain", which is characterised by the exodus of highly prepared nurse educators, weakens the capacity of schools in running innovative education programmes;

- demand on human and material resources: problem-based learning requires more classrooms, nurse educators to manage small groups, and learning materials to foster active learning and group discussions;
- limited expertise in relevant assessment strategies: assessment in problem-based learning requires people with expertise in assessment strategies that addresses the learning process skills as well as the application of subject matter. We argue that developing the triple jump assessment strategies and training staff and students in this approach is one way of addressing this issue.

Assessment of Learning Using a Triple Jump Problem-solving Exercise

Assessment in problem-based learning is underpinned by the premise that learning and assessment are inextricably linked and assessment should be aligned to the teaching methodology used (McTiernan, Leahy, Walsh, Sloane, & Smith, 2007). Learning in PBL is knowledge- and process-based, which means that the assessment method used should also share these characteristics. According to Lee and Brysiewicz (2009), the problem-solving process in PBL tutorials resembles the process followed in the triple jump assessment. As with problem-based learning, the triple jump assesses hypothesis generation, use of resources, application of knowledge to problem solve, and self-directed learning. Ragachari (2002), cited in McTiernan et al. (2007), stated that students who are active in their process of learning should be active participants in the assessment of their acquired knowledge.

The triple jump, a three-stage assessment developed at McMaster University in 1974, is one approach that is used to assess learning in problem-based learning. Triple jump, according to Von Bergmann, Dalrymple, Wong, and Shuler (2007), is a problem-analysis exercise and a problem-solving exercise, which assesses the application of knowledge to a clinical situation in a controlled setting outside of the clinical environment. Research that has been conducted in this area (Rideout, 2001; Matthes, Look, Hahne, Tekian, & Herzig, 2008) has led to variations in the triple jump instruments.

Theoretical Foundations of Triple Jump

Triple jump incorporates the values and philosophical ideologies underpinning problem-based learning. Authors, such as Barrett (2005), report on the philosophical ideologies of problem-based learning and present PBL values. The philosophical principles and values reflected in the triple jump process include:

- constructivism: learning is a constructive process where students build new knowledge on prior knowledge;

- metacognitivism: use of problems that engage inquiry learning, and deep thinking;
- authenticity: use of problems that are presented in the same format as in the workplace or real-life situation;
- integrated knowledge base: use of problems that require knowledge that cuts across disciplines;
- student centredness: use of problems that facilitate self-directed learning from the students;
- collaborative learning: learning takes place in small groups using problems that are complex enough to enable students to work in collaboration with one another, taking advantage of collective knowledge;
- problematisation: the students are presented with an ill-structured problem, with no clear solution in order to stimulate critical thinking;
- dialogue: a process of bringing together the community of learners in creating and recreating new knowledge;
- contextualisation of knowledge: knowledge is viewed as fluid and context-driven;
- structural thinking: scientific process of analysing and solving or addressing a problem in a logical manner;
- cognitivism: requires that students engage in the process of accessing prior knowledge, making connections between the old and new concepts, and using an elaboration of relationships to engage in theory construction, as stated in Schmidt (1993).

Models of Triple Jump

Although there are a number of triple jump models, this chapter will present only two versions. In the first model, which is commonly used during formative assessment, the triple jump assessment is administered to a group of students who approach the assessment as a group and only attend to the last step of the process as individuals. In the second model, commonly used during the summative assessment phase, the triple jump assessment is administered to the individual student.

The process of assessment is the same in both models. The first step is that of encountering and defining the problem, the second step is the self-study phase, and the third step is the reassessment stage. Within each stage are a number of phases or activities.

Preparations before the Triple Jump Assessment

The preparation before conducting the assessment is critical and includes preparing materials for assessment and attending to the logistics related to conducting triple jump assessments. These preparations include:

- learning resources which are organised with the help of the librarian;
- a holding or waiting area for the students before the examination;
- a writing area is required for "Step 3" of the triple jump process;
- a timetable with the names of the students, their assessors, and the time for interviews that should be communicated to the students a day before the examinations;
- a co-ordinator who will organise the whole examination process and be a timekeeper;
- presenting problems or scenarios to be given to the students during the interview period;
- a document with more information about the case or presenting situation that will be given to the tutors or examiners on the day of the assessment;
- free writing paper with an official school stamp that may be used by the students to write on;
- training of assessors for executing triple jump assessment, especially those with limited expertise in conducting this assessment.

Step One: Encountering and Defining the Problem

The first step is an oral examination phase, where a tutor conducts an interview with each student in a private or controlled space; this step takes about 30 minutes. The tutor is expected to capture all of the information from the student as fast as possible while attending to the student. This first step consists of five phases.

The first phase during this step is that of hypothesis generation. A short problem scenario, written on a piece of paper (with minimal information), is presented to the student. The problem is presented in the same way that it would present itself in a real-life situation. The content of the triggering scenario can easily be adapted to reflect different professional contexts, clinical and non-clinical alike. The scenario should outline the main actors, the context of the interaction and the profession-related descriptors that form or suggest a problem. Figure 14.2 provides a problem scenario developed for a child public health context.

The student's first task is to generate hypotheses from this presenting situation and their likely connections, using previous knowledge or experience.

> Sindi, a 7-year-old girl, is at the Primary Health Care clinic, brought in by her grandmother.
>
> She presents with swelling of the body and face, lethargy, diarrhoea, vomiting, and cold extremities.

Figure 14.2 Presenting situation.

The student reads the scenario and highlights the key concepts that will be used to generate hypotheses. The tutor assesses the student's ability to identify relevant issues in the presenting situation.

The second phase is that of collecting more information about the presenting situation and interpreting the evidence provided. The tutor has additional information about the case which she/he offers in response to the student's questions. Students are required to interrogate the presenting scenario using discipline-specific frameworks. For example, in the case of clinical nursing, the student exploring the scenario of Sindi requires the following comprehensive history-taking skills:

- logic in asking questions;
- ability to provide rationale guiding the questions asked; and
- ability to integrate knowledge from other subjects (see Figure 14.3).

In all instances or disciplines, the tutor assesses the following:

- ability to generate appropriate and accurate questions based on basic disciplinary assumptions and concepts. In the case of Sindi, the nurse is required to base questions on the biological–sociological–psychological framework of nursing;
- data gathering; this should be done in a systematic manner, using the issues generated during the first step as the starting point. The student should use the gathered data as cues for further data collection and should be able to state the knowledge which guides the data collection;
- ability to interrelate concepts and explain underlying mechanisms when analysing data and the ability to think through unfamiliar concepts.

The third phase is that of problem formulation. On the basis of the information collected, the student summarises the major problems and issues related to the presenting situation. This summary should include findings that support the claims made and the reasons for identifying these factors as problems. At this stage, the student makes a problem list or problem statement(s) or diagnosis, depending on how the discipline conceptualises issues. A diagnosis, a nursing diagnosis may be "undernourished child" because the body mass index is below 18.5. The normal body index is between 18.5 and 24.9; lowered body temperature (hypothermia) because the temperature was 35° C; dehydration because of diarrhoea and vomiting; poor skin turgor. The student is required to list the problems in the order of their priority and to provide a rationale for this order. The tutor assesses the student's ability to outline the problems in an accurate and precise manner.

1. Social history

1.1 Why is Sindi brought to the clinic by her grandmother? Where is her mother?

I am asking these questions to determine Sindi's family situation. Grandparent-headed households are common in South Africa because of the impact of HIV/Aids on the adult population.

1.2 Is there food in the household and who cares for Sindi's nutritional needs in the home?

I am asking these questions because Sindi presents with symptoms of undernourishment and this may be due to a lack of food (poverty), and/or preparation methods.

2. Vital signs

2.1 What was Sindi's temperature?

As she had cold feet, perhaps she has hypothermia, which is a serious problem because it lowers the body metabolism and may affect mental functioning.

3. Physical examination (from head to toe)

3.1 What was the colour and texture of Sindi's hair?

Children with Kwashiorkor have reddish coloured, coarse-textured hair.

3.2 For how long did Sindi have body swelling?

Because this is one of the signs of undernourishment where the body does not have enough proteins in the blood to pull the fluid from the tissues to the blood. The swelling may be due to loss of potassium because of diarrhoea, thus creating an imbalance between potassium and sodium in the body.

3.3 How was the skin turgor (skin elasticity)?

Because Sindi had a history of diarrhoea and vomiting. Skin that is pinched and released should immediately go back to its normal shape but in dehydrated cases the skin stays folded longer before returning to its shape.

Figure 14.3 Generation of information.

The fourth phase is that of developing initial actions or interventions guided by the list of problems generated. These interventions should be in line with how the problems are prioritised and with the discipline's knowledge base. The student should indicate which problem should be attended to first and the reason for attending to that problem first. The tutor assesses whether the student is able to describe the most important initial actions and to provide a rationale.

The fifth phase is the self-assessment phase. The student should be able to identify gaps in his/her knowledge, taking into consideration all five of the phases in the first step, and any additional information required to analyse the presenting situation. The gaps identified should be very specific. For example, the student in the scenario of Sindi might want to know more about the normal values for potassium and sodium and the part played by these two electrolytes in cases with diarrhoea and vomiting, appropriate investigations in undernourished cases, how to manage hypothermia, and how swelling of the body is managed in undernourished children. Assessment in the fifth phase focuses on the student's ability to identify gaps in his/her knowledge; this self-assessment by the student should be accurate, clear, and relevant. The tutor concludes the first step by giving instructions for step three which is after self-study (step two).

The tutor uses the time between interviewing candidates to mark and rate performance of the student in the first step using a structured marking guide which is provided. The rating scale use ranges from one to five. There are two statements, reflecting the two extremes: poorly done and excellent. Figure 14.4 presents a section of the instrument that is used by one of the academic institutions to evaluate Phases One, Two, and Three of Step One.

Step Two: Self-directed Learning Phase (Accessing, Evaluating, and Utilising Information)

The second step, according to Feletti and Ryan (1994), allows the student time to pursue research by finding relevant information, checking its reliability and whether the information is helpful to formulate an appropriate response to the original question. The student locates and consults relevant resources which may be a material resources or a list of subject experts, main players or actors (e.g. patients and or families). The student reads critically and interprets text in the light of the presenting situation and information obtained during the data-collection stage. Experts and main players may be consulted to verify information that is not clear. The skills required in the second step include resourcefulness and ability to critically appraise resources and information obtained from the resources used (Feletti & Ryan, 1994).

Step Three: Synthesis and Feedback Stage

At the third step, the student synthesises all of the information and returns to present a resolution to the problem (McTiernan et al., 2007). The student constructs the new knowledge to resolve the presenting problem. How the third step is conducted depends on the institution; the tutor may require the student to give either a written or an oral report. Feletti and Ryan (1994) note that both of these models use pre-specified criteria for evaluating the student's performance, taking into consideration the students' structural thinking skills, and the research conducted during the self-study period. At this final stage, it is expected that the students know more about the problem and will be able to apply new knowledge to the problem, validating or refuting the initial hypotheses generated during the initial encounter.

1. Issue identification

Statement 1
Unable to identify relevant issues in the situation.

Statement 2
Identifies relevant issues in the situation.

Essentially like 1	More like 1 than 2	Between 1 and 2	More like 2 than 1	Essentially like 2

2. Question generation

Statement 1
Major gaps in questions generated.

Statement 2
Accurate and appropriate initial questions generated – include psychological, physical, and social concepts.

Essentially like 1	More like 1 than 2	Between 1 and 2	More like 2 than 1	Essentially like 2

3. Data gathering

Statement 1
Unsystematic data collection. Does not use gathered data as cues for further data collection.

Statement 2
Systematic data collection. Proceeds from the client's presenting problem and priority issues. Uses gathered data as cues for further data collection.

Essentially like 1	More like 1 than 2	Between 1 and 2	More like 2 than 1	Essentially like 2

Figure 14.4 Marking guide.

The third step consists of two phases: problem formulation and describing a nursing intervention for one of the identified problems. During the first (problem formulation) phase, the student revises the initial problem list using additional information, provides accurate explanations for problem formulation using concepts, theory and/or nursing models, and ranks the problems in order of priority and support. A rationale for the ranking reflects the student's ability to recognise the interrelationship among problems. The second phase involves describing interventions specific to one of the identified problems. In the case of nursing, an intervention should resolve more than one patient problem. For example, in the scenario with Sindi, the student may choose planning a nursing intervention for undernourishment. The tutor assesses the student's ability:

a. to describe interventions which are related to the problem formulation, goals, and context;
b. to plan individualised interventions;
c. to identify interventions that will resolve more than one problem; and
d. to provide theoretical explanations for selected interventions based on how they address the problem.

The tutor uses a structured assessment tool to rate the performance of the student on Steps One, Two, and Three. Once the examination process is completed, the examiners come together to do cross marking. The tutors present how they rated each student and provide a rationale for why they rated the student in that way. The rating is debated until the tutors reach a consensus on the performance of each student.

Validity and Reliability

Validity is considered to be high in triple jump assessment, especially face validity, as triple jump assessment mirrors problem-based learning or the tutorial process (Cunnington, 2002). Content validity is enhanced by having a team of experts develop the material together and/or by subjecting the developed material to the scrutiny of experts before using it to get their input.

Reliability is achieved through the process of cross marking of the written section by different markers. This practice of cross marking, according to Feletti and Ryan (1994), enables a check on inter-rater reliability and on rater consistency. The training of assessors for conducting triple jump and a marking guide detailing expected responses from the student improves the chances of reliability, while also ensuring consistency in marking. However, Hoon and Gwee (2003) have cautioned that reliability may be low in triple jump assessment for a number of reasons, including subjectivity in the assessment process, the lack of peer checking in the interview phase, the loss of information if the tutor cannot capture data fast enough during the interviews, the quality of the material (case) used for assessment, the candidate's personality, and the preparation of tutors or assessors for conducting the triple jump assessment. Therefore, the proper preparation of assessors and students and the monitoring of the process of assessment is crucial to improve the chances of reliability in the process.

Summary

Assessment should be aligned to the curricula goals and the teaching methods used. Problem-based learning engages students in their own learning, with the aim of facilitating acquisition of relevant knowledge and development of critical life skills. Triple jump is one of the assessment methods used in problem-based learning because it shares similar principles with PBL; it places an emphasis on identifying a problem and critically analysing it, with the aim of establishing key issues and questions, researching important issues, evaluating literature used as evidence, applying proposed solutions to a particular context, and communicating these solutions. In short, triple jump assesses the mastery of relevant content in a specific context and the mastery of the PBL process.

References

Barrett, T. (2005). Understanding problem-based learning. In T. Barrett, I. Mac Labhrainn, & H. Fallon (Eds.), *Handbook of enquiry and problem-based learning: Irish case studies and international perspectives* (pp. 13–25). Galway: National University of Ireland Galway and All Ireland Society for Higher Education. Retrieved from: www.nuigalway.ie/celt/pblbook/chapter2.

Barrows, H.S. (1986). Taxonomy of problem-based learning methods. *Medical Education, 20*, 481–486.

Feletti, G., & Ryan, G. (1994). The triple jump exercise in inquiry-based learning: A case study showing directions for further research. *Assessment and Evaluation in Higher Education, 19*(3), 225–234.

Gwele, N.S. (1997). The development of staff concerns during the implementation of problem-based learning in a nursing programme. *Medical Teacher, 19*(4), 275–285.

Hoon, T.C., & Gwee, C.E. (2003). *Student assessment in problem-based-learning: A challenge beyond reliability and validity.* Centre for Development of Teaching and Learning, National University of Singapore CDTL Brief 6(3). Retrieved from: www.cdtl.nus.edu.sg/brief/v6n3/sec3.asp.

Iputo, J.E., & Kwizera, E. (2005). Problem-based learning improves the academic performance of medical students in South Africa. *Medical Education, 39*, 388–393.

Lee, M., & Brysiewicz, P. (2009). Enhancing problem solving and nursing diagnosis in year III Bachelor of Nursing. *Nurse Education Today, 29*(4), 389–397.

McTiernan, K., Leahy, M., Walsh, I., Sloane, P., & Smith, M. (2007). The triple jump assessment in problem-based learning: An evaluative method used in the appraisal of both knowledge acquisition and problem solving skills. In G. O'Neill, S. Huntley-Moore, & P. Race (Eds.), *Case studies of good practices in assessment of students' learning in higher education* (pp. 116–119). Dublin: All Ireland Society for Higher Education. Retrieved from: www.aishe.org/readings/2007-1/No-19.html.

Matthes, J., Look, A., Hahne, A.K., Tekian, A., & Herzig, S. (2008). The semi-structured triple jump: A new assessment tool reflects qualifications of tutors in a PBL course on basic pharmacology. *Naunyn-Schmiedeberg's Archives of Pharmacology, 377*(1), 55–63.

Mtshali, N.G. (2009). Implementing community-based education in basic nursing education programs in South Africa. *Curationis, 32*(1), 25–32.

Murray-Harvey, R., Curtis, D.D., Cattley, G., & Phillip, T. (2005). Enhancing teacher education students' generic skills through problem-based learning. *Teaching Education, 16*(3), 257–273.

Rideout, E. (2001). Evaluating student learning. In E. Rideout (Ed.), *Nursing education through problem-based learning* (pp. 215–238). London: Jones & Bartlett Publishers.

Schmidt, H.G. (1993) Foundations of problem-based learning: Some explanatory notes. *Medical Education, 27*, 422–432.

South African Qualifications Authority. (1995). Act 58. Retrieved from: http://qspe.saqa.org.za/showUnitStandard.php?id=116929.

Veldman, F.J., de Wet, M.A., Mokhele, N.E., & Bouwer, W.A.J. (2008). Can engineering education in South Africa afford to avoid problem-based-learning as a didactic approach? *European Journal of Engineering Education, 33*(5–6), 551–559.

Von Bergmann, H., Dalrymple, K.R., Wong, S., & Shuler, C.F. (2007) Investigating the relationship between PBL process grades and content acquisition performance in a PBL dental programme. *Journal of Dental Education, 71*(9), 1160–1171.

Part III

Sustainability and Building Capacity in Problem-based Learning Initiatives

15

Planning and Building Capacity for a Major PBL Initiative

Paul Finucane, Peter McCrorie, and David Prideaux

Introduction

Planning a PBL approach needs organisational energy and a strategic systems approach. This chapter draws on the development of three major medical education PBL initiatives across the globe, and uses those first-hand experiences to provide lessons that PBL practitioners from any discipline can learn from.

Our story begins in the early 1990s, when Flinders University in Adelaide radically revised its medical programme, replacing a 6-year school-entry programme with a 4-year graduate-entry course. In the process, the Flinders medical programme adopted PBL as the cornerstone for teaching and learning in the first 2 years. Until that time, the University of Newcastle was the only Australian medical school with a PBL curriculum. The factors that led to this change have been described in detail elsewhere (Sefton, Prideaux, & Price, 1999). In short, Flinders realised that its existing course was becoming increasingly irrelevant to societal needs and wished to respond to a national goal of providing diverse pathways to medicine. When its new curriculum was introduced in 1996, Flinders offered Australia's first graduate-entry medical programme (GEMP). A year later, broadly similar but independent graduate-entry and PBL-based medical courses were introduced by the University of Sydney and the University of Queensland. The introduction of these changes began a period of reform and expansion in Australian medical education with the result that all schools now use some form of PBL or case-based learning.

A few years later, and at a time when basic medical education in the UK was in the process of expanding, St George's, University of London decided to establish the UK's first graduate-entry medical programme. Rather than developing PBL materials *de novo*, it sought to establish a partnership with an existing medical school and to use that partner's course material, particularly material relating to PBL for its new stream. St George's delivered its new course in parallel with its existing 5-year, school-entry, and more traditional course. Its international search for a partner focused on Australia and settled on the thriving Flinders programme. In 2000, St George's had the first intake of students into its Graduate Entry Programme (GEP) (McCrorie, 2001).

The story moves forward to 2005 and the decision by the University of Limerick (UL) to tender for a medical school at a time when Ireland was planning to double its medical student numbers. Unlike Flinders and St George's, UL had no existing medical school, although it had a growing interest in the health sciences. UL was keen to adopt new approaches to medical education, including PBL, which was not yet used by any of Ireland's five existing medical schools. In developing its curriculum, UL developed a partnership with St George's, which allowed access to the St George's/Flinders curriculum. In 2007, a medical school at UL received government approval and the first students were admitted 5 months later.

The three medical schools, though united by a common curriculum, have diverse origins and operate in very different geographical, political, cultural, and economic landscapes; these factors have profoundly influenced the building of capacity for PBL. We now describe the generic issues that arose when building capacity to deliver PBL, together with the specific challenges that faced each institution, and our ways of managing these. Though we focus on PBL in the context of medical education and while some issues have particular relevance to medicine, we believe that most are generic and apply to PBL in wider educational contexts.

Chapter Overview

This chapter will explore:

- how PBL is delivered in our contexts;
- key considerations for building PBL capacity;
- PBL challenges and solutions within three different international contexts.

How We Deliver PBL

The manner in which PBL is delivered critically determines the need for resources. At our three schools, each week we deliver three tutorials over a total of 5 or 6 hours; to maximise efficiency, we run Tutorial 3 and Tutorial 1 back-to-back, so that the conclusion of one case (Tutorial 3) is immediately followed by the start of a new case (Tutorial 1). This approach also allows a gap of at least 3 days between Tutorials 1 and 2 and between Tutorials 2 and 3, thus maximising the opportunities for self-directed learning. Each tutorial group has 7–10 students and a tutor is present at all times. The three schools use the *Progressive Release* version of PBL (Kaufman, 1985).

Building Capacity for PBL: General Considerations

The resources to deliver PBL can be categorised into those required in the initial phase and in the maintenance phase.

Resources Required in the Initial Phase

PBL Case Material

PBL case material refers to the text of the cases, together with the photographs and other images, video-clips, and assorted materials that contribute to the cases week-on-week; it is a critical factor in determining the quality of PBL and nothing will compensate for poor-quality cases. Writing cases *de novo* is no easy task. In the medical context, the best cases tend to be written jointly by clinicians and basic scientists. The cases work best if they are as true to life as possible, so clinicians need to create the overall scenario, with a presentation, diagnosis, management plan, and outcome. The co-authors can then tease out the scientific, psychosocial, ethical, and other principles to be covered in the case.

Following an initial broad, non-specific presentation that allows students to generate hypotheses, the case can be developed in more detail to cover history-taking, physical examination, investigations, diagnosis, management, and outcome. That is the easy part. A greater challenge lies in writing tutor notes in sufficient detail to cover what students are likely to discuss, but in plain, carefully phrased language that allows a non-expert tutor to understand the basic principles. A first draft should be reviewed by a PBL committee, a group of experts in the PBL process, where fresh eyes can spot inconsistencies or lack of clarity. The case is then returned to the case writers for modification. Several such iterations may be required.

It follows that the effort involved in generating good cases and in fine-tuning the end product is time-consuming. It took Flinders some 6 years to generate and repeatedly redraft the 66 PBL cases that underpin the curriculum at our three medical schools. In the early years, each PBL case was carefully evaluated by students, tutors, and course organisers at the end of the relevant week. Practically all of the cases were modified in the light of experience and quite a few had to be discarded and replaced.

Though St George's and UL sourced ready-made PBL case material, they were then obliged to refine it to suit local needs. Across our three schools, we have had to make some modifications to almost all PBL cases, to substantially rewrite some and to discard and replace one or two. However, the resources required to modify cases is a tiny fraction of what is required for their genesis. It follows that PBL case material constitutes valuable intellectual property and schools are increasingly placing a monetary value on this.

Student and Tutor Guides

As the name implies, the Student and Tutor Guides contain the information that allow the students to progress through the PBL cases and that allow tutors to stay abreast of and to guide student learning. The Tutor Guides used across our three institutions are substantial documents, often running to 50 or more pages; this is because PBL tutors are not always medically qualified or do not have relevant content expertise. The Tutor Guide also contains the prescribed learning outcomes (LOs) for the relevant week and it is essential that tutors are fully aware of the LOs, in advance, if they are to successfully guide their students through the PBL process.

Significant changes were made to the Tutor Guides when the Flinders cases were adopted by St George's and UL. At Flinders, the Tutor Guides were concise, but were accompanied by extensive additional reading material and lengthy extracts from books and journals. St George's incorporated this material into the text of the Tutor Guides in a more condensed form, making them easier to follow and reducing the amount of reading time required. Tutors also formally met with the case writers prior to every new PBL case, allowing any difficulties with the material to be discussed.

Tutors: Recruitment and Training

An adequate number of tutors must be recruited and trained; the number required depends on the approach taken to the delivery of PBL. While some schools recruit dedicated PBL tutors for the full academic year, others have a relay system, with individuals delivering relatively short blocks of tutoring. The planned or unplanned absence of tutors must be factored into any recruitment process. It is, therefore, essential to train more tutors than will be required at any given time.

Tutor training is an important part of capacity-building, and having an initial cohort of skilled and confident tutors gets PBL off to a good start and generates confidence in the process. The converse is equally true as those who have been involved in attempting to resuscitate an ailing PBL process will confirm. In each of our institutions we insist on formal training before people are allowed to tutor in PBL. We believe that tutor training can only be delivered by people with experience with the process and with a background in educational theory relevant to PBL.

The essential and desirable attributes of PBL tutors have long been debated. Although a detailed discussion of this debate is outside the scope of this chapter, it is important to note that, in recruiting PBL tutors, two key attributes need particular consideration: content expertise and process expertise. There is no doubt that effective tutors require good PBL process skills. While the three schools have some very good tutors with limited content expertise, such expertise does confer advantage when reading and understanding Tutor Guides. Specialist content expertise is not required, however, and many tutors prefer to work in cases outside of their specialist area.

Tutorial Rooms

With our students and tutors spending 5 or 6 hours per week in PBL tutorials, an adequate environment is essential. The size and configuration of tutorial rooms is critical. We have found that, for tutorial groups involving up to 10 people, at least 24 m² of space is required. Adequate lighting and ventilation is essential. We facilitate social integration by encouraging students to bring food and beverages to tutorials. Therefore, the provision of kettles, crockery, and access to water should be considered. Furniture should be comfortable. The students need to be able to describe and explain their knowledge, ideas, and thought processes to other group members. Therefore, the walls of the room should be literally covered in whiteboards on which students can write, draw diagrams, construct flow charts, etc. A TV screen or interactive whiteboard, linked to a computer, is essential for web-based delivery of cases. At our three schools, we maximise efficiency by having each tutorial room shared, at different times, by at least two PBL groups. Rooms are used for other activities at other times, but PBL always has priority.

Systems for Quality Assurance: Feedback

It is important to evaluate the quality of all PBLs. There are many ways of doing this, such as weekly online feedback, when individuals or groups of students use a Likert Scale to indicate how the course delivered on each of its learning outcomes for the week.

Just as a meeting of tutors occurs *prior* to each PBL, a second meeting *post* PBL allows tutors to discuss its strengths and weaknesses with the case writer. Thus, concerns can be addressed immediately and corrected for the following year. Alternatively, when tutors' time is at a premium, they can complete a feedback form for each case. At the end of each teaching module, it is useful to convene a larger meeting, involving both tutors and students, to review all aspects of the module.

Associated Needs

The use of PBL as an educational strategy generates a knock-on demand for other resources. For example, PBL is highly reliant on self-directed learning and e-learning and these approaches require significant library and IT resources. Furthermore, administrative resources are required to support PBL in such areas as the formulation of PBL groups, the assignment of tutors, the preparation and circulation of Tutor and Student Guides, the analysis of feedback, and the organisation of tutor training. It is difficult to quantify the resources required for these essential activities.

Resources Required in the Maintenance Phase

Funding

For any PBL-based curriculum, the ongoing financial cost of its delivery is a major consideration. At UL, which employs sessional staff as PBL tutors, the cost of delivering PBL in 2008 was estimated at almost €3,000 per student per year, with 89% of the cost relating to tutor payments (Finucane, Shannon, &

McGrath, 2009). Although this direct cost will not apply to schools that rely on existing staff to teach, the indirect costs of using tenured staff can easily outweigh the direct cost of sessional tutors. Flinders has now moved to a mixed model of sessional and existing staff to deliver PBL. Even within a mixed model, the budget for sessional staff is significant – the equivalent of €1,000 per student per year. At St George's, the majority of tutors are now sessional and peer tutors (i.e. other students) are also regularly employed. Peer tutors receive payment, but at a lower rate.

Ongoing Tutor Recruitment, Monitoring, and Staff Development

Even if sufficient tutors have been recruited for the initial phase of a PBL curriculum, maintaining adequate numbers can be challenging. With expanding student numbers, more tutors will be required to deal with students and there will, inevitably, be some tutor attrition. The recruitment of new tutors will, therefore, be a never-ending task and with this undertaking comes the ongoing need for training for novice tutors. This training can usefully be linked to strategies to enhance the skills of existing tutors; thus, basic and advanced PBL tutor training can go hand in hand. The monitoring of tutor performance is essential and requires the expertise of experienced fellow tutors, preferably those with some formal training in medical education.

Systems for Quality Assurance

Like all educational processes, PBL will only thrive if it is continually evaluated and modified. New diseases emerge, as do new perspectives on existing diseases, and with advances in medical knowledge, PBL cases become outdated. For this reason, it is essential to have a formal process for reviewing PBL cases at least every 2 or 3 years. We prominently record the date of the last case review in our Tutor Guides, so that everybody is aware of the currency of the case.

The PBL tutors also have an important role in ensuring the content of PBL cases and in monitoring the manner in which the case succeeds in generating the desired learning outcomes and in stimulating student learning. In our three schools, we have a formal process of getting tutor feedback on each and every PBL case and this information is fed back to the case reviewers. Tutors are also formally responsible for monitoring student attendance at PBL tutorials and the contribution that individual students make to the process. At Flinders and Limerick, tutors hold regular formal meetings with individual students throughout the year to give them one-on-one feedback on their performance within PBL. At St George's, group feedback is preferred. We also ask our students to systematically review the PBL cases on a weekly basis and the performance of PBL tutors on a module basis and use the information received to enhance the quality of cases and the quality of tutor performance.

Associated Needs

As with capacity building in the initial stages, as described earlier, PBL also has particular associated needs in its maintenance phase. The need for library and IT support is substantial and ongoing, as is the need for administrative support.

Challenges and Solutions at Three Different Institutions

Challenges and Solutions in Building Capacity at Flinders

The Initial Phase

It is difficult to separate out the challenges in moving to PBL at Flinders from moving to a 4-year graduate-entry course because both processes occurred simultaneously. The move to PBL was seen as the more challenging, particularly as there had been a decision not to proceed with this approach some years previously (Prideaux & McCrorie, 2004). A key step was to invite a PBL group and tutor from Newcastle to deliver a tutorial in front of a large audience of staff. This demonstration of the power of PBL to stimulate student reasoning and the subsequent discussion with the students convinced the Flinders staff to adopt PBL (Prideaux, Farmer, & Rolfe, 1994).

The real challenge was to construct the 36 PBL cases for each of Years 1 and 2 and to train a cohort of staff to be tutors, while simultaneously designing new student selection processes and translating the curriculum content of a 6-year course to a 4-year one. Fortunately, Flinders received two crucial supports. At the time, the Australian government wished to sponsor reform in medical education and granted developmental funds to three schools: Flinders, Sydney, and Queensland. This enabled the schools to develop admissions tests, to form a consortium for co-operative planning and to establish medical education units; at the time, such units were rare in Australian medical schools. The government also allowed the schools to suspend student admissions for 2 years while retaining funding, thus giving staff valuable time for case writing.

Flinders devised several unique solutions in meeting the challenges and building capacity. The first was to recruit a new Dean from the University of Newcastle to lead the curriculum change and to provide the skills and vision to drive reform. A new participatory decision-making structure enabled staff to volunteer for the committees and working parties of their choice, thus fostering ownership and commitment to the new course (Prideaux & Lyons-Reid, 2000).

The existing 6-year course at Flinders was structured around blocks of integrated body systems and these were translated into the new course. Both clinicians and basic scientists were involved in case writing for each block. A key feature was a commitment to faculty development and staff members were encouraged to visit successful PBL medical schools such as McMaster,

Maastricht, and Harvard. A medical education fellowship enabled international staff to spend significant periods of time at Flinders. The case writing and tutor training process was heavily influenced by Stewart Mennin from the University of New Mexico, who took the Foundation Waterman Visiting Fellowship in Medical Education at Flinders. Tutor training was, and continues to be, a key investment. A 2-day programme involving observation, direct experience, and input from experienced tutors was developed and continues to this day.

Finally, the school obtained a commitment and dedicated funds from the university to invest in new infrastructure, including purpose-built tutorial rooms, robust IT systems, and additional library resources. Having PBL as part of a major reform, together with a move to graduate-entry, facilitated access to this funding.

The Maintenance Phase

The Flinders programme has now operated for 14 years and PBL remains a key element. The intensive system of working parties and committees was not sustainable as the school moved from initial implementation to maintenance; it has been replaced by year-level committees reporting to an overall curriculum committee. Tutor training continues and, with the employment of more sessional staff, this remains a priority.

Continued case review and modification is essential for the cases to maintain currency and clinical relevance. From the very beginning, Flinders put evaluation and feedback mechanisms in place to underpin the processes of case review. Maintaining this has been a significant challenge as original case writers have moved on and teaching loads have increased. Flinders has been significantly aided in the review process by its partnerships with other medical schools; the PBL cases have been used at St George's and Limerick and the school has licensed two new Australian medical schools at Griffith and Deakin to use its whole curriculum. In providing curriculum materials, including PBL cases, to other schools, there is an imperative to ensure that they are current.

The increased use of information technology and flexible learning has also facilitated active review of PBL. Flinders first used printed versions of its PBL material, but now delivers all the cases online, with savings of paper and more flexible access for students. Many students bring wireless-enabled laptops to tutorials allowing greater flexibility for searches and access to Internet-based resources. Initially, this provided a challenge, as there was concern about students giving more attention to their laptops than to the PBL process; it is now considered a process issue for tutors and students to negotiate.

Currently, Flinders is undergoing a review of its whole curriculum. While this review is focused on the school's commitment to social accountability and engagement with health service partners, a review of PBL is also a key component. Flinders is also observing developments at some of the PBL pioneers (McMaster and Maastricht) as it examines its own model of PBL. So far, one clear commitment has been a decision to give students more responsibility for the conduct of tutorials as they become more experienced with PBL. Some of the later blocks in the course have reduced tutor time and encourage more student-led tutorials. This renews and refreshes student interest and involvement. Some final-year students have taken a medical education elective that includes tutor training, and have proved to be effective tutors.

In the school's view, PBL is not, nor should it be, static and unchanging; to remain a key educational strategy, it needs to incorporate new theories and approaches to learning. In particular, PBL needs to adapt to the learning styles of new students who enter medical schools with an increased understanding and ability to use information communication technology in its many forms.

Challenges and Solutions in Building Capacity at St George's
The Initial Phase
St George's was lucky from two perspectives. First, the graduate-entry programme was new to St George's – indeed new to the UK. For this reason, quite a number of external staff was recruited specifically to take part in a PBL course. With only 35 initial students, a small number of tutors was required and these were hand-picked, partly from the new staff, partly from enthusiastic existing staff. Second, the school had the benefit of 2 weeks of tailored faculty development delivered by experts and enthusiasts from Flinders; they provided training on the principles and process of PBL, on facilitating PBL, on writing PBL cases, on assessing and evaluating a PBL programme, and on dealing with difficult students. Furthermore, the enthusiasm of both the new and existing staff enabled cases to be updated, revised, and rewritten with surprising ease. There was even sufficient energy for the time-consuming task of developing new cases.

The Maintenance Phase
St George's problems came later, particularly in maintaining the interest and commitment of staff. Eight years after the course began, not a single person who was actively and enthusiastically tutoring in 2000 remained as a PBL tutor. This was due to staff leaving, assuming other responsibilities, and/or burnout. In addition, tutors repeatedly dropped out of facilitating individual sessions, resulting in a real lack of continuity for the students. Consequently, one group had a different tutor for every session in an entire module. This was unacceptable.

Three approaches were taken. First, tutors who were unable to commit to a full term's teaching of 6 hours per week were *paired* with each other. Second, St George's employed an increasing number of senior students as peer tutors; this had its good and bad points. Students learned really useful skills, revisited their knowledge base, understood the clinical perspective of all of the cases, were paid, and made very popular facilitators. On the negative side, they missed out on 6 hours *each week* of their clinical programme, which is short enough in a 4-year fast-track programme. By being selective about which students were used, the benefits generally outweighed the disadvantages.

The third solution was the most successful – the employment of *sessional tutors*. Being paid by the hour solely for being a PBL facilitator ensured commitment, enthusiasm, and almost 100% attendance. Therefore, St George's gained much greater stability among its tutors without the need to rely wholly on full-time staff. However, all of this came at a price. The salaries of full-time staff were covered in the school's existing budget, while the employment of sessional tutors required new expenditure. The sessional tutors are considerably cheaper than the full-time staff, since they have little in the way of overheads. The argument against recruiting full-time staff as PBL tutors is that they can do more harm than good, if they are not committed and enthusiastic. However, there are contrary views and some resent the need to spend yet more money on teaching.

Over time, aside from the difficulty in maintaining PBL tutors, other carefully thought out ideas have fallen by the wayside, owing to exhaustion and apathy. The pre- and post-PBL briefings, so useful at the start of the course, eventually became a bit of a chore and attendance dropped off until there became little point in holding them.

Challenges and Solutions in Building Capacity at UL

The Initial Phase

Building initial capacity to deliver PBL was a particular challenge for UL, as its medical school received government approval just 5 months before the first student intake. However, UL had earlier reached agreement with St George's to use the SGUL/Flinders curriculum and, with it, had access to the PBL cases. There was something of a race against time to customise the cases to the Irish setting. By the time of the first UL student intake, the cases had been in use for 11 years at Flinders and for 7 years at St George's, so that the cases and the associated Student and Tutor Guides were well developed and required little modification. For most of the cases, input from one or two people, over a few hours, was sufficient to have them ready for use. This contrasts with the need for a team of people working on each case for several months at Flinders, before the cases were even ready to be trialled. At UL there was no particular pressure to have all of the cases fully revised before the first student intake.

The task at UL was also made appreciably easier through having just 32 students in four PBL groups in its first intake. The recruitment of four PBL tutors for the first year was relatively easy, though the school ensured that those recruited were of high calibre, both in terms of their content and process expertise. Furthermore, we sourced an experienced tutor trainer from

Flinders, who worked with the first group of tutors over a 3-month period to develop their tutoring skills and to enhance their self-confidence. At the start of the second year, the same tutor trainer returned to UL, this time training both novice and experienced tutors in the PBL process. By the start of the third year, UL had built up sufficient expertise in PBL to be able to dispense with the need for an overseas tutor trainer.

The need for tutorial rooms was also incremental, with just two rooms being required in the first year and four in the second year. Here again, UL had little difficulty in sourcing and equipping the space that it required. Administrative support for PBL was estimated at less than one full-time person in the first year and less than two people in the second year.

The Maintenance Phase

At the time of writing, the Graduate Entry Medical School at UL is still very much in development. However, it is now possible to accurately predict the school's structure and the manner in which it will function in the years ahead. In its third year, the need for PBL tutors increased to 18 and, ultimately, 30 tutors will be required. To date, unsolicited approaches from people seeking to tutor in PBL has greatly exceeded our requirements. There are, perhaps, a number of reasons for this. First and, perhaps, most important, we have benchmarked the rate of pay for our sessional staff against payment rates for principals in General Practice. Thus, we have removed any financial disincentive that clinicians would otherwise face in being PBL tutors. Second, our academic year in Years 1 and 2 runs for 33 weeks only, with relatively long breaks over traditional holiday periods. This makes PBL tutoring particularly attractive to people with family and other commitments. Third, our tutors constantly tell us that they find PBL to be immensely enjoyable and rewarding. This positive view of PBL is disseminated to other potential tutors largely by word of mouth.

Final Considerations

In many respects what has been outlined here is only part of the story. The adoption of PBL has a ripple effect on other parts of the curriculum. The PBL process can be subverted by assessment methods which concentrate on factual recall. Thus, the initial phase of adoption of PBL is likely to involve more than just the implementation of PBL. It may well require an overhaul of assessment to find ways of assessing knowledge that is compatible with the PBL process. All three schools have adopted non-grading policies in the early years of their courses to counter excessive competition which may hinder group processes.

There are also important issues in the maintenance period. One issue is fostering critical debate about PBL and not allowing it to become an unquestioned orthodoxy. Problem-based learning was first created before the electronic revolution; it now needs to incorporate the new learning approaches that students bring to their studies. St George's has already embarked on such directions with the incorporation of virtual patients (VPs) into their cases. There are significant advances in our understanding of learning theory and the development of clinical reasoning. Problem-based learning needs to remain flexible in order to incorporate new developments in learning.

One of the main messages of this chapter is that initial and maintenance issues are challenging but not insurmountable, and addressing these issues is aided by collaboration. The success of the Flinders, St George's, and UL partnership now extends to two other Australian medical schools at Griffith and Deakin Universities. This is a good example of how hard work and energy at one institution can be shared by others while retaining the freedom to adapt and modify cases. While the task of revising cases is significant, it is not in the same league as starting from scratch. The fact that the Flinders cases have easily "translated" across 10,000 miles is surely proof that the globalisation of education works. Furthermore, the flow of cases is not just in one direction. When adapting a PBL curriculum, schools inevitably seek to improve the course and the changes made are worth feeding back to the original source. The same argument applies to other educational resources. St George's has produced extensive educational materials, mainly in electronic format, which have been made available to both UL and Flinders.

Progressive release PBL is a successful learning method for graduate entrants to medicine. There is much to be gained from a collaborative approach to its development and implementation.

References

Finucane, P., Shannon, W., & McGrath, D. (2009). The financial costs of delivering problem-based learning in a new, graduate-entry medical programme. *Medical Education, 43*, 594–598.

Kaufman, A. (1985). *Implementing problem-based education: Lessons from successful innovations.* New York, Springer.

McCrorie, P. (2001). Tales from Tooting: Reflections on the first year of the MBBS graduate entry programme at St George's Hospital Medical School. *Medical Education, 35*, 1144–1149.

Prideaux, D., & Lyons-Reid, A. (2000). Is participation in curriculum change sufficient? Towards a culture for change in medical education. *Focus on Health Professional Education, 2*(1), 58–66.

Prideaux, D., & McCrorie, P. (2004). Models for the development of graduate entry medical courses: Two case studies. *Medical Education, 38*, 1169–1175.

Prideaux, D., Farmer, E., & Rolfe, I. (1994). Faculty development in problem based learning. *ANZAME Bulletin, 21*, 17–20.

Sefton, A., Prideaux, D., & Price, D. (1999). Decisions in problem-based learning: Experiences from three Australian medical schools. *Focus on Health Professional Education, 1*, 1–16.

Further Resources

PBL discussion list

You can put a question to the discussion group on the following link: to find out who around the world is using PBL in your discipline: www.jiscmail.ac.uk/cgi-bin/wa.exe?SUBED1=pbl&A=1.

16

Empowering Tutors

Strategies for Inspired and Effective Facilitation of PBL Learning

Deirdre Connolly and Charlotte Silén

Introduction

Guiding students through the problem-based learning (PBL) process is often a challenging element of PBL. The range of literature and research on the effect of different tutoring styles on students' learning, on group functioning, and group dynamics all point to the important influence of the tutor in the PBL process (Barrows, 1988; Connolly, 2009; Neville, 1999; Savin-Baden & Howell Major, 2004; Schmidt & Moust, 2000; Silén, 2006). In this chapter, we bring our knowledge, experiences, and research of PBL tutoring together and suggest some useful strategies for inspired and effective tutoring. This chapter focuses on four elements of the PBL process that tutors need to consider and understand, namely: problem analysis, the group process, students' learning processes and developing students' metacognitive processes. New concepts of tutoring are introduced, such as the tutors' ability to be "present" during the tutorials, along with strategies to achieve attentiveness during tutorials. Research on students' evaluations and perceptions of their PBL tutors also provide fresh insights into tutor behaviours.

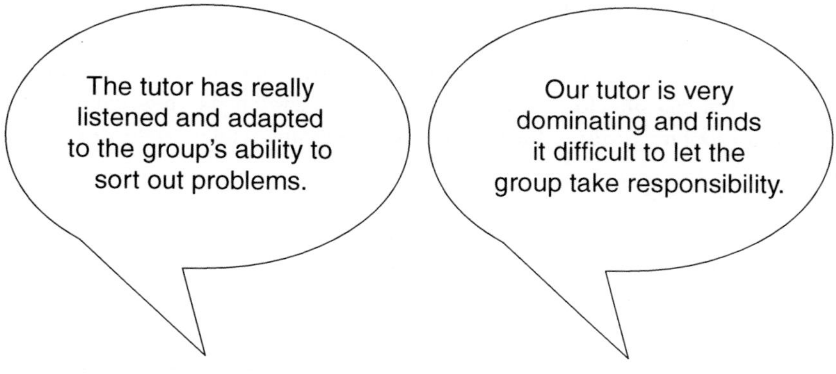

> The tutor has really listened and adapted to the group's ability to sort out problems.

> Our tutor is very dominating and finds it difficult to let the group take responsibility.

Figure 16.1 Students' perceptions of their tutor (Silén, 2006, p. 375).

Chapter Overview

This chapter is presented in three sections:

1. theoretical dimensions of PBL tutoring;
2. transferable practices and principles of PBL tutoring; and
3. a strategy for developing PBL tutor facilitation skills.

Theoretical Dimensions of PBL Tutoring

Learning Processes in PBL

In PBL, students formulate problems, identify learning needs, search for knowledge, study, and apply their knowledge. The centre of the learning context is the small tutorial group, comprising six to nine students and a tutor. The tutor's function is that of facilitator – someone who builds on and guides the students' own learning processes. The tutor needs to function on a metacognitive level: challenging and encouraging inquiry, stimulating reflection, and helping students to engage in critical appraisal (Barrows, 1988; Boud & Feletti, 1997; Dolmans, 1994; Rideout, 2001; Savin-Baden, 2003; Wilkerson, 1995).

In PBL, the students' analytical learning strategies, aimed at self-directedness in learning, is emphasised. The theoretical underpinning of PBL and self-directed learning has its roots in adult education (Candy, 1991; Knowles, 1984), pragmatism (Dewey, 1911, 1916), cognitive psychology (Boekaerts, 1997; Gijselaers, 1996; Norman & Schmidt, 1992), meaningful learning (Marton & Booth, 1997; Marton, Hounsell, & Entwistle, 1997; Ramsden, 2003), and social constructivism (Boud, 1988; Säljö, 1997). Silén (2003) argues that the process of self-directed learning should be looked on as a joint process in which students, tutors, and curriculum developers are all engaged. These different parties should each play a role in the process and interaction between teachers, students, and curriculum designers is essential. This interaction includes communication, dialogue, reflection, negotiations, and active participation in constructing the learning context, and the development of meta-cognitive competencies in relation to learning. Chapter 9 discussed the theoretical and practical implications of conceptualising the PBL tutorial as a potential site for dialogic knowing. Chapter 11 highlighted the importance of maximising the tutorial for developing student reflection.

The Tutorial Session

In the tutorial session, several intertwined processes occur: problem analysis, the group process, students' learning processes, and students' struggling for metacognitive awareness (Silén, 2009; Silén & Uhlin, 2008). The reality-based situations presented in the group, such as a patient case, a public health problem, or an interprofessional issue, are the core of the enquiry process. This enquiry process springs from and evolves according to the approach taken by the students to the reality-based situation. Thus, these situations form a basis for thinking and learning that is concrete and meaningful and allow the students to see clearly what the focus of interpretation and analysis should be. The students' learning processes become visible in their reasoning, problem solving, critical thinking, and behaviour. In the tutorial session, students analyse, explain, and appraise phenomena based on theory and apply their theory to a real situation.

Generally, one of the key ways in which learning processes can be made more meaningful and effective is to provide opportunities for learners to grasp relationships between parts and wholes by providing a meaningful context for learning (Fyrenius, Wirell, & Silén, 2007; Marton & Booth, 1997; Marton et al., 1997). And, as explored earlier in Parts I and II of this book, the importance of meaningful learning is constantly emphasised within the PBL context.

Learning can be made more meaningful by enhancing the relevance, significance, value, and usefulness of learning. Meaningfulness is closely linked to the concept of "preunderstanding" (Marton & Booth, 1997) which refers to knowledge, conceptions, and perceptions carried by the learner encountering new situations. These perceptions influence the learner's approach in a learning situation and also constitute the basis for creating meaning. All these dimensions of meaningfulness depend on the learner having the opportunity to relate to a context that is interesting, valued, and that somehow stimulates the will to learn. In PBL, the realistic situations used in tutorials are meant to serve as meaningful contexts for the students' learning – and the benefits of using these situations, as learning triggers, have been explored from a range of perspectives throughout this book.

Tutoring

The tutor's own understanding of PBL influences his/her readiness to intervene and facilitate in the processes described above. According to Silén (2006), PBL processes need tutors who are extremely engaged, responsive, and fully present while in the learning group. Tutors need to base their activities and interventions on what the students do; in order to do this, the tutor must focus attention on the students and what is happening in the group. The tutor concentrates on what the students do and say, and on what they do *not* do and say – and, by keeping a distance and trying to remain objective, observes the mood in the group. This approach creates opportunities for the tutor to pay attention to the way students analyse the problem, the group processes, the students' learning processes, and their metacognitive awareness. Based on such observations, the tutor can respond to and build on the students' ongoing learning activities.

How does a tutor become engaged, responsive, and fully present in order to facilitate the students' learning processes? We believe that it is necessary for tutors to recognise that the development of these skills is an ongoing learning process. Tutor training cannot be a single event; instead, it must be offered on a regular basis and be guided by the existing knowledge about student-centred learning and PBL. The principles and philosophy of PBL and the underlying theories must be activated in the tutor. In addition to acquiring strategies to manage group dynamics, it is also essential to experience the learning processes in PBL, both as a learner and as a tutor. Feedback from students and colleagues and continuous reflection on the tutor's function are also essential elements of tutor development. In the next section, we will present:

- examples of typical tutorial situations and elaborate how these situations have informed the writers' tutoring practices;
- a strategy for development of tutor functioning and facilitation skills.

Transferable Principles and Practices of PBL Tutoring

Transferable principles and practices for tutoring, are discussed in relation to four elements of PBL, namely: problem analysis, the group process, students' learning processes, and developing students' metacognitive awareness. In addition to the authors' experiences of tutoring, this section is informed by research carried out with occupational therapy students on their evaluations and perceptions of their PBL tutors.

Problem Analysis

In our experiences of PBL tutoring, we have found that students new to PBL often tend to rush through the PBL process. Sometimes the students hurry through the initial analysis and discussion of a trigger/scenario and, instead, focus on identifying goals for their independent study periods. Students often need to be encouraged to recognise the importance of using the full time allotted during tutorials to consider the problem. Instead of diving in to solve the problem, they sometimes need to be given the confidence to activate their own relevant prior knowledge and apply this knowledge to the problem/ trigger. Students may also need assistance in recognising that they have a wealth of prior knowledge, both through formal learning experiences and through their own personal and life experiences. The tutor can facilitate this recognition by asking questions that will assist students to activate relevant prior knowledge.

Within the PBL process, other important activities are identifying and deciding on learning goals, which should also help to direct the students' self-study periods. The difficulties that we have observed with this element of the process include the students setting learning goals that are broad and/or ambiguous. This situation can occur when students identify general areas for study rather than identifying specific components of a topic to be studied.

Consequently, the students then gather very different levels of information on a broad topic. Some PBL students have reported inconsistencies in the tutors' involvement in setting learning goals and have found it helpful when the tutor asks the students to formulate specific goals as opposed to identifying general areas of practice to be researched:

> Some of the tutors would say put that into a proper sentence to make it clear for everyone. It did actually help to make it specific and helped to identify what was the most important thing to spend the most amount of study time on. It was also helpful if they indicated where the majority of reading should be.
>
> **(Connolly, 2009, p. 6)**

Assisting students in establishing clearly stated learning goals helps direct the students to the type of information that they need to acquire for the follow-up PBL tutorial. It also helps the students to identify which elements of the learning goals to focus on during their independent study periods. In our experience, ambiguous and non-specific learning goals can result in students returning to subsequent tutorials with very fragmented areas of knowledge, which can then result in disjointed discussions. Students, therefore, have fewer opportunities to integrate their own knowledge with that of other students or to actively construct new understandings of knowledge as facilitated through group discussions (Hmelo-Silver, 2004; Norman & Schmidt, 1992). Discussions in groups where students have not had a clear understanding of their learning goals results in the superficial understanding of knowledge (Schmidt, 1993).

Group Process

In PBL, the students' active participation in tutorial discussions is important for two reasons. First, it provides an opportunity for students to elaborate their understanding of their knowledge (active construction of knowledge). Second, it provides a range of perspectives on knowledge gained through self-study which helps to increase the students' understanding of the newly acquired knowledge.

Some PBL students identified differences in the tutors' abilities to encourage all of the students to participate actively in tutorial discussions (Connolly, 2009). One of the roles of the student chairperson is to ensure that all students have an opportunity to contribute their knowledge and understanding of the triggers (Savin-Baden & Howell Major, 2004). Engaging all students may require some interventions that restrict the contributions of dominant students so that the quieter students have opportunities to contribute. In this study, the students stated that they had difficulty in managing dominant students who were also their peers and friends. One approach to managing this is for tutors to articulate for the students the differences between the role of the tutor and that of the chairperson. The tutor is there as a guide to facilitate student learning (Barrows, 1986). If students are clearly informed about the expectations of the chairperson, this may eliminate personal issues and enable the chairperson to manage their peers in a way that supports group functioning.

Students, who are new to PBL may require more guidance from tutors. The students may need a role model to help them consider what to do in difficult group situations. In this respect, tutors can model behaviours that are effective in containing dominant students and encouraging non-participating students. Students can then apply these behaviours and strategies, refining them over time, to suit their own personal group facilitation style. In order for students to appreciate the importance of developing these skills, the tutors can emphasise the necessity of these skills for the students' future professional practice and identify the PBL environment as an opportunity to practise these skills.

Schmidt and Moust (2000) contend that, to stimulate the students' participation in tutorials, a tutor should have an interest in the interpersonal dynamics of the group, be sensitive to group development processes, and be able to manage interpersonal conflicts. One approach in helping to manage group dynamics is to give feedback to the group regarding their performance from both a group perspective and individually. Students often state that they require feedback in relation to their contributions to the group process:

> Give more feedback regarding personal performance in the group; give more positive feedback to students when they contribute to the group and give individual and group feedback to enable students to have some degree of knowledge of their performance in the group.
>
> **(Connolly, 2009, p. 8)**

Feedback should be given to students on a regular basis. Tutors have a responsibility to ensure that adequate time is allocated regularly in order to provide constructive feedback to the group on how they are functioning as a group and in managing the PBL process. Sloboda (2001) explains that students cannot improve their performance unless they have a means of judging their present performance and receive guidance on how to make the necessary changes. Rogers (2001) provided a guide for giving student feedback and maintained that such feedback should be specific, timely, relevant, objective, balanced, and enthusiastic. In Figure 16.2, we present some useful guidelines for giving student feedback during the PBL process.

Tutor interest in the students' activities is recognised as an important element of tutoring (Dolmans, DeGrave, Wolfhagen, & van den Vleuten, 2005). In an occupational therapy study, the students identified tutor behaviours that they found confusing and distracting; some of the behaviours cited by the study's participants included tutors appearing withdrawn and

Specific: Support feedback with clear examples of student performance during tutorials.
Timely: Feedback should be given regularly such as at the end of each tutorial or every other tutorial.
Relevant: Feedback should clearly relate to students' learning activities within the PBL process.
Objective: Feedback should focus on how performance impacts on individual and group learning.
Balanced: Feedback should include effective and non-effective aspects of student and group performance.
Enthusiastic: Clearly explain to students how feedback can help with PBL and their future professional practice.

Figure 16.2 Guidelines for student feedback in PBL tutorials.

uninterested, tutors not making eye contact with whoever was speaking, and tutors making notes during the tutorial discussions. Students discussed the impact of these behaviours:

> Sometimes, the tutor can seem like they are not listening at all. They can seem totally withdrawn. Sometimes that can be off-putting when you are trying to say something and you think you are saying something wrong or irrelevant because he or she is not listening.
>
> **(Connolly, 2003, p. 11)**

A common concern for PBL students is whether they have acquired relevant and sufficient knowledge and, therefore, often they rely on the tutor to validate their learning (Connolly & Donovan, 2002; Raine & Symons, 2005; Silén, 2001). Occupational therapy students recommended that this could be achieved, for example, by the tutor giving some form of non-verbal confirmation during student contributions (Connolly, 2009). Schmidt and Moust (2000) contend that the interpersonal qualities of the tutor have an important influence on student learning. Without genuine and personal interest in the students' learning, tutors would not have the necessary motivation to help the students achieve their learning tasks.

Student Learning Processes

In PBL, an important aspect of student learning is the discussions that occur within tutorials. The literature indicates that it is through group discussion that students consolidate their learning and put newly acquired knowledge in context with a range of knowledge brought forward by all students (Dolmans & Schmidt, 2000; Hmelo-Silver, 2004, 2009). Elaboration of knowledge and opportunities to clarify understanding of the group learning goals assist in retention of knowledge and the ability to apply this knowledge to other contexts (Norman & Schmidt, 1992). In our experiences as tutors, we have observed that students are reluctant to question their peers on their contributions or enter into debates regarding the relevance of knowledge discussed in tutorials. Students often state that, as the group members are their peers, they view this form of debate as antagonistic as opposed to an appropriate aspect of group discussions. In order to prepare students for this aspect of PBL, during their induction, students should be informed of the importance of questioning and debating with their peers. In the initial stages of implementing PBL, tutors can also role model these behaviours and demonstrate to students how to pose questions that encourage debate without incurring negative reactions from their peers.

The PBL literature gives much attention to the impact of tutors providing knowledge and relating their professional experiences during group tutorials (Davis & Harden, 1999; Dolmans et al., 2002; Schmidt, 1994). Neville (1999) maintained that students who are new to PBL require more input than students who are experienced in the process. The occupational therapy students valued the input from tutors regarding their professional experiences and sharing information regarding the realities of professional practice. However, they also requested that these interventions be short and focused, as tutors who over-contributed to the group discussion deflected the discussion away from the direction in which the students wished to bring it:

> Sometimes the tutor intervenes and gives their tuppence worth, or whatever, but then goes on and on and on and everyone else is sitting there and listening to this example. It takes over from everyone else giving their points of view.
>
> **(Connolly, 2009, p. 6)**

For students to manage over-contributing tutors, they require the necessary skills and confidence to manage these situations. This can be a difficult task for students, particularly if the tutors concerned are also involved in their assessment. During the student preparation sessions, tutors should discuss with the students how the chairperson can monitor the contributions from the tutors in relation to knowledge input, so as not to interfere with the flow of the student discussions. By doing this, the tutors are informing the students about what is expected of them and are providing them with "permission" to interrupt tutors. During the PBL preparation sessions, the tutors can add more weight to the necessity for students doing this by relating these skills to their future professional work practices.

Developing Student Metacognitive Processes

Zimmerman (2002, p. 65) defines metacognition as "an awareness and knowledge of one's own thinking and learning" and contends that the students' difficulties in learning are often related to a lack of metacognitive awareness of their learning limitations. In his book *The Idea of Higher Education*, Barnett (1990) maintained that higher education processes must promote the students' abilities to critically evaluate their learning performances and achievements in order to justify the title of "higher education". Originally, problem-based learning was designed to facilitate the students' development of their metacognitive skills. Barrows defines self-evaluation and reflection on learning activities as a critical element of the PBL process (Barrows, 1988).

An important role of a PBL tutor, therefore, is to foster the students' commitment and ability to evaluate their learning activities. However, in order for students to undertake this process, they must first acquire the necessary skills to evaluate (1) how they learn and (2) the effectiveness of their learning strategies and activities. In the initial stages, the tutor can act as a role-model by posing questions which facilitate the students' awareness and evaluation of their learning. Such questions should focus on the type of learning activities in which the students are engaged and on how effective they perceive these approaches to be in achieving the group's learning goals. Figure 16.3 provides examples of the types of questions tutors can ask students at the end of the tutorial. Hmelo-Silver (2004) stresses that a PBL tutor must model the types of questions that the students need to ask themselves in order to evaluate their learning. She stated that, in doing so, the tutor externalises self-reflection which ultimately facilitates the development of metacognitive skills.

Miflin, Campbell, and Price (2000) noted that adults often do not want to decide on how and what they should learn, particularly when they are in unfamiliar learning environments. Students who have previously been exposed to traditional methods of teaching and learning may have difficulty adapting to this new way of learning. Savin-Baden and Howell Major (2004)

• How did you approach your learning?
• What have you learned?
• What did you contribute to the learning?
• What learning resources did you use?
• How effective were these learning strategies?
• What would/could you do differently to improve your learning?

Figure 16.3 Questions to facilitate development of metacognitive processes.

contend that students have to make philosophical and behavioural changes in order to participate in student-centred and active approaches to learning, thus highlighting the importance of adequately preparing students for engaging in PBL methods. Student preparation should include an understanding of the underlying principles of PBL and the expectations placed on students when participating in PBL. In particular, the necessity for students to learn how to learn within an increasingly changing and contestable world should be emphasised.

A Strategy for Development of PBL Facilitation Skills: Spaces for Reflection

As discussed earlier, development of facilitation skills should be an ongoing learning process for the tutor. Based on our experiences and research, we believe that an important element of a tutors' learning is reflection on their tutorial experiences. The tutor, as a learner, needs to construct his/her own understanding of being a tutor. Therefore, tutoring experiences need to be analysed, linked to theory, and applied to future tutorial functioning. Our suggestion for a strategy to empower and enhance tutor functioning builds on the idea of creating and recognising "spaces for reflection" (Savin-Baden, 2007).

One important space for reflection occurs during the tutorial itself. At the end of a tutorial, the students' feedback is a valuable source for reflection and there are many ways to elicit student feedback. For example, feedback can be included in the regular tutorial evaluation by asking students specific questions such as whether the questions asked were helpful to their learning process. Students can also give written feedback to the tutor at regular intervals which can be general or may focus on certain issues such as whether tutor interventions were appropriate or helpful. The tutorial session, as a space for reflection, becomes "richer" if the tutor discusses with students their own reflections and self-evaluations of their tutoring approaches. The quality of the students' feedback on these reflections will depend on the tutor's ability to create a climate in which the students feel safe and motivated to give honest feedback. Students usually do not, and should not, focus on what the tutor is doing, but on how this influences their own learning. Inviting a colleague, as a learning partner, to a tutorial session creates another opportunity both for input from another perspective and for reflection. This learning partner can observe the tutor's behaviours in relation to the students' learning. Feedback from a learning partner can be used in combination with the students' feedback as a space for reflection.

PBL tutors can also create spaces for reflection through reflective teams. For example, one tutor may present a tutorial situation to other tutors. The group then asks questions of the tutor and discusses the problem, while the tutor listens without making any further comments or input. The session ends with an open discussion between the tutor and the group. A variation of reflective teams is the situation in which a number of tutors role-play a tutorial session to other tutors which is then followed by discussion and reflections regarding the tutors' approaches.

Data from the tutorial sessions can also be brought to the tutors' meetings, where tutor functioning is discussed. This creates a different space for reflection. The data might consist of written or oral reports from students or the tutor themselves and may, with the students' permission, also include audio- or video-recordings of a tutorial.

As shown in Figure 16.4, the spaces for reflection described above are not stand-alone strategies. Each space for reflection can be used alongside another in order to inform discussions and reflections on PBL tutoring. Our suggestions are intended to demonstrate possibilities for individual tutors and groups of tutors to create spaces for reflection with different characteristics and are not meant to be exhaustive.

Conclusion

The purpose of this chapter is to empower PBL tutors to develop and revitalise their tutoring practices. We set about this by debating current knowledge about learning processes related to PBL tutorials, presenting four elements of

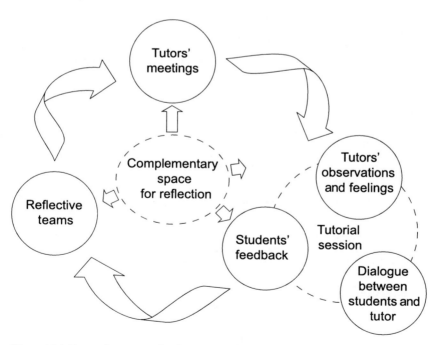

Figure 16.4 Spaces for tutor reflection processes.

tutor functioning and a strategy for tutor development. The notion of creating spaces for reflection, as a way to inspire tutors is consistent with learning in PBL. These spaces for development of PBL tutors are important in creating sustainable PBL initiatives. Tutors are provided with tools and "food" for thinking about tutoring, which can be used during tutorial sessions. From a staff development perspective, tutor empowerment is an ongoing process that is achieved through continuous reflection and dialogue with students and other PBL tutors.

Finally, we ask you to revisit the student quotations at the beginning of this chapter (Figure 16.1):

- What do you think about these student quotations now?
- How can you use the chapter contents to understand your tutoring practices and to develop your own and your curriculum teams' practice?

References

Barnett, R. (1990). *The idea of higher education*. Buckingham: Society for Research into Higher Education and Open University Press.

Barrows, H.S. (1986). A taxonomy of problem based learning methods. *Medical Education, 20*, 481–486.

Barrows, H.S. (1988). *The tutorial process*. Springfield, IL: Southern Illinois University Press.

Boekaerts, M. (1997). Self-regulated learning: A new concept embraced by researchers, policy makers, educators, teachers and students. *Learning and Instruction, 7*(2), 161–186.

Boud, D. (Ed.). (1988). *Developing student autonomy in learning* (2nd ed.). London: Kogan Page.

Candy, P. (1991). *Self-direction for lifelong learning*. San Francisco: Jossey-Bass Publishers.

Connolly, D. (2003). *The role of problem-based learning tutors in an occupational therapy curriculum*. Unpublished doctoral paper, University of Lancaster.

Connolly, D. (2009). PBL tutors facilitating active learning: What do students value? In *Proceedings, Improving University Teaching*, Vancouver, 14–17 July.

Connolly, D., & Donovan, M. (2002). Introducing a problem-based learning module into an occupational therapy course. *Learning in Health and Social Care, 1*(3), 150–157.

Davis, M.H., & Harden R.M. (1999). AMEE Medical Education Guide No. 15: Problem-based learning: A practical guide. *Medical Teacher, 21*(2), 130–140.

Dewey, J. (1911). *How we think*. New York: Prometheus Books.

Dewey, J. (1916). *Democracy and education*. New York: Macmillan.

Dolmans, D.H.J., & Schmidt, H. (2000). What directs self-directed learning in a problem-based learning curriculum? In D.H. Evensen & C.E. Hmelo (Eds.), *Problem-based learning: A research perspective on learning interactions* (pp. 251–262). London: Lawrence Erlbaum Associates.

Dolmans, D.H.J., DeGrave, W., Wolfhagen, I.H.A.P., & van der Vleuten, C.P.M. (2005). Problem-based learning: Future challenges for educational practice and research. *Medical Education, 39*, 732–741.

Dolmans, D., Gijselaers, W.H., Moust, J.H.C., de Grave, W.S., Wolfhagen, I., & van der Vleuten, C.P.M. (2002). Trends in research on the tutor in problem-based learning: Conclusions and implications for educational practice and research. *Medical Teacher, 24*(2), 173–180.

Fyrenius, A., Wirell, S., & Silén, C. (2007). Student approaches to achieving understanding: Approaches to learning revisited. *Studies in Higher Education, 32*(2), 149–165.

Gijselaers, W. (1996). Connecting problem-based practices with educational theory. In L. Wilkerson & W. Gijselaers (Eds.), *Bringing problem-based learning to higher education: Theory and practice. New Directions for Teaching and Learning* (nn. 68, 13–21). San Francisco: Jossey-Bass Publishers.

Hmelo-Silver, C.E. (2004). Problem-based learning: What and how do students learn? *Educational Psychology Review, 16*(3), 235–266.

Hmelo-Silver, C.E. (2009). What do we know about problem-based learning? Current status and future prospects. Keynote paper. In G. O'Grady (Ed.), *The 2nd International PBL Symposium proceedings. What are we learning about learning?* (pp. 2–19). Singapore: Republic Polytechnic, Centre for Education.

Knowles, M. (1984). *The adult learner: A neglected species* (3rd ed.). Houston: Gulf Publishing Company.

Marton, F., & Booth, S. (1997). *Learning and awareness.* Mahwah, NJ: Lawrence Erlbaum Associates.

Marton, F., Hounsell, D., & Entwistle, N. (1997). *The experience of learning* (2nd ed.). Edinburgh: Scottish Academic Press.

Miflin, B.M., Campbell, C.B., & Price, D.A. (2000). A conceptual framework to guide the development of self-directed, lifelong learning in a problem-based medical curriculum. *Medical Education, 34,* 299–306.

Neville, A.J. (1999). The problem-based learning tutor: Teacher? Facilitator? Evaluator? *Medical Teacher, 21*(4), 393–401.

Norman, G.R., & Schmidt, H.G. (1992). The psychological basis of problem-based learning: A review of the evidence. *Academic Medicine, 67*(9), 557–565.

Raine, D., & Symons, S. (2005). Experiences of PBL in physics in UK higher education. In E. Poikela & S. Poikela (Eds.), *PBL in context: Bridging work and Education* (pp. 67–78). Tampere: Tampere University Press.

Ramsden, P. (2003). *Learning to teach in higher education* (2nd ed.). London: Routledge Falmer.

Rogers, J. (2001). *Adults learning.* Buckingham: Society for Research into Higher Education and Open University Press.

Säljö, R. (1997). *Learning and discourse: A sociocultural perspective.* UK: British Psychological Society.

Savin-Baden, M. (2007). *Learning spaces: Creating opportunities for knowledge creation in academic life.* Buckingham: Open University Press.

Savin-Baden, M., & Howell Major, C. (2004). *Foundations of problem-based learning.* Buckingham: Society for Research into Higher Education and Open University Press.

Schmidt, H.G. (1993). Foundations of problem-based learning: Some explanatory notes. *Medical Education, 27,* 422–432.

Schmidt, H.G. (1994). Resolving inconsistencies in tutor expertise research: Does lack of structure cause students to seek tutor guidance? *Academic Medicine, 69*(8), 656–662.

Schmidt, H.G., & Moust, J.H.C. (2000). Factors affecting small-group tutorial learning: A review of research. In D.H. Evensen & C.E. Hmelo (Eds.), *Problem-based learning: A research perspective on learning interactions* (pp. 19–51). London: Lawrence Erlbaum Associates.

Silén, C. (2001). Between chaos and cosmos: A driving force for responsibility and independence in learning. In P. Little & P. Kandlbinder (Eds.), *The power of problem-based learning* (pp. 126–133). Newcastle, Australia: PROBLARC, The University of Newcastle.

Silén, C. (2003). Responsibility and independence in learning: What is the role of the educators and the framework of the educational programme? In C. Rust (Ed.), *Improving student learning: Theory, research and practice* (pp. 249–262). Oxford: The Oxford Centre for Staff and Learning Development.

Silén, C. (2006). The tutor's approach in base groups (PBL): A phenomenological approach. *Higher Education, 51*(3), 373–385.

Silén, C. (2009). Self-directed learning as learning process and a learning outcome. In G. O'Grady (Ed.), *The 2nd International PBL Symposium Proceedings* (pp. 112–120). Singapore: Republic Polytechnic, Centre for Education.

Silén, C., & Uhlin, L. (2008). Self-directed learning: A learning issue for students and faculty. *Teaching in Higher Education, 13*(4), 461–475.

Sloboda, J. (2001). What is skill and how is it acquired? In C. Paechter, M. Preedy, D. Scott, & J. Soler, J. (Eds.), *Knowledge, power and learning* (pp. 89–108). London: Sage.

Zimmerman, B.J. (2002). Becoming a self-regulated learner: An overview. *Theory into Practice, 41*(2), 64–70.

Further Resources

Centre for Excellence in Enquiry-Based Learning, The University of Manchester: www.manchester.ac.uk/ceebl/resources/evaluation.

The website provides a range of resources for students and staff using enquiry and problem-based learning. There is a pdf guide on facilitating small-group learning with useful information on helping students "go deeper" and giving student feedback.

University of Colorado, Centre for Instructional Support: www.uchsc.edu/CIS/PBLchkList.html;
www.uchsc.edu/CIS/SmGpchkList.html.
Both of these websites have checklists with a number of factors to consider during the
planning and implementation stages of PBL tutorials and small-group learning.
Centre for Leadership in Learning, McMaster University: www.mcmaster.ca/cll/inquiry/inquiry.
resources.htm#Problem.
This website provides a range of resources and other web links for many elements of the
PBL process, including a section on tutoring tips.

17

PBL Challenges Both Curriculum and Teaching

Sari Poikela and Ivan Moore

Introduction

Problem-based learning curriculum development requires commitment and collaboration from a wide range of people within any educational system if it is to be sustainable. Drawing on our own experience and research, we highlight, in particular, how important it is to identify essential core competences when starting to design PBL curricula.

As a total approach to education, PBL means not only the design of PBL curricula but also requires an exploration of:

- the teachers' orientations and ways of working collaboratively;
- the culture of the organisation; and
- the structuring of the learning environment and resources.

Chapter Overview

Drawing on a study in which teachers on a PBL programme were interviewed (S. Poikela, 2005) and on our combined PBL practice, we explore the insights and ideas of academics from a wide range of different disciplines (engineering, forestry, nursing, physiotherapy, information sciences, arts, and social sciences), and use these insights to discuss:

- the curriculum development issues that are crucial to the development of PBL;
- the issues of culture and climate; and
- the challenges that PBL presents for teachers' identities and roles.

Constructing Problem-based Curricula and Identifying Professional Core Competences

Savin-Badin (2000) identified five models of problem-based learning. These models are ideal types and are useful to us as PBL practitioners not only for locating our current PBL practice models in relation to these models but for identifying where on this spectrum we would like to situate the model for our future PBL initiatives. Savin-Baden (2000) identifies these five models as follows:

Model 1: PBL for Epistemological Competence;
Model 2: PBL for Professional Action;
Model 3: PBL for Interdisciplinary Learning;
Model 4: PBL for Transdisciplinary Learning;
Model 5: PBL for Critical Contestability.

In addition to these ideal types, Savin-Baden (2003, p. 4) has identified "modes of curriculum practice which are not ideal types of problem-based learning, but, instead, are understandings of what it is that we actually see going on inside curricula that utilize problem-based learning". These modes are very useful for categorising your current PBL practice and for future curriculum planning of new PBL initiatives. It helps you to clarify exactly what form of PBL you are using or would like to use. Seven modes of problem-based learning are named and described by Savin-Baden (2003) as follows:

Mode 1: Single Module Approach – one PBL module in final year of programme;
Mode 2: Problem-based Learning on a Shoestring – only some lecturers use PBL in a limited number of modules. This is done at minimal cost and there is no overall approach to PBL in the programme;
Mode 3: The Funnel Approach – PBL is used for the full final year of the programme;
Mode 4: The Foundation Approach – students are introduced to concepts and principles in the first year and then limited aspects of PBL followed by using a full PBL approach in the final year;
Mode 5: The Two-strand Approach – this approach combines a PBL approach with a mixed learning methods approach;
Mode 6: Patchwork Problem-based Learning – in this approach PBL is used in all modules but there is no comprehensive integrated framework for the programme;
Mode 7: The Integrated Approach – the whole programme uses PBL in an integrated comprehensive framework.

A completely integrated curriculum allows PBL to be implemented on a macro level across the entire curriculum. In particular, a cross-disciplinary approach is ideal as it allows problems to be linked with each other and is a strategy for transforming curricula. At its best, this integrated approach leads to fundamental pedagogical changes, the redirecting of teachers' work, and a transformation of the whole learning culture (Barrett, 2005; Chen, 2000; S. Poikela, 2003, 2005).

One of the key issues in this change process from a traditional curriculum to a PBL curriculum is the commitment of participants in an organisation, but even when commitment has been secured, change is never easy. In the words of one of the participants:

I think there have been as many difficulties as good experiences on the way. This is not easy in any way but the commitment is the most important question.

The idea of a long-term commitment to pedagogical changes was discussed closely among participants (S. Poikela, 2005). One of the informants evocatively compared the experience of pedagogical change to having a "cold shower" – which eloquently reflected what many people talk about when engaged in the transformation to a PBL curriculum – it is refreshing and stimulating, while at the same time feeling uncomfortable. There are fresh insights to be gained when colleagues or students start to question the sense of PBL-related changes, but it almost always requires people to step out of their comfort zones and to take a metaphorical cold shower in the process. Some of the informants came to realise that, even when highly motivated, it can take a long time to reorganise the idea and structure of the whole curriculum or even a single PBL module. There are many challenges faced by teachers new to PBL.

Seven Key Challenges for Teachers New to PBL

Challenge 1: Reorienting the Curriculum around Professional Competences

One of the main challenges PBL tutors face is to identify professional core competences and to put these competences, rather than their subject specialisms, at the core of the curriculum. This challenge often requires a shift in teaching and learning culture, identity, and practice.

Our research suggests repeatedly that teachers were often surprised by how difficult they experienced the reorientation and redesign of the curriculum. The identification of the most essential core competences, within any profession, even by experienced educators, seems to require careful thinking and substantial negotiation. Introducing a PBL curriculum often operates as a stimulus to facilitate the educators to articulate the really important competences that students need to develop.

Challenge 2: Shifting Roles – From Lecturer to PBL Tutor

Teachers who are moving to PBL often identify the increased demands on the nature of the PBL tutoring role. As one teacher put it:

[PBL] demands more from the teacher. It was much easier to just lecture one course for several groups of students and then just read their exams or essays. But in this case you need to be actively present and co-operate with the students for the longer period of time. You need also to face the difficulties appearing in a group and to face your own tiredness sometimes and even failures.

Teachers need support, training, and reflective spaces to help them develop as PBL tutors. Chapter 16 explored strategies for developing effective and inspiring PBL tutors.

Challenge 3: Supporting Self-directed Learning

In PBL curricula, the students need more guidance with independent studying, especially at the beginning of their studies. Self-directed learning requires practice by the students and more proactive engagement by learners (Poikela & Poikela, 2006); it also, crucially, requires support and scaffolding by PBL tutors. This support and scaffolding was described vividly by one of the engineering teachers:

> When we started with PBL we thought that students are so clever we only need to let them loose and they will do the job somehow. Then we realised nothing is happening.

Unless the range of resources are actively identified, and students become aware of and comfortable with drawing on the "total" learning environment, they may experience the PBL process as unstructured and frustrating. Teachers have to grapple with the idea of helping students develop and utilise a wide range of problem-solving strategies and sources.

Another fundamental element of PBL is a self-directed study period between tutorials, when students utilise several kinds of information resources. Common and shared information seeking focuses on theoretical and professional knowledge resources. The aim of this information seeking is to reach a sufficient understanding in order to allow closer exploration of the phenomena at hand. Information seeking can also be shared between participants by interviewing experts, seeking information on the Internet, or acquiring other knowledge based on experience (Poikela, 2001). Chapter 10 explored strategies for students developing information literacy in PBL programmes.

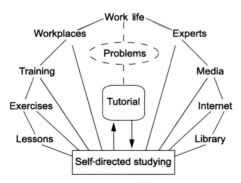

Figure 17.1 The PBL curriculum as a knowledge and learning environment (Poikela & Poikela, 2006, p. 76).

The result of this new way of integrating shared and self-study is to reduce the time spent in lectures and to increase the time for independent study and information seeking. Lectures become a learning resource, like any other type of study including professional literature, work-based training periods, and exercises. New kinds of demands are placed on the quality of the lectures and the exercises – they need to be tailored and timed according to the process of problem-based learning.

> I think a lecture can act as an awakening to information acquisition. Its aim is certainly not to provide answers. There was a time when we almost tried to avoid lectures but now we have realised what is the meaning of a lecture. I mean in its real and genuine sense as an important resource.

Challenge 4: Making PBL-based Pedagogical Connections with the Workplace

When work placement is part of the students' programme of study, it is essential that PBL tutors familiarise the workplace supervisors with the principles of PBL (Poikela, Vuoskoski, & Kärnä, 2009). It is often challenging to ensure that the work-based supervisors are fully briefed about the stages and schedules of the PBL process, and even for supervisors who are not involved; their role in assisting alignment can either enhance or diminish the impact of PBL.

> Supervisors of training periods are now interested in PBL as well. They want to know how it affects the time students spend at work. So, it is not only our university interested in PBL but the surrounding work life as well. We have started development projects involved in this.

See Chapters 3 and 7 for strategies for involving employers in PBL initiatives.

Challenge 5: Facilitating Deep Learning

Within the PBL tutorial, the capacity for deep learning is strong (Poikela, 2003; Silén, 2004). But if that capacity is to be authentically realised, the requirements of tutor engagement are substantial. Some new PBL tutors may mechanistically stick to the structured PBL process (see Figure 17.2), rather than creatively and flexibly using the tutorial process for meaningful, deep learning.

The tutorial phases in PBL are not designed to be rigid structures, though novice PBL practitioners may risk using them in this way. One respondent referred to the experience of a PBL tutorial process feeling more like an act ("a tutorial circus") rather than a place "where you could get a taste of real learning".

So, like anyone learning new skills, novice PBL tutors experience challenges and may approach their early PBL experiences in a way that risks being rigid

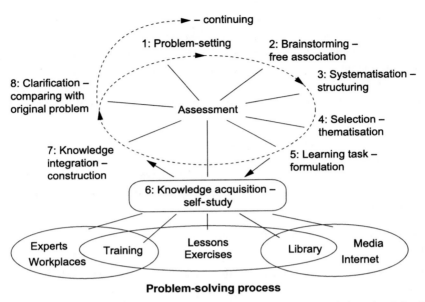

Figure 17.2 Problem-based learning cycle and knowledge acquisition (Poikela & Poikela, 2006, p. 78).

and non-responsive. Becoming a skilful tutor means also reflecting on earlier practices and unlearning how to teach (McWilliam, 2008). The development of responsive, vigilant, accomplished flexibility within the PBL process may be one of the most fundamental professional development challenges for PBL practitioners (S. Poikela, 2005). Chapter 9 discussed maximising the PBL tutorial for dialogic knowing.

Challenge 6: Confronting Resource Requirements

In the PBL curricula, the quality, relevance, and accessibility of learning resources are highly important as PBL students are working on current professional practice problems. From the earliest days of their studies, their access to relevant material, ideas, research, and tools is a major factor in the maintenance of their learning momentum. PBL tutors often find that they come face-to-face with resourcing difficulties and often talk about having to find creative ways of ensuring that their students' PBL resource needs are met.

Challenge 7: Matching Assessment Strategies with PBL Pedagogy

If the methods of assessment used do not align with the principles of PBL, the new pedagogy loses credibility. For example, if the values and practices of group work are supported throughout the programme, but assessments are conducted on an individual basis only, the consistency of the underlying values becomes confused and contradictory. Another challenge of PBL is to design assessments that are both PBL-compatible and drive learning in relation to the core professional competences identified. Students study according to what and how they are assessed. Designing appropriate and effective assessments is one of the biggest challenges in developing PBL curricula. Specific strategies for meeting these assessment challenges are discussed in Chapters 13 and 14.

PBL Curricula as Knowledge and Learning Environments

This section explores PBL as a knowledge and learning environment affecting various aspects of teachers' work collaboratively and individually, designing curricula, students' style of working, and using different knowledge resources. The problem-based curriculum can be understood as an integrated knowledge and learning environment which can be researched from many points of view including psychological, technological, cultural, and pragmatic. Psychological factors are connected to hidden beliefs regarding how individuals gain, organise, and use their knowledge and competence. Technological expectations focus on actions, methods, and infrastructures of the learning environment created by advanced technological possibilities such as virtual learning environments. A cultural perspective reflects existing educational beliefs and organisational values and roles (Hannafin & Land, 1997; Poikela & Portimojärvi, 2004).

In the context of PBL, knowledge is not only an object for memorising, it is a subject and tool for observing, analysing, integrating, and synthesising. The construction of shared knowledge starts from facing the problem; it is an essential element for producing scientific and multiprofessional competences. Independent knowledge acquisition (individual learning between tutorials) and shared knowledge construction (during reflective discussions in tutorials) are separated chronologically. Together, these processes of learning and reflection lead to deep learning and competence. It is important that teachers recognise these connections and see the whole learning and knowledge environment rather than only some parts of it. Time, place, and other situational factors need to be considered during the problem-solving process. Lectures, exercises, and other types of teaching take place but their timing and content is designed according to the needs of the students' problem solving.

The PBL curriculum can be simplified in the form of a proto-model (see Figure 17.2). The dynamo of learning is the tutorial, namely a group session of seven to nine students and a teacher acting as a tutor. The tutorials are usually held once or twice a week, with the same participants, during the whole study module or semester. The importance of tutorials as a construction site of knowledge was recognised by the informants

New demands are placed on the qualities of learning materials, too. For instance, the web-based material available needs to be useful for problem solving. Useful material, relevant literature, and established theories need to be updated simultaneously. The importance of material produced by the students themselves increases because the learning processes are shared and co-operative.

The PBL curriculum requires broad co-operation among staff in various positions within the organisation. Teachers cannot handle the curriculum by themselves, because PBL demands collaboration in planning and implementing the teaching and learning programme.

The Problem-Solving Process

The process of problem solving may be structured in different ways. One of the most famous models was developed by Barrows (1985) at the University of McMaster in Canada. Another well-known model is Schmidt's (1983) "seven jump" model from the University of Maastricht in the Netherlands and its variations in many universities. The cyclical model developed at the University of Linköping, Sweden has also been applied in many places. It is not possible or desirable to identify a single model for the PBL tutorial process that should be applied in all contexts (Barrett, 2005; Poikela, 2003; Savin-Baden & Howell Major, 2004).

Figure 17.2 shows the phases of a cyclical model of the PBL tutorial process. The idea of a cyclical model has been developed further over ten years in Finland and, at the moment, is the most common procedure or script to organise the learning process taking place in tutorials in Finland (Poikela & Poikela, 2006). Problem-based learning offers a procedure for structuring and facilitating learning and group processes based on problem solving. Carefully designed work-related problems create a solid base for learning (Poikela, 2003). The tutor facilitates the problem-solving process during tutorials that last for different time periods according to the context.

During the first phase of the tutorial the students have to find a shared understanding of perspectives and conceptions of the problem. The purpose of the second phase is to elicit and elaborate former knowledge about the problem phenomena which is achieved by brainstorming ideas about possible ways of dealing with the problem. The third phase starts with connecting similar types of ideas together into separate categories and naming them. During the fourth phase, the most important and actual problem areas (the named categories) are negotiated. The fifth phase culminates in the first tutorial session with the aim being that students decide the learning task and the objects of study.

The sixth phase is a period of information seeking and self-study between tutorials. The students work both alone and in small groups depending on the learning tasks and aims. The seventh phase begins in the second tutorial and is a practical test for using new knowledge. Freshly acquired knowledge is used to tackle the learning task and applied in constructing the problem in a new manner. New knowledge will be synthesised and integrated at a more advanced level and it provides a basis for learning to be continued. During the eighth phase, the whole process of problem solving and the learning process are clarified and reflected on in light of the original problem. It is essential that the tutorial closes with a period of feedback and assessment discussion. In this way, the students receive the necessary information and feedback about their own learning, group processes, and problem-solving skills.

Conclusions

Research suggests the more students are exposed to PBL the greater effect on student learning and the more students are oriented to a meaning perspective than a reproducing perspective (Sadlo & Richardson, 2003). This would support the argument for macro-level implementation of PBL. Also macro-level implementations applied simultaneously across the entire curriculum means that difficulties are encountered in "one go".

However, sometimes it is not possible or desirable to have a full PBL programme. Piloting PBL with one module can sometimes be a practical way to begin.

References

Barrett, T. (2005). Understanding problem-based learning. In T. Barrett, I. MacLabhraim, & H. Fallon (Eds.), *Handbook of enquiry and problem-based learning. Irish case studies and international perspectives* (pp. 13–25). Galway: CELT, National University of Ireland Galway and All Ireland Society of Higher Education.

Barrows, H. (1985). *How to design a problem-based curriculum for the preclinical years.* New York: Springer.

Chen, S.E. (2000). Problem-based learning: Educational tool or philosophy? In O.S. Tan, P. Little, S.Y. Hee, & J. Conway (Eds.), *Problem-based learning: Educational innovations across disciplines. A collection of selected papers. 2nd Asia-Pacific Conference on Problem-based Learning* (pp. 210–219). Singapore: Temasek Centre for Problem-based Learning.

Hannafin, M., & Land, S. (1997). The foundations and assumption of technology-enhanced student-centered environment. *Instructional Science, 25,* 167–202.

McWilliam, E. (2008). Unlearning how to teach. *Innovations in Education and Teaching International, 45*(3), 263–269.

Poikela, E. (2001). Ongelmaperustainen oppiminen yliopistossa. In E. Poikela & S. Öystilä (Eds.), *Tutkiminen on oppimista: ja oppiminen tutkimista* (pp. 101–117). Tampere: Tampere University Press.

Poikela, E. (2005). Työssä oppimisen prosessimalli. In E. Poikela (Ed.), *Osaaminen ja kokemus* (pp. 21–41). Tampere: Tampere University Press.

Poikela, E., & Poikela, S. (2006). Problem-based curricula: Theory, development and design. In E. Poikela & A.R. Nummenmaa (Eds.), *Understanding problem-based learning* (pp. 71–90). Tampere: Tampere University Press.

Poikela, S. (2003). *Ongelmaperustainen pedagogiikka ja tutorin osaaminen.* Tampere: Tampere University Press.

Poikela, S. (2005). Learning at work as a tutor: The processes of producing, creating and sharing knowledge in a work community. In E. Poikela & S. Poikela (Eds.), *Problem-based learning in context: Bridging work and education* (pp. 177–194). Tampere: Tampere University Press.

Poikela, S., & Portimojärvi, T. (2004). Opettajana verkossa. Ongelmaperustainen pedagogiikka verkko-oppimisympäristöjen toimijoiden haasteena. In V. Korhonen (Ed.), *Verkko-oppiminen ja yliopistopedagogiikka* (pp. 93–112). Tampere: Tampere University Press.

Poikela, S., Vuoskoski, P., & Kärnä, M. (2009). Developing creative learning environments in problem-based learning. In Tan Oon-Seng (Ed.), *Problem-based learning and creativity* (pp. 67–85). Singapore: Cengage Learning.

Sadlo, G., & Richardson, J. (2003). Approaches to studying and perceptions of the academic environment in students following problem-based and subject-based curricula. *Higher Education Research and Development, 22*(3), 253–274.

Savin-Baden, M. (2000). *Problem-based learning in higher education: Untold stories*. Buckingham: Society for Research into Higher Education and Open University Press.

Savin-Baden, M. (2003). Disciplinary differences or modes of curriculum practice? Who promised to deliver what in problem-based learning? *Biochemistry and Molecular Biology Education, 31*(5), 338–343.

Savin-Baden, M., & Howell Major, C. (2004). *Foundations of problem-based learning*. London: Open University Press.

Schmidt, H.G. (1983). Problem-based learning: Rationale and description. *Medical Education, 17*(1), 11–16.

Silén, C. (2004). Does problem-based learning make students to "go meta"? In M. Savin-Baden & K. Wilkie (Eds.), *Challenging research in problem-based learning* (pp. 144–155). London: Society for Research into Higher Education and Open University Press.

Further Resources

Jackson, N., & Shaw, M. *Conceptions and Visual Representations of the Curriculum* (Part l). LTSN Generic Centre: www.palatine.ac.uk/files/1048pdf.

Jackson, N., & Shaw, M. *Conceptions and Visual Representations of the Curriculum* (Part 2). LTSN Generic Centre: www.palatine.ac.uk/files/1047pdf.

18

A PBL Response to the Digital Native Dilemma

Timo Portimojärvi and Roisin Donnelly

Introduction

The purpose of the chapter is to delve into the growing imbalance between the educational technology widely supported by higher education institutions and today's digitally cognisant student body. The authors argue that technology, such as Learning Management Systems (LMS), are not meeting the needs of current students, commonly referred to as "digital natives", and that a disparity exists between how the students choose to communicate, in general, and how they are encouraged or required to communicate in accredited courses.

This chapter draws on the writers' experiences and research together with studies on problem-based learning (PBL) supported and enhanced with technology. The key issues discussed include resolving the dichotomy between the technology needs of higher education students and the systems that institutions are providing to support their learning environments. The main thrust of the chapter is to highlight the strongest points where PBL and modern technology meet which will be illustrated using current examples from Ireland, Finland, and other countries.

As stated by John Dewey (1938), "If we teach today as we taught yesterday, we rob our students of tomorrow". In writing about digital natives and digital immigrants specifically, Prensky (2001a, p. 1), one of the leading proponents of this theme, argues that "our students have changed radically. Today's students are no longer the people our education system was designed to teach" and that "[o]ur digital immigrant instructors who speak an outdated language (of the pre-digital age) are struggling to teach a population that speaks an entirely new language" (Prensky, 2001a, p. 2). Bayne and Ross (2007) warn that serious critique of this discourse is long overdue as there is comparatively little published literature that examines Prensky's assumptions in a sustained way.

While Dewey (1938) and Prensky (2001a) are not writing about problem-based learning or simply technology, both are looking to the future and are seeing education as continuing preparation for that future. The views of Dewey and Prensky create a grounding for this chapter, in which we discuss the tensions and possibilities in using information and communication technology (ICT) with PBL, and present a framework for future development.

Traditionally, PBL has usually been conducted in a face-to-face setting. Recently, there has been a growing interest in PBL and technology among educational researchers (Dennis, 2003; Donnelly, 2007; Portimojärvi, 2006; Savin-Baden, 2003; Savin-Baden & Wilkie, 2006; Uden & Beaumont, 2006). There have been several attempts to define terms for the combination of e-learning and PBL. However, these attempts are seen as problematic since they offer little indication about the ways in which technology is being used, the areas of student interaction, the quality of the learning materials or the extent to which any of these factors are integrated with PBL. In this chapter, we subscribe to the idea of enriching the essential components of PBL with media and integrating technology, as a natural part of PBL. The context and the need set the limits as to whether technology is used just to enrich classroom practices or to create fully virtual applications. We already know that even a full implementation of online PBL with a dispersed group is possible when needed.

Chapter Overview

In this chapter, we return to pragmatic, basic views: the tools and practices used in learning should be selected and developed to achieve the learning goals needed in life and work.

This chapter:

- discusses key emerging issues;
- explores reflection and digital tools;
- outlines a framework for the future; and
- provides a list of useful further resources for integrating technology and PBL.

Context

This section of the chapter details the context of a triad of perspectives of teacher education at tertiary level and outlines the authors' argument on the lack of alignment therein. Three issues are explored:

1. the culture and tools of digital natives;
2. the current use of ICTs in educational contexts; and
3. work culture.

Digital Natives and Immigrants

The generation born from the beginning of the 1980s has been characterised as "digital natives" (Prensky, 2001a) or the "net generation" (Tapscott, 1998) and are also referred to in the literature as the "NetGen" or "digital learners" (Oblinger, 2006) because of their familiarity with and reliance on ICT. Digital natives are seen as having grown up in mediated environments surrounded by and using computers, video games, digital music players, video cameras, mobile phones, and all the other toys and tools of the digital age (Prensky, 2001a).

Manathunga and Donnelly (2008), echoing the sentiments of many educationalists, have argued that the learning preferences and styles of the so-called digital natives are extremely important to take into account when designing any course involving learning technologies. The aptitudes, attitudes, expectations, and learning styles of these NetGen students reflect the environment in which they were raised – one that is decidedly different from that which existed when the academic staff were growing up (Oblinger & Oblinger, 2005). As Oblinger (2006) continues to argue, today's younger student learners are digital, connected, experiential, immediate, and social, with preferences for learning, which include peer-to-peer interaction and engagement, and for learning resources that are visual and relevant.

This technological immersion is described as so complete that young people either do not consider computers as technology any more or are not able to distinguish the real world from the digital one. These young people are the native speakers of the digital language of computers, video games, and the Internet. Those individuals who were not born into the digital world, but have later adopted many aspects of the new technology are compared to them and called "digital immigrants" (Prensky, 2001a).

Prensky (2001b) grounds his idea in neurobiology, social psychology, and in studies conducted with children using games for learning. Neurobiologists and social psychologists agree that the brain can and does change with new input. Teachers of students with disabilities and the military are already using custom-designed computer and video games as a way of reaching digital natives. However, the majority of today's educational establishment remains bound to more traditional means of delivering instruction.

The divide between digital natives and digital immigrants over-simplifies the differences between the users. Students have the skills to use new kinds of applications and new forms of technology, and their ICT skills are wide but their working habits might still require much development and support (Ilomäki, 2008). Age, ICT skills, and the availability of digital media are not interdependent, and Prensky's argument does have weaknesses. The divide remains strongly debated (see Bennett, Maton, & Kervin, 2008).

The findings of Margaryan and Littlejohn (2008), from their study of students' use of technology in two British universities, tend to contradict the prevailing view of the "digital native" as a sophisticated user of technology who has a fundamentally different approach to learning. In more detail, they report:

Students use a limited range of technologies for both learning and socialisation. For learning, mainly established ICTs are used – institutional VLE, Google and Wikipedia and mobile phones. Students make limited, recreational use of social technologies such as media sharing tools and social networking sites ... the findings point to a low level of use of and familiarity with collaborative knowledge creation tools, virtual worlds, personal web publishing, and other emergent social technologies.

(Margaryan & Littlejohn, 2008, p. 625)

A recent study (Joint Information Systems Committee [JISC], 2007) notes that, while use of Internet technology, particularly for social networking, is almost ubiquitous among 16–18 year olds, this does not translate into a desire among this age group for more technologically focused approaches to teaching and learning at university.

While the existence of this debate is recognised here, it illustrates the bigger picture that can be seen in the practice of many academic staff today.

ICT in Educational Contexts

What is the role of technology in our classrooms? Is it to support the teaching paradigm? Is it the means for developing media literacy skills in action? Is it the leading force in educational development? Inherent in a discussion of the function of ICT in education is the position of LMS, institutional views, and centralised systems.

The use of technology in education brings a series of huge expectations, with many success stories, but also at least as many failures and frustrations. It has two major roots: computer-aided instruction and distance education, both of which still have a remarkable impact on education. Media and technology change rapidly, as we have seen, but the dominant paradigms seem to remain active, even if the old paradigms and new media collide with each other.

In opposition to the discourse of digital natives, other researchers (van Braak, 2004; Rajab & Baqain, 2005) report that the main use of computers among students is still word processing, as it used to be 15 years ago. We have to keep in mind that the research of educational technology does not often converge with the research of the new media cultures of youth. However, the notion of word processing being the main activity reveals that educational settings are still based on some traditional instructional practices.

During the last 10 years, dominant educational technologies are virtual learning environments (VLEs) or, more precisely, learning management systems (LMSs) such as WebCT, Blackboard, Moodle, and Sakai. These systems are typically centralised, maintained within an organisation's IT sector, and are focussed specifically on educational purposes, supporting the systematic hierarchies and structures of courses. In other words, LMSs are institution- and teacher-centred systems for managing courses, students, materials, discussions, assignments, and examinations. And here we have the central paradox between the system and the objectives.

LMSs, such as Moodle and Blackboard, do not always meet natural ways of communicating, saving, sharing, and editing. When students or teachers are asked which media they use for education and which media they use in their informal daily life, the difference is clear. Tønnessen (2008), in a longitudinal study looking at recent media development from a generational perspective with school children, reports that they seem to relate differently to formal and informal paths of learning. The findings indicate that knowledge of ICT and its use is developed mainly outside school in informal learning communities.

LMSs do not seem to have any use outside of educational contexts; this gap is particularly evident when "digital natives" are expected to use these LMSs. In the literature, many small-scale studies are available which describe the use of an LMS to support student learning; only for formal courses. There is little indication of the LMSs being used for informal activities, even if this option is available. Students are increasingly digital natives, who are familiar with social media such as Facebook, Wikipedia, Twitter, Ning, blogs, wikis, Jaiku, Skype, etc.

Learner management systems have the potential to bring students' increasing social networking skills more firmly into the realm of learning. This potential is still quite under-exploited in many learning settings, and PBL is an ideal learning context in which to develop and maximise the benefits that learning technologies can bring to the quality and dynamism of student learning.

Even if the divide between digital natives and digital immigrants were sustainable, the need for teaching ICT skills, media literacy, or ethical issues does not disappear. Calling students digital natives is not an excuse for not actually teaching them about technology. While the variety and fragmentation on mediated culture increases, it becomes more complex to organise teaching and learning in ways that use media, if taught. Instead, a teacher traditionally may be forced to admit he/she cannot be an expert of all media practices. Such an instance provides the perfect opportunity to empower students to direct and steer the learning dynamics in ways that align with the skills and orientations they bring, both within and beyond the classroom.

Students need to be given opportunities to use technology in college. This issue of technology use in college is less about teachers mastering specific tools or techniques than their being willing to allow students to use these tools to find information and create products. Many teachers resist being taught to use technology:

because it is not they who should be using the technology to teach students, but rather their students who should be using it, as tools to teach themselves. The teacher's role should not be a technological one, but an intellectual one – to provide the students with context, quality assurance, and individualized help.

(Prensky, 2008a, p. 2)

Work Cultures

We have been discussing the discontinuity in using ICT between the digital natives' informal life and formal education; however, this is not the only possible gap. Another critical point is the shift from education to working life and the induction phase at work. One of the main strengths of PBL is often said to be the development of relevant transferable skills (such as time management, teamwork, independent learning, decision-making, problem solving, and communicating ideas and results) needed in work.

However, even if we can provide students with a range of transferable skills and more comprehensive disciplinary knowledge, we also question whether technology-bound communicative processes and tools meet the real standards used in work, especially now that there are new challenges of working across traditional time, geographic, and organisational boundaries, while information and communication technologies are transforming traditional workplaces into virtual workspaces.

Globalisation and virtuality are common trends in work and education. Information and communication technology has a central role in the post-modern society (Castells, 1996). Over the last 10 years, the change in education and working practice and tools has been truly remarkable. In today's so-called "knowledge society", where there now exist new technologies and new structures for knowledge construction, new challenges emerge. Working in geographically dispersed groups needs effective computer-mediated communication tools to enable the group action in spite of the distance (Hildreth, Kimble, & Wright, 2000; Vartiainen, Kokko, & Hakonen, 2003).

Yet, we can recognise the difference between different fields. In many branches of business, technology or medicine, the continuum in using ICT is clear, when the same technologies are used in both education and work. The professional development of teachers in ICT is a central educational imperative that presents financial and strategic challenges. While many teachers are now integrating ICT in innovative and pedagogically appropriate ways, there is still a significant number of teachers who are resistant to using technology in their teaching.

Colleges, as communities, are slow in implementing changes, even in well organised projects. There is evidence that special pedagogical ICT projects have led to true changes in learning practices and to student-centred, collaborative, inquiry-oriented, and authentic teaching practices (Ilomäki, 2008, p. 4).

Main Issues

What, then, is the role of problem-based learning with this critical view of educational technologies and the paradox between students as digital natives and teachers as digital immigrants? Online PBL, as practice-driven theory-informed learning, is similar in many ways to everyday informal learning. What is being proposed here is that a way forward with online PBL is an easy, affordable, and sustainable solution that is already in use outside of formal education.

Prensky's view that we need a totally new pedagogical approach may be quite confusing. We would argue that it depends on the current approach to learning and teaching. As McWilliam (2008) states, there are three popular metaphors in use in the literature: "Sage on the stage", a metaphor for a substance expert teacher, who relies on a transmission model of teaching; "Guide on the side" is a metaphor which has a transactional perspective. However, she states that this is not enough, and presents a third metaphor, "meddler in the middle" which positions the teacher and student as mutually involved in assembling and re-assembling cultural products. This metaphor of meddler in the middle is bound to sociocultural approaches, which emphasise participation and transformation in the same way that has been identified in using social media.

It is well recognised that there are many approaches to online problem-based learning (Savin-Baden & Wilkie, 2004). The main approach is establishing the role of a tutor, as well as the role of technology. If PBL is to be understood as truly student-centred and as a group-intensive way of learning, arguably the best metaphor for a tutor would be "a meddler in the middle".

Earlier, we described LMSs as artificial "out-of-the-real-world" systems. In the same way, traditional teacher- and subject-centred teaching is unaligned with current information society. We have learned that PBL is something else. Problem-based learning begins with a real or authentic problem, goes through natural processes of enquiry such as questioning, sourcing information, communicating, analysing – with the group as the active element initiating rich discussion, meaning negotiation, and information practices. And those processes are under constant assessment and development.

This description, again, has the same characteristics with social media practices of the "digital natives". Here we see the focal point, which leads us to develop the use of technology with PBL further and towards the use of "natural", easy, affordable, and sustainable media choices and practices.

Reflection and Digital Tools

Reflection enables us to generalise mental models from our experience; it is the process of learning from experience. Chapter 11 explores how PBL can be used to develop student reflection. The digital world is described as fast, hectic, and having less and less time and opportunity for reflection. This development concerns many people. In teaching digital natives, it seems important to figure out and invent ways to include reflection and critical thinking in the learning process, either built into the instruction or through a process of instructor-led debriefing (Prensky, 2001b).

The learning groups in PBL can benefit from "blending" virtual and physical resources, examples of which include combinations of technology-based materials and traditional print materials. The fact that the Internet is a complex repository, containing an enormous maze of information from a variety of sources, has impacted on the PBL landscape, in that it has become a prominent source of information for multidisciplinary groups. The use of online communication technologies also provides many ways in which distance educators can facilitate flexible tutorial support to groups of students (Fox, 2005).

Prensky (2008b) gives us three simple practices which help teachers make education relevant to students' lives and truly prepare students for the future. First, it is vital to give students the opportunity to use technology in school. Second, this opportunity to use technology needs to be followed by finding out how students want to be taught and connecting students to the world. Finally, we need to understand where students are going and help them to get there. Prensky (2008b) also tells us to "Work with both students and teachers to implement the new 'kids teaching themselves with guidance' model". Inherent in this is the elimination of lectures and busywork from schools and asking teachers, who use active learning, to share their practices with their colleagues. While Prensky does not refer to PBL, this is following Dewey and seems to have the same basic ideas and principles that are present in PBL.

In terms of exploring the crossover and boundaries of informal and formal education events and technology tools to support them, there has been much debate in the literature as to the nature of formal, informal, and non-formal learning. The locus of this debate is centred on arguments for "the inherent superiority of one or the other" (Colley, Hodkinson, & Malcolm, 2002, p. 2) and "it is difficult to make a clear distinction between formal and informal learning as there is often a crossover between the two" (McGivney, 1999, p. 1).

One tool that is making great progress in bridging this crossover is the use of a blog with group access. Bull et al. (2008) reports on the effectiveness of the dynamic dialogue generated by blogs, but in order to translate informal use of communication technologies outside college into applied activities inside college, educators must consider content and the pedagogies best suited for bridging these in- and out-of-college uses of technology.

Other social media tools which reflect new opportunities and outlets for creativity are wikis, instant messaging, and texting in the realm of writing, podcasting in audio, countless sites such as Flickr for distribution and sharing of images, and video shared via YouTube.

While constraints remain in colleges in today's challenging global economic climate, more than ever, Sterling (2008) suggests that the energy and creativity emerging outside colleges should be harnessed and linked to the academic enterprise within colleges. The fact exists that the ubiquitous spread of social media outside college has yet to be employed with equal effectiveness inside colleges.

Personal Development Planning (PDP) is a key component of today's life-long learner's continuous professional development. Jackson (2001) argues that through this process there is an emphasis on learners making sense of what they are learning and how they are learning it and, ultimately, taking responsibility for what they learn. Increasingly, in higher education, e-portfolios are being used to help students realise the many skills that they have developed during their time in formal education and to provide them with a vehicle to help them plan ahead for their personal and continuing professional development. Within formal education, the e-portfolio is a collection of computer-based files organised into a personal website that is representative of coursework that the participants produce in their courses. It can be based on assignments and activities completed in and out of class to demonstrate the participant skills and knowledge related to the subject discipline. There are a variety of e-portfolio system tools available today, such as PebblePad and Mahara.

The development of an e-portfolio can help students synthesise much of what they have learned on their course, as well as creating one cohesive package that demonstrates the skills and knowledge that they bring back to their professional practice and working context. In essence, the e-portfolio can serve as a record of what each student has learned during his/her course. Undergoing an e-portfolio development process can provide students with distinct benefits; it captures the complexities of their learning in a discipline and, from the teacher's perspective, it matches assessment to the teaching style of each course.

From a networking perspective, e-portfolios can promote new conversation about e-learning practice around higher education institutions. It has the potential to create a culture in which "*thoughtful discourse*" about e-learning becomes the norm. Over time, e-portfolios can create a concrete evidence of learning by documenting the development or "*unfolding of expertise*" in a subject discipline. It also gives a profile of student abilities by enabling them to show quality work that is done with the help of resources, reference material and collaboration with others. A wide range of skills can be demonstrated and it shows efforts to improve and develop and demonstrates progress over time.

The e-portfolio is a tool for assessing a variety of skills; written as well as oral and graphic products being easily included. In addition, it develops an awareness of the students' own learning as they have to reflect on their own progress and the quality of work in relation to known goals. The e-portfolio also caters to individuals in the heterogeneous class; since it is open-ended, students can show work on their own level. Since there is a choice, the e-portfolio caters to different learning styles and allows expression of different strengths. Finally, it develops independent and active learners: students must select and justify e-portfolio choices, monitor their own progress and set learning goals. However, from the authors' experience, as teacher educators, encouraging reflective writing among students can be challenging, alongside ensuring that adequate support is provided in the area of academic writing.

Framework for the Future and Conclusion

Problem-based learning offers online learning a structure and pedagogical grounding and a motivating and effective way of learning. Over time, we anticipate that our understanding of online PBL and its outcomes will mature and that measures of effectiveness will continue to develop and improve.

Donnelly and Portimojärvi (2006) have argued that technology offers PBL more flexible environments, limited on some aspects, but enriched on others. The workload that active participation in online PBL places on students should not be underestimated when the decision is being made to pursue this style of education.

The advanced combinations of problem-based learning and online learning provide effective tools for virtual teams and virtual communities of practice. However, the development of higher levels of skills in the use of online communications is an important consideration in the design of PBL online. Figure 18.1 illustrates a number of key factors for effectively implementing PBL in a virtual environment, including the function of the PBL group online

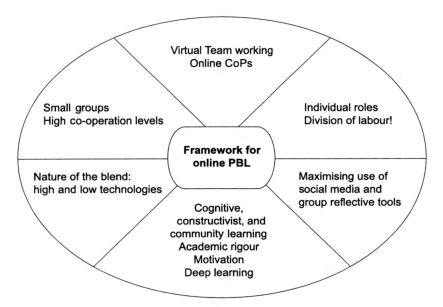

Figure 18.1 Proposed factors for aligning the digital native dilemma.

and how ultimately and successfully this can lead to an online community of practice (CoP); within this is the division of labour for the individual roles, the size of the group, and the level of co-operation and collaboration between members. The nature of the blend of technologies is also an important consideration; Graham (2006) has coined asynchronous interaction as *low-fidelity*, and it is argued here that the blend of high and low technologies needs to be explored in relation to how they affect the problem-based learning experience. A range of psychological variables need to be balanced in an implementation of online PBL including cognitive, constructivist, and community learning alongside motivation, rigour, and deep learning strategies. Finally, the role of the different, relevant technologies needs to be considered including the role of social media and group reflection tools.

References

Bayne, S., & Ross, J. (2007, December). *The "digital native" and "digital immigrant": A dangerous opposition*. Paper presented at the Annual Conference of the Society for Research into Higher Education (SRHE), Edinburgh, Scotland.

Bennett, S., Maton, K., & Kervin, L. (2008). The "digital natives" debate: A critical review of the evidence. *British Journal of Educational Technology, 39*(5), 775–786.

Bull, G., Thompson, A., Searson, M., Garofalo, J., Park, J., Young, C., & Lee, J. (2008). Connecting informal and formal learning: Experiences in the age of participatory media. *Contemporary Issues in Technology and Teacher Education, 8*(2). Retrieved from: www.citejournal.org/vol8/iss2/editorial/article1.cfm.

Castells, M. (1996). *The rise of the network society*. Oxford: Blackwell.

Colley, H., Hodkinson, P., & Malcolm J. (2002). *Non-formal learning: Mapping the conceptual terrain. A consultation report*. Retrieved 1 June 2010 from: www.infed.org/archives/e-texts/colley_informal_learning.htm.

Dennis, J.K. (2003). Problem-based learning in online vs. face-to-face environments. *Education for Health, 16*(2), 198–209.

Dewey, J. (1938). *Experience and education*. New York: Collier Books.

Donnelly, R. (2007). Virtual problem-based learning communities of practice for teachers and teacher educators: An Irish higher education perspective. In C. Kimble & P. Hildreth (Eds.), *Communities of practice: Creating learning environments for educators* (pp. 162–173). Charlotte, NC: Information Age Publishing.

Donnelly, R., & Portimojärvi, T. (2006). Shifting perceptions within online problem-based learning. *Encyclopedia of Distance Learning*. Tampere: Tampere University Press.

Fox, S. (2005, September). *Reflections of the benefits of the use of the new learning technologies in higher distance education through the prism of a case study*. Paper presented at the 11th Cambridge International Conference on Open and Distance Learning.

Graham, C. (2006). Blended learning systems: Definition, current trends, and future directions. In C.J. Bonk & C.R. Graham (Eds.), *The handbook of blended learning: Global perspectives, local designs* (pp. 3–21). San Francisco, CA: Pfeiffer.

Hildreth, P., Kimble, C., & Wright, P. (2000). Communities of practice in the distributed international environment. *Journal of Knowledge Management, 4*(1), 27–37.

Ilomäki, L. (2008). *The effects of ICT on school: Teachers' and students' perspectives*. Academic dissertation, University of Turku, Turku, Finland. Retrieved from: https://oa.doria.fi/bitstream/handle/10024/42311/B314.pdf?sequence=3.

Jackson, N. (2001). *Personal development planning: What does it mean?* Retrieved from: www.heacademy.ac.uk/resources/detail/resource_database/id65_Personal_Development_Planning_What_does_it_mean.

Joint Information Systems Committee (JISC). (2007). *Student expectations study*. Retrieved from: www.jisc.ac.uk/media/documents/publications/studentexpectations.pdf.

McGivney, V. (1999). *Informal learning in the community: A trigger for change and development*. Leicester: National Institute of Adult Continuing Education.

McWilliam, E. (2008). Unlearning how to teach. *Innovations in Education and Teaching international, 45*(3), 263–269.

Manathunga, C., & Donnelly, R. (2008). Opening online academic development programmes to international perspectives and dialogue. In R. Donnelly & F. McSweeney (Eds.), *Applied eLearning and eTeaching in higher education* (pp. 84–107). Hershey, PA: Information Science Reference.

Margaryan, A., & Littlejohn, A. (2008). *Are digital natives a myth or reality? Students' use of technologies for learning.* Brighton: Higher Education Academy.

Oblinger, D. (2006, September). *Listening to what we're seeing.* Keynote presentation at ALT-C, Edinburgh, Scotland.

Oblinger, D., & Oblinger, J. (Eds.). (2005). *Educating the net generation.* Boulder, CO: EDUCAUSE.

Portimojärvi, T. (Ed.). (2006). *Ongelmaperustaisen oppimisen verkko [The network of problem-based learning].* Tampere: Tampere University Press.

Prensky, M. (2001a, October). Digital natives, digital immigrants. *On the Horizon, 9*(5). www.marcprensky.com/writing/Prensky%20-%20Digital%20Natives,%20Digital%20Immigrants%20-%20Part1.pdf

Prensky, M. (2001b, December). Digital natives, digital immigrants, Part II: Do they really *think* differently? *On the Horizon, 9*(6). www.marcprensky.com/writing/Prensky%20-%20Digital%20Natives,%20Digital%20Immigrants%20-%20Part2.pdf

Prensky, M. (2008a, November–December). The role of technology in teaching and the classroom. *Educational Technology.* Retrieved from: www.marcprensky.com/writing/Prensky-The_Role_of_Technology-ET-11-12-08.pdf.

Prensky, M. (2008b). Turning on the lights: Reaching the reluctant learner. *Educational Leadership, 65*(6), 40–45. Retrieved from: www.ascd.org/publications/educational_leadership/mar08/vol65/num06/Turning_On_the_Lights.aspx.

Rajab, L., & Baqain, Z. (2005). Use of information and communication technology among dental students at the University of Jordan. *International Perspectives on Dental Education, 69*(3), 387–398.

Savin-Baden, M. (2003). *Facilitating problem-based learning: Illuminating perspectives.* Buckingham: Society for Research into Higher Education and Open University Press.

Savin-Baden, M., & Wilkie, K. (Eds.). (2004). *Challenging research in problem-based learning.* Maidenhead: Open University Press.

Savin-Baden, M., & Wilkie, K. (Eds.). (2006). *Problem-based learning online.* Maidenhead: Open University Press.

Sterling, R. (2008). *Writing, technology, and teenagers.* Retrieved from: http://wamu.org/programs/kn/08/04/29.php.

Tapscott, D. (1998). *Growing up digital: The rise of the net generation.* New York: McGraw-Hill.

Tønnessen, E. (2008, June). *ICT(s) and socialization: The role of the school and teachers.* Contribution to OECD Expert Meeting, Oslo, Norway.

Uden, L., & Beaumont, C. (2006). *Technology and problem-based learning.* Hershey, PA: Information Science Publishing.

van Braak, J.P. (2004). Domains and determinants of university students' self-perceived computer competence. *Computers & Education, 43*(3), 299–312.

Vartiainen, M., Kokko, N., & Hakonen, M. (2003). Competences in virtual organizations. In *Proceedings of the 3rd International Conference on Researching Work and Learning* (Book I, pp. 209–219). Tampere, Finland.

Further Resources

In this final section, we provide an annotated list of web-based resources that are relevant for the practitioner wishing to integrate technology with problem-based learning.

An annotated list of online PBL resources from Central Queensland University: http://pbl.cqu.edu.au/content/online_resources.htm.

Online PBL: models, processes and tools for creating collaborative learning environments: www.elearningguild.com/olf/olfarchives/index.cfm?id=452&action=viewonly.

An annotated list of online PBL resources from the University of British Columbia: http://web.ubc.ca/okanagan/ctl/support/practice/pbl/PBL_Resources.html.

Tools for delivering scenario-based e-learning: PBL Interactive is a newly developed suite of tools designed to enable teachers, lecturers, and others working in training or education to create and deliver interactive problem-based scenarios as an aid to the PBL instructional method: http://pbl.massey.ac.nz/pbl-interactive.htm.

Special Interest Group in PBL: The context and problem-based learning (C/PBL) SIG is a forum for people with an interest in the use of C/PBL to support teaching and learning: www.heacademy.ac.uk/physsci/home/networking/sig/CPBL.

Eduforge Learning Resources: http://eduforge.org/wiki/wiki/eduforge/?pagename=LearningResources.

PBL online: http://pbl-online.org/LearnOnline/elearn.htm.

E-learning scenarios including PBL: www.eduhub.ch/info/elearningscenarios.

19

Rethinking Supervision of PhD Work Processes

ProBell Research Group Walking the PBL Talk

Anna Raija Nummenmaa and Merja Alanko-Turunen

Introduction

This chapter will explore the question:

> How can we adapt PBL work processes in the supervision of PhD students?

The supervision of doctoral students has traditionally focused on guiding the production of a research-based dissertation. The main tasks associated with supervision have been the scientific problem-solving processes related to the contents and methods of scientific research and writing in the specific discipline. General work processes such as planning, motivation, information gathering, reflection, and assessment, as well as study and learning processes, have received less attention, even though they are vital processes in the completion of PhD research. Furthermore, we argue that being part of a PhD student group is a beneficial and often under-utilised learning resource for PhD supervision. In this chapter, our aim is to conceptualise and dialogically explore the meanings and roles of research and the conceptions of the PhD supervision process. We reconstruct a process of PhD supervision by exploring the methods and practices employed in the ProBell research group for problem-based learning in Finnish higher education (www.uta.fi/eduta/probell). This research group was made up of doctorate students researching problem-based learning and senior researchers who were their supervisors. We offer the reader an opportunity to reflect on and assess how the practices of PBL can be transferred to the supervision of PhD work processes. We suggest that the epistemological practices embedded in a PBL approach are powerful and effective. We show how such practices can contribute to enlightened and engaged supervision of the work processes of PhD students.

Chapter Overview

The scientific research process is often referred to as a journey. Indeed, applying the metaphor of the traveller to researchers may be particularly appropriate as they start with a destination in mind, they need various kinds of equipment and resources to ensure the success of the journey, and they meet obstacles and surprises along the way – some pleasant, some not so pleasant. Journeys have a structure to them, but there are many unpredictable things that happen while they are underway.

The supervisor can be considered as a travelling companion, whose job it is to accompany the student and to guide him/her in choosing particular routes, in making particular choices, or in tackling particular obstacles – thus, giving support and motivation to help the student reach his/her destination.

This chapter describes the journey of a research group of PhD students where the goal of each student was to complete a dissertation. This group of PhD students concentrated on studying problem-based learning from different perspectives in higher education. Our focus is to examine the supervision of these PhD students from two specific points of view: the group as a resource for learning and supervision and the general work processes as objects of supervision. These two elements are also essential when tutoring a group in problem-based learning. We are especially interested in discussing commitment, planning, motivation, and the role of feedback during the research process. Both of us are members of the ProBell research group; Anna Raija Nummenmaa supervised the doctoral students and Merja Alanko-Turunen is a member in the ProBell research group and completed her dissertation in 2005 (Alanko-Turunen, 2005). Figure 19.1

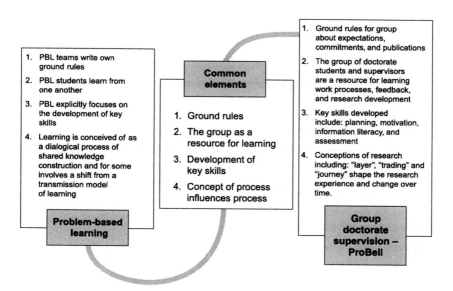

Figure 19.1 Common elements of both problem-based learning and group supervision of doctorate students in the ProBell Group.

highlights some of the common key elements of both problem-based learning and group supervision of doctorate students in the ProBell group that are discussed in this chapter.

Negotiating the Meaning of Research

The way that a supervisor conceptualises research is likely to have a strong influence on the ways in which she/he guides the research of her/his students. We have already shown how the journey metaphor might influence the ways in which supervisors interact with their students; however, there are other lenses through which research (and the supervision of research) can be viewed. Brew (2001) shows that in addition to conceptualising research as a journey, there are other dominant metaphors among senior researchers including the domino conception (where one atomistic step leads to another), the layer conception (where research involves uncovering layers of hidden meaning), and the trading conception (where there are transactions involving products, publications, grants, and social networks)

The Domino Conception

Researchers who perceive their research work as *domino* are described as understanding their research as a series of separate tasks, incidents, problems, things, experiments, and ideas. As a metaphor, domino includes the idea that even though it is important to link various separate phases, they can be combined in numerous patterns. The domino conception involves "an external product orientation" which is established by combining separate phases to solve practical problems or by obtaining answers to research questions.

The Trading Conception

Research categorised using the metaphor of *trading* involves the conception of understanding research as a social phenomenon. In the foreground are the products of research including publications, grants, and social networks, which are produced and then exchanged in a social situation for money, status, or recognition. Thus, there is an external product orientation to research, and while describing the research process, there is a strong focus on scientific reading and writing. Doing research is interpreted as operating in a kind of a marketplace.

The Layer Conception

Research understood as the *layer* conception represents a more internal orientation to research where the focus is on pondering the ontological premises. These researchers have their own ideas, concepts, and methods, and research is interpreted as a process of discovering, uncovering, and creating underlying meanings instead of giving evidence.

The Journey Conception

Categorising research as a *journey* signifies the idea of research as a process of discovery possibly leading to the transformation and growth of the researcher. The awareness and the development of the researcher are the focus of the process. Our research group shared this last conception of research and for us the journey metaphor is an evocative operating concept. However, like Brew (2001), we recognise that this metaphor is not the only one.

In both the group supervision of doctorate students and the facilitation of PBL students, conceptions of the educational process influence that process and can change over time.

On the Way: in a Group and Together

Increasingly, the world of work requires multidisciplinary, shared expertise that breaks the boundaries of the various fields. Based on this perspective of boundary breaking, it is assumed that expertise is a social process or a mechanism where the actor appropriates diverse practices, norms, and ideas (e.g. Lave & Wenger, 1991) and does not reside only in individual skills. It has also been suggested that expertise is a relational concept that is socially and discursively constituted. Educators and supervisors need to help people to learn to collaborate, share, and create information together in the doctoral education processes.

Tightly interacting groups of people can solve more difficult problems than they could solve individually (Hakkarainen, 2003; John-Steiner, 2000). Based on this notion of interactive problem solving, our ProBell research group, as a multidisciplinary group, formed a creative forum for the development of shared expertise; this collaborative partnership has also been a strength in supporting our research group.

Problem-based learning has acted both as the object of our research and the pedagogical base for our practice. PBL has given us a structure and ideological approach to learning to become a researcher. We have built on the similarities of the PhD research process and the problem-based learning approach. The core of the PBL process is learning, collaboration, and joint knowledge creation.

Our research group has included senior researchers, who conducted their own research work related to our project, and doctoral students. Although the diversity of the project group has been a strength, it has also brought some learning challenges for both the supervisors and the doctoral students. The supervision of our doctoral students has occurred mainly as group supervision in the regular meetings of the project group and in seminars. The research cluster has been defined by the following genuine group characteristics (Johnson & Johnson, 1982, 1987):

- it possesses shared goals and interests;
- participants have felt part of the group;
- membership of the group has been experienced as rewarding;

- the operation of the group is characterised by strong and regular interaction; and
- the group has had mutually agreed, although loose, working rules.

All of these features have contributed to the group's ability to act as a beneficial supervision resource. As mentioned above, the core of doctoral education is often seen as the target-oriented dissertation that answers a scientific question. Our endeavour has extended this focus of doctoral education by paying explicit attention to the more general processes associated with research. By participating in various activities that support work processes and making them visible and by encouraging students to think about and engage with other researchers' projects, our doctoral students have become substantially more aware of, for example, their own planning, time-management, and motivation. Furthermore, these students have been encouraged to evaluate their own know-how continually and have studied their own practices in receiving and using feedback. In many ways, shared reflection and collegial feedback has been the core of the supervision.

In addition to the topic-specific work and skills, we have placed much emphasis on the development of general, transferable work and life-relevant skills which involve paying attention to: planning, motivation, information gathering, reflecting and assessment processes, and study and learning processes. It is these general work processes that often cause problems and lead to delays in the students' progress or pose a threat to the completion of their work. In the work of a doctoral student, these scientific and general work processes are closely connected to the preparation of the PhD dissertation. Both the ProBell group and problem-based learning emphasise the development of key transferable skills.

The primary purpose of our research supervision, focusing on general work processes, is to move away from seeing the "dissertation as an object" and towards utilising the dissertation challenge and study processes as something that recognises the student as a living, feeling, and acting subject (Nummenmaa, 2006) – and that approach facilitates learning and development in a range of processes rather than simply the production of an output.

Whereas a dissertation and research processes are often described as logical and linear, work processes overlap, recur, and relate to each other in unexpected ways. One of the goals of the supervisory focus on general work processes is to facilitate the mobilisation of the learner's own resources. In this way, peer groups form an essential resource for supervision for this purpose. Our aim has been to construct a new sociocultural space for studying and learning in the supervision of work processes (Nummenmaa & Lautamatti, 2004).

Starting the Journey: Clarifying and Setting the Goals for Learning

As the doctoral education and dissertation is lengthy and future-oriented, it is vital, from the start, to activate the students' motivation, planning, and self-evaluation processes. We encourage dialogue at the early stages so that students have the opportunity to contemplate how they will keep their interest alive, how they will deal with their hopes, fears, and concerns about their capabilities, and how they will plan their education to be a part of their lives. In this chapter we dialogically explore the meanings and roles of research and the conceptions of the PhD supervision process through sharing our dialogue about these important topics with you.

Dialogue 1

ANNA RAIJA: The supervisor's attitude to this is crucial. When the supervisor understands how intricate and important the beginning is for the students' future work, she can consciously utilise it by contemplating with a student or student group the general and personal goals of studying, such as:

- What kinds of goals do I set for my doctoral education?
- How am I going to reach these goals?
- What kinds of expertise and know-how will I try to achieve and develop during the doctoral education?
- How will I develop this know-how and expertise?
- What kinds of career plans do I have at the moment?

It is useful in the beginning of the process for students to also think about their dissertations as a part of the postgraduate education process. Possible questions are:

- What kinds of thoughts and plans do I have about the forthcoming dissertation process?
- What kind of timetable plan do I have?
- How do I plan my time and other resources in practice?
- How will my dissertation support the development of my know-how and expertise?

MERJA: Your questions are essential in the doctoral process. Usually they are passed as somewhat trivial but they really set the tone to the whole process. And among all these useful questions lies a central question: Why I am doing it and what do I want to accomplish by it?

The questions here were jointly raised and discussed in the ProBell group, sometimes formally, sometimes informally. As a doctoral student and a full-time employee in a demanding role I had to contemplate what kind of practical arrangement needed to be made, what I wanted to get out of the whole postgraduate education process career-wise, would it even have some impact on my career?

I wanted to devote my time for learning challenging new themes as well as PBL, and therefore made some not so obvious and easy choices. I also had to ponder what kinds of scientific communities I needed and wanted to join for the completion of my doctorate dissertation.

I understand the doctoral process as a ritual of socialisation to the scientific community. What I found really interesting was that we were building a new social world or community of practice for PBL research at the University of Tampere. Scientific social worlds are often amorphous, lacking clear-cut boundaries or specified members. Social worlds may cross-cut, or reside in, multiple formal organisations. We were working within universities of applied sciences and universities, having different disciplinary backgrounds. The difference between our social worlds and formal organisational structures made it sometimes a bit problematic (Clarke, 1991, pp. 129–131). Our supervisors with long careers in educational sciences had to take the position of insider. Insiders are those who identify strongly with the social world and exhibit an unusually intense commitment to the maintenance and advancement of social world activities. We, doctoral students, as novices became regulars participating in the social world of a research group (Unruh, 1979).

ANNA RAIJA: Then there is the conception of research – do we understand each other's ways of perceiving the whole process?

MERJA: My conceptions of understanding research and research process was based on my master's and licentiate theses. I was not especially happy with the final stages of my licentiate process and wanted to have a different kind of experience of doing research. Having a business background quite obviously relates to the trading metaphor. In the beginning of the whole PhD process, I have to admit, the idea of doing research reminded me of Brew's metaphor of a layer. In the end of the process my conception had moved more towards to metaphor of a journey. Now, it seems that the trading metaphor is the one emphasised in the university world understanding research as a commodity more than a medium for personal learning.

ANNA RAIJA: On the tactical level, what do you think about the contract between the supervisor and the doctoral candidate? – I might expect certain things from my students, for example that they:

- are prepared when arriving at the supervision situation;
- continuously produce written material and distribute draft material;
- are in regular contact with the supervisor;
- complete the tasks agreed together.

The student, on the other hand, might expect from the supervisor:

- regular supervision;
- oral and written timely feedback;
- a positive and supportive relationship.

We had a discussion about the so-called general work conventions that are needed in the beginning. First, it is important that the supervisor explains her work methods to the students and clarifies how the students need to fit into them. Possible practical questions related to supervision include:

- How often the meetings are held;
- What is the best time for a meeting;
- How the agenda should be agreed beforehand and what the agenda should contain;
- Contact practices;
- Yearly supervision cycle;
- Publication practices and agreements.

It is important to make the principles related to publishing practices explicit in the beginning, especially in research projects that prepare joint publications, to avoid unnecessary disappointments or misunderstandings. (Delamont, Atkinson, & Parry, 1997). As the supervision of dissertations generally include a lot of personal supervision, it is advisable that the supervisor and student make a supervision agreement that can have written into it the jointly set goals, responsibilities of supervisor and student, the plan for completing the dissertation, the amount of time the supervisor reserves for supervision, agreements on contacting and meeting practices, etc. (Lindholm-Ylänne & Nevgi, 2003).

MERJA: The relationships with the supervisors were important. I was lucky enough to have two supervisors who responded quickly to my queries and showed an interest in my research endeavour. Furthermore, having various groups for presenting my research ideas to from the beginning was also important as they gave me valuable feedback and were committed to assisting me in many ways.

Discussion about these various issues helps students to discern their own doctoral education as a target- and future-oriented process. It also creates a basis for the tentative postgraduate education plan prepared by the student and the supervisor. Setting principles and ground rules at the beginning of the research relationship takes time, reflection, and energy. However, we have found that discussing expectations and commitments at the start is enormously helpful in defining aspects of the process, discussing assumptions, and creating a bedrock for the successful development of positive and effective research relationships, processes, and outcomes.

Ground rules are important to both group supervision of doctorate students and facilitation of problem-based learning students. At the start of the PBL process, PBL teams write their own ground rules in order to work and learn effectively together.

Planning Processes

It is said that all work is done at least twice: first in thought and, then, in the final form; this applies especially well to dissertations. While writing their dissertations, students learn new things, work with complex concepts, and the result is realised in a structured format. The use of thinking that involves planning and guided imagination is very important. Furthermore, in this context, it is useful to make the same kind of separation between process and output as in research usually; both the planning process and the plans themselves have their own rules. A student preparing her/his dissertation should know the ways she/he usually plans things and the measures that promote planning, and should also know what form of plans it is necessary to prepare to promote the study. In addition, she/he needs plans related to the structure and content of the study and plans regarding its progress. It is useful for the students to consider what types of plans are the most helpful to them. Plans can be very different and aspects of them can be related to both the study or dissertation process and more widely to the students' personal-life situations.

As well as a strong and structured research plan, we have routinely instructed our students to plan their time management and to generate timetables for both long-term and short-term periods. Regular review of these timetables, including making changes or modifications to them, helps students revise the assumptions that they have made about the time needed for the various operations. By using timetables as tools for their professional development, students learn to become better at predicting forthcoming stages and estimating the time that certain phases and activities will take. Timetables can become operating devices that help to plan, give rise to self-knowledge, and facilitate realistic engagement with all of the aspects of the research process.

Time-management plans may differ from student to student. While all of the plans may have common features (e.g. yearly, monthly, weekly, and daily breakdowns of tasks), individual students may also devise their own unique, creative, and motivating alternatives. What kinds of tasks the timetable includes is a personal matter. It is advisable that a student's week plan includes a peaceful moment of thinking every morning when matters can be set into an order of importance. In more demanding phases, it is good to have space for matters to work out by themselves. The subconscious seems to work best when it has time to be alone; this method also has its own name: the Chinese concept of Wu Wei refers to restraining oneself from action until the right moment comes.

Keeping Motivation Alive

Students often mention that personal interest in the research subject is an important motivator, but they find it hard to know how long this kind of initial interest will last. Among the Finnish PhD students almost 45% had considered withdrawing from their studies at some point (Pyhältö et al., 2008). Students differ from each other according to what levels of their motivation are directed by interior factors, such as personal interests, and what levels are directed by exterior factors. Motivation can depend on career development, personal goals and circumstances, or research interests.

On the one hand, the work process, in itself, can strengthen motivation if the student feels that doing research empowers her/him personally and provides her/him with general and academic working-life skills. On the other hand, even a motivated student has to be prepared for the fact that the working pace changes.

Dialogue 2

ANNA RAIJA: One very important issue keeping motivation going on is the belonging in a research community like the ProBell group. The group needs to have some common aim and also a good coherence.

MERJA: ProBell had regular meetings with pre-agreed presentation agenda. This regularity meant that you had to be ready to share your ongoing research process with others. This gave a boost that you had to have motivation for keeping up with reading and writing. And as the ProBell group shared a common interest in PBL, those discussions were rewarding and I learnt a lot from the methods used in our meetings when sharing our processes and from the topics others were researching. Being a member of a research group meant also actively participating in organising national and international PBL conferences, writing and presenting papers for those conferences, and facilitating PBL workshops for teachers in many institutions around Finland. These activities all contributed to becoming a competent researcher.

Above all, the commitment of the other doctoral students raised my motivation. We had our intensive meetings and seminars in various places with international visitors. This also added some extra flavour to our community. The grant given by the Academy of Finland also was an exterior motivational factor – it was a strong signal to us that others were also appreciating what we were doing and wanted to support us.

ANNA RAIJA: Supervision can support motivation in at least two ways. First, it can help the student to recognise her own motivational state and the factors that affect it. Second, supervision in its different forms can increase the elements that maintain motivation. A well functioning group or support that the group members offer each other in various ways can have this kind of an effect. Various motivating and self-awareness methods can be used such as visualisation, recognition of work rhythm and learning styles, etc. These often help students to recognise their own strengths and possibilities (Nummenmaa & Lautamatti, 2004). For example, one PhD student group was asked to produce personal metaphors by being asked to complete the following sentence "Supervision is like…" After completing the sentence they discussed the meanings of their metaphors together and visualised them.

Figure 19.2 captures one PhD group's conceptualisation of research, as related to the ideas of a journey and of the importance of being a member of a community of practice.

Developing and Revitalising Supervision Practices: Peers as Resource for Learning

Both the ProBell group supervision of doctorate students and the facilitation of problem-based learning stress the group as a key learning resource.

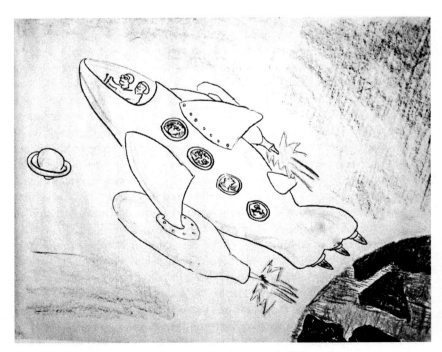

Figure 19.2 Supervision as a journey; a visualisation of a PhD student group.

Chapter 9 discusses student groups maximising the PBL tutorial for dialogic knowing. PhD education is a complex and dynamic process in which success is affected by many different factors. Doctorate studies always take place within a particular context and are influenced by the social practices of the scholarly community in question. The experience of belonging to a scholarly community seems to be a crucial factor in the successful completion of doctorate studies. A scholarly community provides a learning environment that includes various complementary elements such as knowledge, learning, and assessment practices, as well as the physical learning environment. Supervision is an essential part of this environment.

Conclusion

The research group or the supervision group can form a community that, in many different ways, may help individuals during the long journey. Participation in this group encompasses processes in which the students are involved in the practices of the community and construct their identity in relation to this community. Becoming a member of a community of practice shapes the identity construction of the students and also the way that they interpret their own activities within the community (Wenger, 1998).

The experience of belonging to a community supports the study, research, and learning processes. Indeed, not belonging to such a community has been found to lead to more difficulties, lower levels of self-efficacy and a higher likelihood that PhD studies will end before completion (Pyhältö et al., 2008). For a PhD student working alone, fellow PhD students and peer guidance can function as a vital supportive community. There is much evidence to suggest that such community belonging is especially supportive of the development of general work processes and the emergence of strong transferable skills (Lautamatti & Nummenmaa, 2008; Soini, 2008). When planning and developing the learning environments for doctoral education, it is important to consider what kinds of learning and supervision environments would promote not only the development of scientific expertise but also participation to a scientific community.

Meaningful learning is efficiently supported in empowered learning environments that require the student's own initiative, planning, experimentation, and reflection in collaboration with peers and senior members and is based on shared responsibility and control (John-Steiner, 2000; Mandel, Gruber, & Renkel, 1996). This kind of learning environment creates *constructive friction* (Vermunt & Verloop, 1999), that is, the urge to gradually develop more and more sophisticated academic skills and knowledge. ProBell research group has provided a learning environment with constant constructive friction. We have also understood PBL as a threshold concept, as a portal, opening up a new and previously inaccessible way of thinking about something (Meyer & Land, 2003). Problem-based learning supports our continuous journey as lifelong and critical learners. Initiating and developing a PBL research group similar to ProBell is a very effective way of research capacity building and contributes to the sustainability of PBL research and practice.

References

Alanko-Turunen, M. (2005). *Negotiating interdiscursivity in a problem-based learning tutorial site. A case study of an international business programme.* Doctoral dissertation, Tampere: Tampere University Press.

Brew, A. (2001). Conceptions of research: A phenomenographic study. *Studies in Higher Education, 26,* 272–285.

Clarke, A.E. (1991). Social worlds/arenas theory as organizational theory. In D.R. Maines (Ed.), *Social organization and social process: Essays in honor of Anselm Strauss* (pp. 119–158). New York: Aldine de Gruyter.

Delamont, S., Atkinson, P., & Parry, O. (1997). *Supervising the PhD: A guide to success.* Baltimore, MD: Open University Press.

Hakkarainen, K. (2003). Kollektiivinen älykkyys [Collective intelligence]. *Psykologia, 38*(3), 384–401.

Johnson, D.W., & Johnson, R. (1982). *Joining together: Group theory and group skills.* (2nd ed.). Englewood Cliffs, NJ: Prentice-Hall.

Johnson, D.W., & Johnson, R. (1987). *Learning together and alone.* Englewood Cliffs, NJ: Prentice Hall.

John-Steiner, V. (2000). *Creative collaboration.* Oxford: Oxford University Press.

Lautamatti, L., & Nummenmaa, A.R. (2008). Jatko-opiskelun työprosessien ohjaus. In A.R. Nummenmaa, K. Pyhältö, & T. Soini (Eds.), *Hyvä Tohtori. Tohtorikoulutuksen rakenteita ja prosesseja [A Good Doctor. The Structures and Processes of PhD Education]* (pp. 107–125). Tampere: Tampere University Press.

Lave, J., & Wenger, E. (1991). *Situated learning: Legitimate peripheral participation.* Cambridge: Cambridge University Press.

Lindblom-Ylänne, S., & Nevgi, A. (Eds.). *Yliopisto- ja korkeakouluopettajan käsikirja. [Handbook for a university teacher].* Helsinki: WSOY.

Mandel, H., Gruber, H., & Renkel, A. (1996). Communities of practice toward expertise: Social foundation of university instruction. In P. Baltes & U. Staudinger (Eds.), *Interactive minds. Life-span perspectives on the social foundation of cognition* (pp. 394–412). Cambridge: Cambridge University Press.

Meyer, J., & Land, R. (2003, May). *Threshold concepts and troublesome knowledge: Linkages to ways of thinking and practicing within the disciplines.* Occasional Report 4. Retrieved from: www.etl.tla.ed.ac.uk//docs/ETLreport4.pdf.

Nummenmaa, A.R. (2006). Process-oriented supervision in doctoral education. In E. Poikela & A.R. Nummenmaa (Eds.), *Understanding problem-based learning* (pp. 291–302). Tampere: Tampere University Press.

Nummenmaa, A.R., & Lautamatti, L. (2004). *Ohjaajana opinnäytetöiden työprosesseissa. Ryhmäohjauksen käytäntöä ja teoriaa [As a supervisor in the work processes of final papers].* Tampere: Tampere University Press.

Pyhältö, K., Soini, T., Lonka, K. Stubb, J., Nummenmaa, A.R., & Soini, H. (2008). *Doctoral students' perceptions about their learning environment and their experienced stress.* Paper in roundtable discussion, EARLI SIG Higher Education conference, Lontoo.

Soini, H. (2008). Vertaisohjaus akateemisen ohjauksen työtapana. In A.R. Nummenmaa, K. Pyhältö, & T. Soini (Eds.), *Hyvä Tohtori. Tohtorikoulutuksen rakenteita ja prosesseja [A Good Doctor. The Structures and Processes of PhD Education]* (pp. 127–137). Tampere: Tampere University Press.

Unruh, D.R. (1979). Characteristics and types of participation in social worlds. *Symbolic Interaction, 2,* 115–127.

Vermunt, J.D., & Verloop, N. (1999). Congruence and friction between learning and teaching. *Learning and Instruction, 9*(3), 257–280.

Wenger, E. (1998). *Communities of practice: Learning, meaning and identity.* Cambridge: Cambridge University Press.

Further Resources

Probell (the Finnish PBL Network) Web resources:
Probell – The Finnish Society for Problem-based Learning: www.probell.fi.
For the materials used in group supervision: www.uta.fi/eduta/probell.
For the publications of ProBell, including online books on PBL research: www.uta.fi/eduta/probell/research.html.

20

How We Wrote This Book

A PBL Approach to Collaborative Writing

Sarah Moore and Terry Barrett

> It is the discourse, with its projects and agendas that determines what writers can and will do.
>
> **(Bartolomae, 1985, p. 160)**

Introduction

Academic writing is not a problem-free activity even though its processes, characteristics, requirements, and rituals are important for us to understand in educational contexts (Moore, 2008). Academics and teachers do not always find writing easy, nor are they often provided with opportunities to talk about their writing activities. These issues with writing persist despite the fact that academics' standing and reputation within their field of expertise often depends on writing, as increasingly do key aspects of their career progression (Murray & Moore, 2006). Furthermore, in higher education, teachers and their students are usually under significant pressure to write. Writing in particular kinds of ways, for a particular type of audience, are assumed to be a central and unassailable dimension of professional development. In learning contexts, writing is a tangible and highly valued symptom and output of the thinking, analysis, interpretation, and understanding that develops in research and relates to ideas, data, and experiences in learning and academic environments.

It is encouraging, then, to see more recent calls for academics and teachers to be less silent about the processes that they use to write and to explore some of the conditions under which academic writing can be seen as an inherent, creative, and pleasurable part of the processes of learning and knowledge development (Elbow & Belanoff, 2000). We believe that these calls to clarify the writing process are worth responding to, and that the writing activities and phases that characterised the production of this text deserve some explicit attention.

Chapter Overview

This chapter draws on data from focus groups with the contributors to the book and reflections by the editors in order to discuss:

- the phases of development in writing this book;
- the key values, features, and principles of the collaborative writing process;
- how the problem-based learning processes were applied to the process of writing this PBL text.

The Phases of Development of Writing this Book

In this section, we share our own reflections on the writing process that unfolded as we wrote this book, collaborated with and listened to our colleagues, and as we discovered how to move from one phase of the process to the next, using many of the same principles and values that underpin PBL including brainstorming, defining the kernel of the problem, dialogic knowing, and team working.

We were concerned, from the outset of this project, that we would try, as much as possible, to ensure that the writing of this book reflected the same processes that we apply to PBL in our teaching and learning contexts. We have seen that mapping out how outputs are achieved is helpful and illuminating for people new to any process and, of course, a focus on process also reflects the dimensions of PBL that make its potential so strong as a total approach to teaching and learning.

As we review how we wrote this book, we are conscious that, in the review phase of a PBL tutorial, for example, the students are often encouraged to reflect on the development of the learning process and on their particular role and contribution both in terms of specific strengths and plans for the future. And we have seen how working in groups, creating communities of learning, and engaging in discourse and dialogue seems essential to the active and engaged learning that we are committed to fostering. We tried to incorporate these activities and beliefs into the writing of this book by initiating and working through the phases of the book's development which are discussed below.

We now briefly summarise the seven phases through which the development of this book occurred:

Phase 1: Idea Generation

Phase 1 involved sketching out the idea for a book. Terry Barrett was the joint co-ordinator of the Enquiry and Problem-based Learning Project, led by University College Dublin and funded by the Strategic Innovation Fund of the Higher Education Authority (Ireland). It was Terry's idea to write a book for PBL practitioners, drawing on the wealth of PBL practice and research of the four partner organisations and their colleagues.

Phase 2: Book Proposal Generation

Phase 2 traced the proposal generation and involved decisions associated with gathering our team of writers who would contribute to this book. The four networks of international partners at the heart of the team were:

1. The Enquiry and Problem-based Learning Project at University College Dublin;
2. The University of Limerick;
3. The Centre for Excellence in Enquiry Based Learning at The University of Manchester; and
4. ProBell, the Finnish PBL network.

Through these networks we also drew in other colleagues beyond these groups.

At this proposal generation stage, we had two residential writers' retreats for contributors: one in Westmeath, Ireland and the other in Monni, Finland. This gave us great opportunities to brainstorm our ideas about the book. During this phase, we clarified that the main audience for the book would be both new and experienced PBL practitioners. We decided that the purpose of the book would be to share our experiences of problem-based learning practice informed by research and theory. By the end of this phase, we were very clear that PBL practice would be in the foreground of the chapters of the book with the research and theory that informed this practice acting as a backdrop. We then defined the kernel of our problem as: "How do we write a book for PBL practitioners that focuses on PBL practice but is also informed by research and theory?" We spent a lot of time brainstorming and discussing this question in PBL mode. However, we were also very clear that this phase needed to produce clear outputs in the form of a draft book proposal with peer-reviewed abstracts for each chapter. The production of these outputs marked the end of the proposal writing phase.

Phase 3: Finalising the Book Proposal

Phase 3 was the stage during which we finalised the proposal using editorial experience and building a strong editorial partnership. Now, as we are at the end of the process of editing and writing, we have reflected on the dynamics of our editorial partnership. Sarah brought much experience in the editing and authoring of academic texts, together with her background in organisational psychology and pedagogy. Terry brought her experience in the design and facilitation of PBL initiatives, along with her PBL research. Both of us brought our experiences of working as education developers and facilitating writers' retreats and an interest in creative and academic writing. We worked together to ensure that the project benefited from these different strands of experience. We deliberately worked face-to-face at key stages and we consider that this added to the dynamic of the editorial partnership and the creativity of the book.

We were also conscious that we wanted to create a space for this book to legitimise the importance of using time and space to think about teaching and learning in creative, playful, and reflective ways in order to produce outputs that enhanced both students' learning and teachers' teaching.

Phase 4: Signing the Book Contract

Phase 4 involved revising the proposal, based on the comments from international reviewers and the commissioning editor. In this phase, we finalised some of the essential features that we wanted to permeate through each chapter and the tone and style that we wanted the authors to observe. We, as the editors, acted as mediators between the goals of the publishers and the spirit and convictions of our authors. We wanted to ensure that the people's voices and experiences, including the student perspective, were protected, but we also recognised the goals, focus, and priorities of the publishers. This mediation was a particularly valuable part of the process because it allowed us to see how the concerns of both the authors and the publishers could be aligned, while keeping the focus of the book on PBL practitioners. Another key aspect of this phase was to emphasise the importance of visual images to illustrate, elaborate, depict, and bring alive the accounts by authors of their PBL practice. We are proud that the publishers recognised the vibrant role that visuals can play in communicating key messages and, of course, this is one of the insights that underpin PBL practice and good pedagogy in general. This phase ended in the signing of our book contract.

Phase 5: Writing the Chapters

Phase 5 involved simply getting down to the writing, now that the chapters had been sketched out and agreed. In this phase, we worked on draft chapters as individuals, in pairs and in groups; some of this phase occurred in residential, collaborative settings. We tried to make sure that many of the authors who were working remotely were, where possible, writing with a co-author who attended one of these sessions. At some point in the process, most of the authors met the editors and many (though not all) of them joined the residential writers' retreats and workshops that formed an essential part in the production of this book. During this writing phase, we had a writers' retreat in Monni, Finland and two peer-reviewing workshops: one in Tampere, Finland and one in University College Dublin, Ireland. We think that this high level of collaboration gave this book a sense of coherence and co-ownership that would have been difficult to create using a more traditional editing process, where people typically work alone on chapters, with minimal input/interaction with the rest of the authors. As one of the contributors commented:

there's a real continuity and connection about this book, and we've achieved that through collaboration, by staying connected, by keeping the dialogue active, even at the times when we're working on our chapters alone.

(Catherine Pettigrew (Ireland), Peer Review Workshop, UCD)

Phase 6: Revising and Editing Chapters

Phase 6 involved the editing and revision of chapters, often an intensive and difficult phase of any writing project. As editors, we reviewed the chapters, both confirming the strengths and recommending specific revisions. The dynamics of this revision phase included challenging, editing, questioning, and aligning with our agreed style and format. We had discussed and agreed a similar format for every chapter but, as editors, we were still keen to make sure that each author pair/group maintained their own voices, and that they had enough leeway to tell their own stories, to explain their perspectives, and to showcase their insights.

We wanted to foster and preserve the author's individual creativity but we also wanted to achieve consistency across the chapters in a way that would give the book clear rhythms and patterns. This part of the writing/editing process was not always easy and, for us, it involved some negotiation with authors to find a way of combining the perspectives of authors, editors, and publisher requirements. For example, two authors wrote in an email to the editors:

> We have followed your lead in the shape of the chapter but returned to a text more closely aligned to our original one. By adding medical education to the title, perhaps it will be clear to the reader that we have focused on what we have learned by using PBL in that context. We still think that these lessons will transfer to other educational levels and disciplines. Thank you for the opportunity to merge our two perspectives. We look forward to reading the entire book.
>
> **(LuAnn Wilkerson and Tatum Korin (United States))**

Phase 7: Final Editing and Finishing

This final phase focused on reviewing the internal coherence of each chapter, the overall coherence of the book, and making further links between chapters. It included writing the introduction to the book and this final chapter. Writing the introduction to the book was inspired by our discussions with authors, the title of the book, our PBL practice and by the painting by Fiona Aherne that is featured on the cover of the book, together with the Oscar Wilde quotation: "Education is an admirable thing, but it is well to remember from time to time that nothing worth knowing can be taught" (Oscar Wilde (quoted in Ellmann 1969)). Finishing the book involved proofreading and copy-editing.

Figure 20.1 Terry Barrett (Ireland) and Sarah Moore (Ireland) working on editing the book.

Values, Features, and Principles of the Collaborative Writing Process

Throughout all of these phases, we were keen to communicate, in explicit ways, some of the values, features, and principles that the group had discussed from the beginning of the project. These values and principles included the importance of creative engagement, a focus on educational practice and PBL research, the key role of dialogue, a strong sense of community and collaboration, a commitment to total immersion in the writing task, and facilitating a change of setting and creating new spaces in which to write. These values, features, and principles are explored in more detail below.

The Importance of Creative Engagement

Grant and Knowles (2000) have argued that if academic writers were more like creative writers, then we might make progress more quickly and be less hide-bound by some of the rituals and requirements that academic writing has come to be associated with. We certainly believe that there was a need to foster creative and innovative thinking as we worked to develop this book. For example, the authors of Chapter 19 wanted to write the bulk of their chapter in a form of a dialogue and the editors encouraged them to do so. We were also aware that creative expression often occurs with the interaction of ideas and different media and the editors encouraged the authors to play with visuals as a way of expressing and sharing their ideas.

A Focus on Practice, As Well As Research

Creativity came at least as often from insights about our own practice as it did from reviewing evidence or assimilating the work of others. Indeed, in the early phase, one of the breakthrough moments (captured in real time in the photograph in Figure 20.2) happened at the first writers' retreat in Monni, where Charlotte Silén (Sweden) assertively proposed that the insights from our practice as PBL tutors should be a central element of this book. In the photograph, Charlotte, with pen in hand, attends an informal brainstorming session, during which she announces strongly that, as well as writing about our PBL research, we should write about our *PRACTICE* and draw on our considerable experience of PBL.

That may not necessarily seem like a substantial or particularly surprising breakthrough, given the nature of the topic, but the format and the context of the discussions gave it an authenticity and a shared meaning that we believe played a crucial part in the way that the themes of the book unfolded.

> Practical ideas and guidelines for readers are important. Our own PBL experiences are very valuable and will be written about in the chapters. Research is in the background. It is now more alive, practice-based, taking the reader much more into account.
>
> **(Marja-Leena Lähteenmäki (Finland), Monni retreat)**

The Importance of Dialogue

We really wanted the authors to talk actively to each other, to share their ideas about what they were trying to achieve in their chapters, and to provide as many opportunities as practical for these ideas to get an airing. It was not possible for all of the authors to attend the gatherings, so we tried to encourage active dialogue both during and between book project meetings.

Figure 20.2 Charlotte Silén (Sweden) emphasises the importance of authors writing about their PBL practice.

The authors reported real benefits from this dialogic engagement with others at different stages in the process.

At the Monni retreats, the active dialogue helped to create coherence and direction at an early stage in the process. By having debate and dialogue about the title, for example, the discussion at Monni helped to focus on the main skewer of the book: the title, the key themes, the main messages that, as PBL researchers and practitioners, the authors could commit to. Some of the important themes and insights that were explored included the need to negotiate with stakeholders in PBL settings in order to foster activities such as reflection, commitment, listening, and responding. We became certain that we wanted to write a book that talked directly to the reader:

> We want to invite readers to take on an active reading position. We want to write an open book with plenty of opportunity for reader engagement.
> **(Timo Portimojarvi (Finland), Monni retreat)**

This kind of active discussion helped the group to name its values and become more deliberate about what the published text could aim to achieve. Even though not all of the ideas and concepts discussed at this stage found their way into the book's ultimate title, the themes and principles became an integrated and persistent part of the text.

Later in the process, when the authors were editing and redrafting, again, active dialogue and interaction were shown to have been valued and important parts of the process:

> It was very encouraging. It was great to find that people really understood what we had written and it was encouraging and it was lovely.
> **(Emma Gleeson (Ireland), peer-review workshop, UCD)**

Figure 20.3 Marja-Leena Lähteenmäki (Finland) and Lars Uhlin (Sweden) reviewing their work on their chapter at a writers' retreat in Monni, Finland.

And that's so important in the writing process, that somebody understands your ideas even if you haven't articulated them exactly or it isn't polished or shining yet.

(Sarah Moore (Ireland), peer-review workshop facilitator, UCD)

Wherever the opportunity allowed, we tried to encourage the authors to sit with each other and share ideas and review their initial and developing drafts together.

But, of course, there were times when face-to-face dialogue was not practical. The authors were encouraged to find and use effective ways of interacting remotely, using available technology:

We have the document on Google apps and sharing it between the three of us and there's no emailing the latest version, it's just up there and I can go in automatically and see exactly what Yves has changed and what Jean-Louis has changed and they can do the same and you can also edit altogether at the same time. I find that that helped us hugely in that there's – you're not waiting for somebody to send you the latest version of the paper especially with the time difference – it's just up there and you can add one sentence to it, go back and add another paragraph and Yves can do the same and I can see exactly where he's going and where his ideas are developing.

(Siobhán Drohan (Ireland), whose co-authors were Yves Maufette (Canada) and Jean-Louis Allard (France))

A Strong Sense of Community and Collaboration

In introducing the collaborative meetings, we often started off by emphasising the importance of active collaboration and the value that we associated with it:

Writing in academia is often treated as an isolated, competitive, somewhat dysfunctional act – one of our convictions as educational developers over the years is that if you treat writing as a social act then it makes it much more successfully aligned with the principles of effective teaching and learning and pedagogy and … positive learning climates. So [we wanted to] change the dynamics of writing a little bit.

(Sarah Moore (Ireland), introduction, peer-review workshop, UCD)

At a writers' retreat in Monni, we reviewed each draft chapter, in turn, as a group: "We will consciously refer to other chapters. It helps integrate the chapters well" (Ingrid Scholten (Australia), Monni retreat).

A Commitment to Total Immersion

We recognised that, as well as opportunities for interacting with each other, we also needed to encourage writers to spend time alone, developing their ideas, reflecting on their themes and topics, analysing their own research and tapping into their reflections on their own practice.

Figure 20.4 Authors getting down to the work of peer-reviewing chapters at a writers' retreat in Monni, Finland.

Figure 20.5 Merja Alanko-Turunen (Finland) immersed in the task of writing.

I suppose the hardest thing for me to do now is to write! Yes I have the outline but now I have to get down to it.

(Marie Stanton (Ireland), peer-review workshop, UCD)

Csikszentmihalyi (1991) writes about the psychology of optimal performance and that, when people are performing well, they are challenging themselves, they feel in control and they feel safe enough to engage positively and non-defensively in the work that they are doing. We wanted to ensure that we encouraged our team of writers to apply the characteristics of optimal performance to their own writing activity. This involves challenging one another and creating safe spaces in which writers would not feel the anxiety of surveillance that often prevails in academic writing contexts (Grant & Knowles, 2000; Moore, 2003).

A Change of Setting to Foster Reflection: Adopting New Perspectives through Change and Distance

By facilitating writers' retreats in supportive settings and by bringing groups of authors together in places where they do not normally work and write, we attempted to create a "third place", a concept popularised by Oldenburg and Bissett (1983) who have championed the importance of finding and using places outside of the workplace and the home in order to provide people with

Figure 20.6 Anna Raija Nummenmaa (Finland) and Terry Barrett (Ireland) reflecting on the work on the book and the importance of the Monni setting at a writers' retreat in Monni.

alternative social and collaborative contexts in which to think and act. By encouraging authors to gather in these contexts, we aimed to provide the whole project with a new discursive base in which to foster diversity of insights, novelty, expressiveness and perspective. And, by punctuating the project with several gatherings in "third places", we aimed to establish a climate for this project which included helping all of the authors to feel welcome, removing any risk of dysfunctional competition, promoting relaxation and pleasure in the context of hard work, and (we hoped) creating a positive environment that valued people and their feelings and passions, as well as their intellectual contribution.

> Anna Raija made it so comfortable for us by having meals appear from nowhere. All we had to do was enjoy it. The fact that we were in such a beautiful environment, you can underestimate that. It was O.K. to go for a sauna, a walk, pick mushrooms. It enriched the process. Being in a beautiful place was so important for the process. It opens up your thought process. The serenity that helps that happen. You feel validated. When you feel valued you produce valuable work.
>
> **(Ingrid Scholten (Australia), Monni retreat)**

That is not to say that we did not challenge and push one another. We were also eager to harness high levels of energy and high standards, something that recent PBL research work has referred to as "hard fun" (Barrett, 2005). And so, the norms and rigours of feedback, peer review, and critical engagement were also a regular part of the process. The following quotation is representative of how authors valued and used the feedback that they received from their peers during the writing of their chapters:

> It really was very good to see how other people confronted it and got ideas and feedback about the structure and restructure of our draft format into something that aligned better with the whole project, to feel part of the bigger picture. And to get feedback as well on what we had done so far.
>
> **(Siobhan Drohan (Ireland), peer-review workshop, UCD)**

Conclusions

We treated the writing of this book in a way that reflected the PBL process. We pulled together a team of people who, from different perspectives, could contribute to and shape this book within their realms of expertise and experience. Together, we defined and refined the kernel of the problem. We created a process that aimed to provide a collaborative structure in which people could work and learn together.

We have also shown how PBL processes can be effectively used in new contexts, for example, for writing books. This chapter has described how the writing of this book emerged through a PBL-type process and, by doing this, it encourages you to explore the benefits of approaching the task of writing and dissemination using a PBL-based philosophy. Most of all, we have been convinced that treating writing and learning as social and collaborative acts can assist and facilitate positive, creative, and dialogic engagement among groups of people working together.

The initial concept for this book came from the insight that it is worth encouraging many voices to explore and explain their practices in teaching and learning in PBL contexts. We hope that this book provides you with PBL practice resources that contribute to you developing sustainable PBL initiatives. The voices of established practitioners, new PBL tutors, students, teachers, employers, and education developers have been represented in this book. All of them encourage PBL curriculum designers and tutors to revitalise their practice.

References

Barrett, T. (2005). Who said learning couldn't be enjoyable, playful and fun? The voices of PBL students. In E. Poikela & S. Poikela (Eds.), *PBL in context: Bridging work and education* (pp. 159–176). Tampere: Tampere University Press. Retrieved from: www.lpt.fi/pblconference/PBL_In_Context.pdf.

Bartolomae, D. (1985). Inventing the university. In M. Rose (Ed.), *When a writer can't write* (pp. 134–165). New York: Guilford.

Csikszentmihalyi, M. (1991). Flow: The psychology of optimal performance. *Teachers College Record, 93*(1), 184–186.

Elbow, P., & Belanoff, P. (2000). *A community of writers.* San Francisco, CA: Jossey-Bass.

Ellmann, R. (1969). *The artist as critic: Critical writings of Oscar Wilde.* Chicago, IL: Chicago University Press.

Grant, B., & Knowles, S. (2000). Flights of imagination: Academic women becoming writers. *International Journal for Academic Development, 5*(1), 6–19.

Moore, S. (2003). Writers' retreats for academics: Exploring and increasing the motivation to write. *Journal of Further and Higher Education, 27*(3), 333–342.

Moore, S. (2008). *Supporting academic writing among students and academics.* SEDA Special 24. London: SEDA.

Murray, R., & Moore, S. (2006). *The handbook of academic writing: A fresh approach.* Maidenhead: Open University Press.

Oldenburg, R., & Bissett, D. (1983). The third place. *Qualitative Sociology, 5*(4), 265–284.

Further Resources

Teaching academic writing: A toolkit for higher education. ESCALATE: http://escalate.ac.uk/164.

Editors and Contributors

Editors

Terry Barrett (terry.barrett@ucd.ie terrybarrett500@hotmail.com) is a Lecturer in Educational Development at University College Dublin Teaching and Learning. She has 17 years' experience of working with problem-based learning as an education developer, programme coordinator, and tutor. She has worked in the design and implementation of PBL initiatives in a range of disciplines including nursing, physiotherapy, ultrasound, science, English literature, business, community development, education, hospitality, tourism, and policing. She is joint coordinator of the Enquiry and Problem-based learning Project (Strategic Innovation Fund, Ireland) led by University College Dublin. Her doctorate thesis focused on what we can learn about problem-based learning from listening to how PBL students talked about PBL in tutorials. She has presented keynote PBL papers at conferences in Ireland, England, Finland, and Australia. She has published in the areas of academic development, problem-based learning, creativity in higher education, and peer observation of teaching. She was lead editor (with Iain Mac Labhainn and Helen Fallon) of *Handbook of Enquiry and Problem-based Learning: Irish Case Studies and International Perspectives* (Galway: National University of Ireland Galway and AISHE, 2005). Her other publications include: "The problem-based learning process as finding and being in flow", *Innovations in Education & Teaching International*, 2010.

Sarah Moore (sarah.moore@ul.ie) is Associate Vice President and Professor at the University of Limerick where she has led key initiatives in higher education, including the launch of academic writing networks, regional teaching enhancement strategies, innovative learner support systems, and problem-based learning programmes. A teacher and researcher in the area of organisational behaviour and development, she has used the principles of this discipline to help develop effective academic practices and processes both within and beyond her own institution. She has designed and developed many dedicated writers' retreats for academics and postgraduates in Ireland and internationally. Sarah's recent publications include *The Ultimate Study Skills Handbook* (2010) with Colin Nevile, Maura Murphy and Cornelia Connelly; *Teaching at College and University* (2007), with Gary Walsh and Angelica Risquez; *The Handbook of Academic Writing* (2006), co-authored with Rowena Murray; and *How to be a Student* (2005), with Maura Murphy. She has published her research in: *The Journal of Further and Higher Education*;

The International Journal of Academic Development, Innovations in Teaching and Education International, Teaching in Higher Education and *The Journal of Higher Education Policy and Management*, and has been a reviewer for the *Oxford Review of Education*. She is a member of the Higher Education Authority (Ireland).

Contributors

Merja Alanko-Turunen (merja.alanko-turunen@helia.fi) was part of a team that initiated and developed a PBL international business curriculum at HAAGA-HELIA University of Applied Sciences in Finland. She is a senior researcher in the ProBell, the Finnish PBL research group.

Jean-Louis Allard (jlallard@cesi.fr) is the Director of eXia (École Supérieure d'informatique du CESI) and regional Director of CESI Nord-Normandie. He conceived of and directed the implementation of a PBL curriculum for a new school of computing science (eXia) within 13 cities throughout France.

Fred Buining (fred@fredwerk.com) – based in the Netherlands, Fred's international consultancy "Fredwerk" helps organisations to change by discovering and harnessing their creative potential. His clients include multinationals, small enterprises, and universities.

Diane Cashman (diane.cashman@ucd.ie) is an Educational Support Specialist for the Veterinary Science Centre, in the School of Agriculture, Food Science and Veterinary Medicine at University College Dublin. Diane is currently developing taught graduate programmes for the veterinary profession that capitalise on educational technologies to deliver off-campus part-time education.

Deirdre Connolly (deirdre.connolly@tcd.ie) is a lecturer in occupational therapy at the School of Medicine, Trinity College Dublin. She has 8 years' experience in designing, implementing, and evaluating PBL modules with undergraduate, postgraduate, and continuing professional development students.

Lorna Dodd (lorna.dodd@ucd.ie) is a Liaison Librarian in University College Dublin. Her research interest is the impact of PBL on students' information literacy and is currently involved in PBL curriculum development and implementation.

Roisin Donnelly (roisin.donnelly@dit.ie) has been working as a lecturer and researcher in the Learning and Teaching Centre in the Dublin Institute of Technology, where she has been involved in designing and delivering continuous professional development opportunities (both short courses and accredited programmes) for academic staff in Third Level Learning and Teaching. She also delivers eLearning pedagogy workshops and consultations as part of the Institute's eLearning training programme as well as regularly tutoring on international online courses for academic professional development.

Siobhán Drohan (sdrohan@wit.ie) lectures in computing in Waterford Institute of Technology and previously worked as a software engineer for close to a decade. In addition to being a member of academic staff, Siobhán is completing her PhD researching the use of problem-based learning and workplace curricula in the software development workplace.

Eeva-Liisa Eskola (eeskola@abo.fi) is an information specialist at the Library of Turku University of Applied Sciences. She works in the area of information literacy, teaching information literacy skills.

Professor Paul Finucane (Paul.Finucane@ul.ie) is the Foundation Head of the Graduate Medical School at the University of Limerick and is a doctor (geriatrician) by profession. While at Flinders University of South Australia, he played a key role in the introduction of Australia's first graduate-entry and PBL-based medical curriculum.

Emma Gleeson (E.Gleeson@ucc.ie) was a Speech and Language Therapy Student in the Department of Speech and Hearing Sciences, University College Cork when she started co-writing her chapter. She is now a speech and language therapist and a problem-based learning tutor.

Louise Goldring (Louise.Goldring@manchester.ac.uk) was a student within the English and American Studies department undertaking an MA at the University of Manchester when she started co-writing her chapter. She is now Student Engagement Officer with the Centre for Excellence in Enquiry-based Learning at the University of Manchester.

Woei Hung (woei.hung@und.nodak.edu) is currently an Associate Professor in Instructional Design and Technology, in the Department of Teaching and Learning, University ofNorth Dakota, USA. His research interests include problem-based learning, problem solving, types and difficulty levels of problems, systems thinking, and concept formation.

Norman Jackson (norman.jackson@surrey.ac.uk) is Professor of Higher Education and Director of the Surrey Centre for Excellence in Professional Training and Education (SCEPTrE) at the University of Surrey which has formed around the concept of "Learning for a Complex World" in the belief that higher education has a responsibility to prepare students for a lifetime of uncertainty, change, challenge and emergent or self-created opportunity. His interest in enquiry and problem-driven learning in experiential situations stems from a desire to provide more opportunities for learning in the HE curriculum that are closer to real world working and learning situations.

Marja-Leena Lähteenmäki (marja-leena.lahteenmaki@piramk.fi) is a principal lecturer and course leader in physiotherapy at Piramk University of Applied Sciences, and has been involved in PBL since 1996. She has been responsible for curriculum development for a PBL programme as well as working as a tutor.

Tatum Langford Korin (tkorin@mednet.ucla.edu) is an Adjunct Assistant Professor in the Department of Medicine at the David Geffen School of Medicine, University of California Los Angeles (UCLA) in the Office of Education Development and Research and Acting Director of the Instructional Design and Technology Unit. In her role as Director of Faculty Development, she is responsible for PBL tutor training, new faculty training, clinical teacher training, and faculty evaluations.

Majella McCaffery (majella.tonra@ucd.ie) is a Lecturer and Module Leader at University College Dublin. She has been a member of the curriculum design team for a new problem-based learning MSc Ultrasound Programme.

Peter McCrorie (P.mcCrorie@sghms.ac.uk) is Professor of Medical Education at St George's University in London. His main interests are in curriculum development, problem-based learning, and community-oriented medical and dental education and is an internationally recognised authority in PBL for medical education.

Yves Mauffette (mauffette.yves@uqam.ca) is the Dean of the Faculty of Science at Université du Québec à Montréal. He was formerly the Director of the undergraduate programme in biology that underwent a change from a traditional programme to an integrated PBL programme.

Lyn Middleton (middletoni@ukzn.ac.za) is a senior PBL tutor in the Scholl of Nursing, University of KwaZulu-Natal in South Africa. She has specialised in mental health nursing with an emphasis on innovative teaching methods for the discipline.

Ivan Moore (i.moore@shu.ac.uk) is Director of the Centre for Promoting Learner Autonomy (CPLA), which is a national Centre for Excellence in Teaching and Learning (CETL), based at Sheffield Hallam University, England. Ivan was an independent Higher Education Consultant.

Ntombifikile Gloria Mtshali (Mtshalin3@ukzn.ac.za) is a lecturer in the School of Nursing, University of KwaZulu-Natal in South Africa. She has specialised in progressive education and is an experienced PBL tutor who has been involved in a number of PBL curricula reviews.

Anna Raija Nummenmaa (Anna.Raija.Nummenmaa@uta.fi) is Professor of Education at the University of Tampere, and has been a leading PBL practitioner in the area of early childhood education since 1999. She was the leader of the research project "Problem based learning as a strategy for developing knowledge and competence in the context of education and work", financed by the Academy of Finland, 2003–2006.

Marcia Ody (Marcia.Ody@manchester.ac.uk) is the University of Manchester's Senior Students as Partners Officer. Marcia supports and facilitates student-led activity, encouraging students to take a holistic approach to their learning and development, concentrating on the total student experience and championing co-curricular learning opportunities as well as those available through the curriculum.

Geraldine O'Neill (Geraldine.m.oneill@ucd.ie) is a Senior Lecturer in Educational Development at University College Dublin Teaching and Learning. She is joint co-ordinator of the Enquiry and Problem-based learning Project (SIF, Ireland) led by University College Dublin.

Karen O'Rourke (K.orourke@leedsmet.ac.uk) is an Academic Developer at the Institute for Enterprise – a Centre of Excellence in Teaching and Learning at Leeds Metropolitan University. Previously she was the Associate Director of the Centre for Excellence in Enquiry-Based Learning University of Manchester.

Catharine Pettigrew (catepettigrew@hotmail.com) has recently relocated to China and was previously a Lecturer in the Department of Speech and Hearing Sciences, University College Cork. She led the development of the 3rd-year curriculum in the PBL-driven BSc (Hons) in Speech and Language Therapy, and has assisted in the development of PBL-based interdisciplinary student learning collaborations within the Faculty of Medicine and Health.

Sari Poikela (sapoikel@ulapland.fi) is a Senior Lecturer at the University of Lapland, Finland. Her research interests include designing PBL curricula, assessment, and evaluation and teachers' professional development.

Timo Portimojärvi (timo.portimojarvi@uta.fi) has been working as a senior researcher, teacher, tutor, and a project manager in the University of Tampere in Finland. His work on media education, online learning, and problem-based learning has been connected to primary and secondary school teacher education and extension studies of teachers in higher education.

David Prideaux (david.prideaux@flinders.edu.au) is Professor of Medical Education at Flinders University in Australia. He has considerable experience in curriculum development and evaluation of surgery programmes at Flinders.

Ingrid Scholten (ingrid.scholten@flinders.edu.au) is an accomplished educational developer with over 20 years of university teaching experience, and recently led the development of the graduate-entry speech pathology programme at Flinders University of South Australia that has problem-based learning at its core. She is an acclaimed teacher and has produced award-winning multimedia programmes that inspire and enlighten students.

Charlotte Silén (charlotte.silen@ki.se) is an Assistant Professor at Karolinska Institute, Sweden. Previously she worked with PBL for 24 years: planning PBL curricula, tutoring, and facilitating staff development.

Marie Stanton (marie.stanton@ucd.ie) is a Lecturer at University College Dublin and led a curriculum development team in the design of a new problem-based learning MSc Ultrasound Programme. Her research interests include ultrasound safety, ultrasound theory and practice, and the development of critical thinking skills in problem-based learning.

Lars Uhlin (lars.uhlin@imv.liu.se) is an education developer at the Centre for Education Development and Research at the Faculty of Health Sciences, Linkoping University, Sweden. He has 20 years of PBL experience in different positions and contexts.

LuAnn Wilkerson (lwilkerson@mednet.ucla.edu) is currently Professor of Medicine and Senior Associate Dean for Medical Education at the David Geffen School of Medicine at University of California Los Angeles (UCLA). Since 1980, she has assisted thousands of faculty members in the study and improvement of medical education in a variety of settings with a special interest in ambulatory teaching and problem-based learning.

Index

Bold page numbers indicate figures, *italics* indicate tables.